# DYNASTY ESCAPE

Nobu Sue

Published by Subon Publishing

Copyright © 2024 Nobu Sue

All rights reserved, including the right to reproduce this book, or portions thereof in any form. No part of this text may be reproduced, transmitted, downloaded, decompiled, reverse engineered or stored, in any form, or introduced into any information storage and retrieval system, in any form or by any means, whether electronic or mechanical, without the express written permission of the author.

Some names and locations may have been changed for privacy reasons. The author accepts full responsibility for its originality, and warrants the publisher that no part of the book is false or libellous and does not infringe on privacy or duty of confidence or break any relevant law or regulation.

Hardback ISBN: 978-1-7384544-3-3
Paperback black and white ISBN: 978-1-7384544-4-0
Ebook ISBN: 978-1-7384544-5-7
Chinese edition ISBN: 978-1-7384544-6-4

Cover Art: Lauren Frances—www.instagram.com/labhrai
Book Design: www.shakspeareeditorial.org

*To all the people whose lives and human rights have
been affected by the abuse of power.
Will history repeat itself?*

*The Author—Nobu Sue*
photo © Odette Sugerman

# CONTENTS

1. Preface ........................................................................... 1
2. The History ................................................................... 6
3. The Taiwanese Kuomintang Dynasty ............................ 15
4. The Financial Dynasty ................................................. 22
5. The Beginning of the Scam ......................................... 29
6. Big Mama's Invisible Hand .......................................... 38
7. Plan X: Execution Started ........................................... 47
8. Filing Under Chapter 11 on June 20, 2013 .................. 59
9. The Hijacked Loans ..................................................... 67
10. Chapter 11 Bankruptcy: Part II .................................. 79
11. TMT vs Mega Bank ................................................... 89
12. Reverse Engineering in Chapter 11 ............................ 97
13. Selling the Entire Fleet ............................................. 103
14. B Max: The Drama .................................................. 113
15. Shanghai Commercial & Savings Bank Ltd. ............. 149
16. KMT Money Laundering and the China Investment Fund ....................................................................... 157
17. Collusion and Attempt to Destroy Nobu Sue ........... 164

18. Delete and Destroy the Evidence.................................. 172
19. The Samson Wu Story: Fake News? ............................ 177
20. AML: US$180 Million News ...................................... 183
21. Mediation and Truth Coming Out............................. 188
22. Television Exposure and Death Threats ...................... 196
23. Corruption and the Fall of the Ma-Kim Dynasty ...... 203
24. Shipbuilding Fraud ...................................................... 211
25. Panama .......................................................................... 215
26. Star Bulk/KMT/Macquarie Bank Orchestration......... 219
27. Conclusion.................................................................... 225
28. Afterword..................................................................... 230
29. SUMMARY ................................................................. 234
30. Glossary 1 – Terms ...................................................... 236
31. Glossary 2 – People and Participants .......................... 242
32. Acknowledgments ....................................................... 245
33. Appendix of Evidence.................................................. 248
34. Bibliography................................................................. 280
35. Illustrations ................................................................. 281

# PREFACE

> **Definition**: A SWAP is a derivative (a security [tradable financial asset] with a price derived from underlying asset/s) contract through which two parties exchange financial instruments.
>
> Futures
>
> Forwards · Derivatives · Swaps
>
> Options
>
> *P.1: Types of derivatives contract*

THIS IS A true story, it shows why SWAP and other current banking procedures need to be reviewed the world over. The basic story outlines how loans made to Taiwan Maritime Transportation (TMT) Group might have been hijacked to move money away from Taiwanese banks before the impending fall of the Kuomintang (KMT) political dynasty—called Plan X. This might have been done with the help of Mega Bank and McKinney Tsai, under orders from President Ma Ying-jeou and his wife Christine (Madam) Chow, aka 'Big Mama.'

The author, Nobu Sue, is an Asian shipping tycoon and inventor, he owns TMT. He is the first person to file against Section 13.4 in US banking law. His story shows that, if a central banker can manipulate a SWAP agreement, backed by the government, that banker can use it for anything he/she wants to.

## FINANCIAL BACKDROP

The recent socio-economic histories of Taiwan and Korea are unique insofar as the Chaebol system (Korea) and the Dynasty system (Taiwan) are concerned. Taiwan is a small country under the shadow of mainland China—the "One China" policy of the mainland People's Republic of China (PRC) refuses diplomatic relations with any country that recognizes the Republic of China (ROC), aka Taiwan. Today, 20 countries maintain official ties with the ROC, while other states maintain unofficial ties through representative offices and institutions that function as de facto embassies and consulates. Although Taiwan is fully self-governing, most international organizations in which the PRC participates refuse to grant membership to Taiwan and do not allow it to contribute, except in a non-state capacity. Internally, the division in politics is between eventual unification with mainland China or complete Taiwanese independence, although both sides have moderated their positions to broaden their appeal.

So, what places the Taiwanese gross domestic product (GDP) in the world's top 30 and its foreign reserves in the world's top 20? How can a small island of 23 million people on the outskirts of Asia have such financial success? Nobu Sue's family is connected to both Taiwan and Japan, so he has a unique insight into the last 50 years of economic history.

The Asian financial crisis of 1997 started in Thailand, which, at that time, had acquired a burden of foreign debt that made the country bankrupt, then its currency collapsed, and the crisis spread to most of southeast Asia and Japan—with the exception of Taiwan. Fears were raised of a worldwide economic meltdown as currencies slumped, stock markets were devalued, and there was a rise in private debt. Foreign debt-to-GDP ratios shot up beyond 180% during the worst of the crisis, but the newly industrialized Taiwan remained immune. The International Monetary Fund (IMF) finally stepped in and initiated a US$40 billion bailout to stabilize the currencies, growth dropped to zero, people rioted, and governments fell. Since the beginning of the 1990s, despite political differences, the economic ties between Taiwan and the PRC have been very strong. The dynamic, export-driven economy of Taiwan benefited from the awakening of the sleeping giant that was the mainland. Real growth in GDP was averaging 8% and exports provided the impetus for further industrialization. Taiwan's trade surplus was substantial and its total foreign reserves grew to be the world's fifth largest—a miracle for such a small nation.

The island's unique location placed it perfectly to play a leading role in Asian/British banking after the handing back of Hong Kong to China by the UK in 1997. Taiwan's economy also survived when the Western financial crisis hit hard in 2008. The first Western hedge funds arrived in October 2008, as the West was in the throes of that crisis and banks were going under or being bailed out by governments. Royal Bank of Scotland (RBS), HSBC (Hongkong & Shanghai Banking Corporation), Barclays, Standard Chartered, and ANZ (Australia New Zealand) Bank all set up shop. They were intended as commercial banks, with some investment activities. However, the most aggressive of them, the Macquarie Bank (Australia), grew fast and became the group's rising star in the East, funding investment activities on the same scale as Goldman Sachs, Morgan Stanley and Merrill Lynch in the USA—through Sino-centric commodities like coal, iron ore, and so on. Macquarie became the leading investment bank in Taiwan.

It might be useful to point out here that the Australian and New Zealand banking systems are closely related to the establishment systems inherited from British colonialism. Unregulated operations, such as that of the East India Company, contributed to the laissez-faire methodologies of HSBC, Standard Chartered Bank, ANZ Bank, New Zealand Bank, Barclays, and others. They operated under the long established legal/financial mores of the British banking hierarchy.

But let's go back to the Western financial crisis of 2007–2009 for a moment. There were many causes, but greed was the major one. The huge scam performed by the big Western banks is discussed at length in my book *The Gold Man from the East*—it's a story that's never been properly told and I highly recommend it for companion reading and reference with *Dynasty Escape*. From the point of view of this book, RBS overstretched itself when it bought ABN AMRO. The Taiwan branch of ABN AMRO was the best performing bank in the world—it had US$8 billion cash deposits and no derivative business in 2007. All its business was related to cash and a stable real estate market. RBS was in trouble and it was a typical Rothschild-style "good bank/bad bank" enterprise. But RBS was in too deep in the CDO/CDS (Collateralized Debt Obligation/Credit Default SWAP [that S word again]) bubble, which eventually burst, causing chaos and the biggest bailout of Western banks ever seen.

However, after the bailout, the mess had to be cleaned up and the evidence of what really happened during this phenomenal banking scam destroyed. It was done through the Asian banks in 2009–2010. Sydney, Singapore, and other banking centers were highly regulated, but its unique "dynasty" ethos enabled the Taiwanese banking system to play a strategic role in the clean-up. In 2009 the Taiwan Minister of Finance agreed to start trading derivatives for CDO/CDSs that had originated in the Western financial crisis, in order to hide those toxic assets from governments that were introducing new regulatory measures and looking for clues as to what had really happened.

## PREFACE

So, in clearing up the mess of the Western banks after the financial crisis of 2007–2009, Taiwanese banks learned how effective the SWAP could be in irregular financial dealings. They learned that it was a technique they could use to their own advantage—a formula to defraud. The KMT Dynasty that had ruled Taiwan for over 60 years would soon be coming to the end of a reign during which, it is alleged, it had amassed a vast fortune through corruption and fraud. Did it need a way to get that fortune out of Taiwan without anyone knowing or suspecting?

That's where Nobu Sue and his Taiwan Maritime Transportation (TMT) Group come into the story.

*P.2: Nobu Sue with DPP Politician in Mega Case*

# CHAPTER 1
## THE HISTORY

FOLLOWING THE FALL of the Ming Dynasty in 1644, Koxinga (Zheng Chenggong), a Ming loyalist, arrived on the island of Taiwan and expelled the Dutch, who had a military presence there. Koxinga established the Kingdom of Tungning, with his capital at Tainan. It lasted for 21 years (1662–1683) and they continued to launch raids on the southeast coast of mainland China well into the Qing Dynasty. Koxinga and the Zeng family reign continued the tax system of the Dutch and they established schools and religious temples.

Taiwan was regarded by the Qing Dynasty as 'a ball of mud beyond the pale of civilization' and it didn't appear on any map of imperial China until after 1683. Nevertheless, following the defeat of Koxinga's grandson (Zeng Keshuang) by Admiral Shi Lang of southern Fujian, the Qing Dynasty formally annexed Taiwan, placing it under the jurisdiction of Fujian Province. The point of the campaign was to destroy the Zeng family regime, rather than to conquer the island, and Qing ministers advocated repatriating all Chinese to the mainland and abandoning the territory. By 1683 there were only about 7,000 Chinese left on Taiwan and they were people who had married into the indigenous seafaring population that had first settled there.

The Qing imperial government tried to stop piracy and issued a series of edicts to manage immigration and respect the land rights of the indigenous population. But immigrants, mostly from southern Fujian, continued to enter Taiwan. The border between taxpaying lands and "savage" lands shifted eastwards,

# THE HISTORY

with some indigenous people becoming sinicized, while others retreated into the mountains. Attempts to limit immigration by the Qing Dynasty lasted from 1683 to 1760. But these restrictions were lifted in the 1760s and, by 1812, there were more than two million Chinese immigrants in Taiwan.

Empress Cixi of the Manchu Yehenara clan was a Chinese regent who effectively controlled the China of the late Qing Dynasty. Selected as an imperial concubine for the Xianfeng Emperor in her adolescence, she gave birth to a son, Zaichun, in 1856. After the emperor's death in 1861, the young boy became the Tongzhi Emperor and Cixi became the Empress Dowager and assumed the regency. Cixi then consolidated control over the dynasty when she installed her nephew as the Guangxu Emperor after the death of the Tongzhi Emperor in 1875, contrary to the traditional rules of succession of the Qing Dynasty. Cixi's younger brother was a Manchu general and she selected his daughter to marry the Guangxu Emperor because she wanted to strengthen the influence of the Yehenara clan within the imperial family. The girl married the Guangxu Emperor in 1889 and became Empress Xiaodingjing, the last empress of China. However, after the wedding, the empress was ignored by the emperor, who preferred his consort, Zhen of the Tatara clan. But Cixi found out and sent the consort to the 'cold palace,' a place reserved for consorts who fell out of favor—Zhen later drowned in a well within the Forbidden City.

Cixi was firmly opposed to the Guangxu Emperor's Hundred Days Reform program and she had him placed under house arrest in the Summer Palace. Empress Xiaodingjing would spy on the emperor and report his every move to Dowager Cixi, but she was generally regarded as a gracious and pleasant person.

In Taiwan during this time, there were a number of conflicts between groups of Han and Hakka settlers from different regions of southern Fujian, and between Fujian Chinese and indigenous aborigines, and the Qing Dynasty felt that it was a difficult place to govern. Taiwan was also plagued by foreign invasions—in 1841 the British attacked Keelung three times but were repelled each time by Yao Ying, who led the Chinese naval forces in Taiwan. In 1867 an entire invading American crew were killed by the indigenous people. When the Americans launched the Formosa Expedition in retaliation, the aboriginals defeated it as well, forcing the Americans to retreat. Northern Taiwan and the Penghu Islands were the scene of the Sino-French war (1884–1885) and the French occupied Keelung on October 1, 1884. Liu Mingchuan recruited aboriginals, many of whom were still primitive headhunters, to serve alongside the Chinese soldiers. The French were defeated at the Battle of Tamsui and pinned down at Keelung for eight months before they finally withdrew. Because of these incursions, the Qing government began constructing a series of coastal defenses in 1885 and, in 1887, Taiwan was upgraded to a Province with its capital at Taipei. Liu Mingchuan served as the first governor and he divided Taiwan into 11 counties and built a railway from Taipei to Hsinchu, a mine in Keelung, and an arsenal to improve Taiwan's defenses against foreigners.

Japan tried to claim sovereignty over Taiwan, which they called Takasago Koku, as far back as 1592. Sporadic invasion attempts spanning three centuries were unsuccessful, due mainly to disease and resistance by indigenous people on the island. In 1871, Paiwan aboriginal headhunters took the heads of 54 crew members of a shipwrecked Ryukyuan vessel and the Japanese tried to use this incident to legitimize its expansion into Taiwanese territory. The Qing ministers pointed out that Ryukyu (a group of islands between Japan and Taiwan) was under Chinese sovereignty and the incident was none of Japan's business. The Japanese pointed out that the Qing Dynasty had no control over the unnaturalized 'raw barbarians' beyond the reach of its government and customs and used this to justify an expedition of 3,600 soldiers to Mutan village in 1874. The Paiwan headhunters lost 30 men, while the Japanese lost 543

# THE HISTORY

and withdrew before the Qing Dynasty sent three divisions (9,000 soldiers) to reinforce Taiwan.

It wasn't until the defeat of the Chinese navy during the first Sino-Japanese war (1894–1895) that Japan was finally able to gain possession of Taiwan. Japanese colonization went in three stages:

1) An oppressive period of crackdown.

2) A period of *dōka*, treating all races alike.

3) A period of *kōminka*, to make the Taiwanese loyal subjects of the emperor.

The bank of Taiwan was established in 1899 to encourage Japanese private sectors, including Mitsubishi and the Mitsui Group, to invest in Taiwan. By 1905 Taiwan was financially self-sufficient, and the modernization of Keelung and Kaohsiung ports facilitated transport and shipping of raw material and agricultural products. Some people went along with Japanese rule and others were happy to become imperial subjects, but Chinese nationalists wanted to return Taiwan to Chinese rule. From 1897 onwards, they staged many rebellions, the most famous being led by Luo Fuxing, who was executed along with 200 of his comrades. Luo was a member of the Tongmenghui, a precursor to the Kuomintang (KMT).

While the Tongmenghui, or Revolutionary Alliance, weren't able to overcome the Japanese on Taiwan, on mainland China they were able to overthrow the Qing Dynasty and establish a Republic of China. The Guangxu Emperor died in 1908, followed by Dowager Cixi just a few days later, but not before she had appointed Puyi, a two-year-old boy and nephew of the Guangxu Emperor, as the new emperor. Empress Xiaodingjing, who had no children of her own, adopted Puyi and became the Empress Dowager Longyu (meaning Auspicious and Prosperous). Longyu became the leading figure in the Qing government and was consulted on all major decisions until the Xinhai Revolution in 1911, when she agreed to sign an abdication on behalf of five-year-old Puyi.

The KMT, or Nationalist Party of China, was founded by Song Jiaoren and Sun Yat-sen shortly after the Xinhai Revolution of 1911. Sun was revered as the Father of the Nation but he didn't have military power and ceded the provisional presidency of the republic to Yuan Shikai, who arranged the abdication of Puyi, the last emperor, on February 12, 1912. After Sun died in 1925, real power within the KMT fell to Chiang Kai-shek, who was trained in Russia and led the National Revolutionary Army. He succeeded in unifying much of China by 1928 and ended the chaos of the "warlord" era.

By this time, Taiwan had become a major food producer, serving Japan's industrial economy. In October 1935, the Governor-General of Taiwan held an Exposition to Commemorate the 40th Anniversary of the Beginning of Administration in Taiwan, to showcase Taiwan's modernization under Japanese rule. This attracted worldwide attention and the KMT in China sent the Japanese-educated Chen Yi to attend the affair. He expressed his admiration for Japanese efficiency and said how lucky the Taiwanese were to live under such effective administration. Ironically, Chen Yi would later become the ROC's first Chief Executive of Taiwan and would become infamous for the corruption that occurred during his watch.

As Japan embarked on full-scale war with China in 1937, Taiwan's industrial capacity expanded to manufacture war material. By 1939 industrial production exceeded agricultural production. At the same time, the *kōminka* project was under way, to ensure that the Taiwanese remained loyal subjects of the emperor. In 1942, after the United States entered the war on the side of China, the Chinese KMT government renounced all treaties with Japan and made Taiwan's return to China a wartime objective. In 1945 Japan surrendered unconditionally, which ended its rule in Taiwan.

Taiwan was placed under the administrative rule of China by the United Nations and, during the immediate post-war period, the KMT administration was repressive and extremely corrupt compared to the previous Japanese rule. This led to discontent and a crackdown by the KMT known as the White Terror—during which 140,000 people were imprisoned or executed for being perceived as anti-KMT. Many citizens were arrested, tortured, imprisoned, or executed for their real or perceived links to Communism. Since these people were mainly Taiwanese intellectuals, activists, and the social elite, an entire generation of political and social leaders disappeared off the face of the earth. It was comparable to the aftermath of the Tiananmen Square incident in mainland China in 1989.

From the 1930s onwards, the Chinese Civil War had been smoldering on the mainland between Chiang Kai-shek's KMT government and Mao Zedong's Communist Party. When the Communists gained complete control in 1949, two million refugees, predominantly from the KMT, fled to Taiwan. The People's Republic of China (PRC) was established on the mainland and Chiang Kai-shek set up a provisional, or "wartime", Republic of China (ROC) capital in Taipei and moved his government there from Nanjing. In 1949 Chiang Kai-shek declared martial law in Taiwan and, under KMT rule, the mainlanders would dominate Taiwan for many decades to come.

The KMT took control of Taiwan's monopolies that had been owned by the Japanese. They nationalized 17% of Taiwan's gross national product and voided Japanese bond certificates held by Taiwanese investors. Along with many national treasures and foreign currency reserves, the KMT government also moved the entire gold reserve from the Chinese mainland to Taiwan and used it to back the New Taiwan Dollar (NT$), stabilizing the new currency and putting a stop to hyperinflation.

From 1950 to 1965 Taiwan received a total of US$1.5 billion in economic aid and US$2.4 billion in military aid from the United States—mostly because the Americans didn't want the communists to expand their territorial dominance any further. During the 1950s the KMT implemented a far-reaching land reform program, redistributing land among small farmers and compensating large landowners with commodities certificates and stock in state-owned industries. Some turned their compensation into capital and started commercial and industrial enterprises. These entrepreneurs were to become Taiwan's first industrial capitalists and managed the country's transition from an agricultural to a commercial and financial economy. However, it was the KMT elite who benefited most, and many people remained oppressed and left behind by the Asian Tiger economy.

Rumors that have come down over the decades suggest that the combined assets of Chiang Kai-shek, his wife, and the KMT were greater than the entire annual GDP of China, at that time.

*1.1: Chinese Nationalists under Chiang Kai-shek*

*1.2: Chiang Kai-shek and wife*

## HISTORICAL OVERVIEW OF MEGA BANK

Mega International Commercial Bank Co. Ltd. came into being as a result of the merger between The International Commercial Bank of China and Chiao Tung Bank, on August 21 2006. Both banks had a long history in Taiwan and China.

The Bank of China's origins date back to the Ta Ching Bank and its predecessor, the Hupu Bank (under the financial arm of the Qing Dynasty imperial court); it was an agent of the treasury and a note-issuing bank before the establishment of the Central Bank of China in 1928. In 1971 the Bank of China was privatized to become the International Commercial Bank of China Co. Ltd. (ICBC) and, from then on, was a licensed specialized bank for international trade and foreign exchange.

Set up five years before the founding of the ROC (Taiwan), Chiao Tung Bank Co. Ltd. (CTB) was also delegated at the outset of the Republic to act as an agent of the government and as a note-issuing bank in conjunction with the Bank of China,. It transformed from a licensed bank for industry in 1928, to an industrial bank in 1975, and to a development bank in 1979, and turned from a state-controlled bank to a privately owned one in 1999. CTB has since engaged in loan extensions, equity investments, and venture capital.

CTB and International Securities Company formed the CTB Financial Holding Company in 2002. Later, Chung Hsing Bills Finance Corporation and Barits International Securities came under its control. On December 31, 2002, Chung Kuo Insurance Company and ICBC joined forces with CTB Financial Holdings to form a conglomerate called Mega Financial Holding Company.

On August 21, 2006, ICBC and CTB formally merged into one bank under the name of Mega International Commercial Bank Co. Ltd. By the end of 2015, in Taiwan the bank had 107 branches, and abroad it had 22 branches, five sub-branches, and five representative offices. There are also wholly owned bank subsidiaries in Thailand and Canada, bringing the number of overseas establishments to 39 in total. It employs almost 6,000 people and has an aggregate paid-in capital of NT$85.5 billion.

So, you can see how Mega Bank has been under the strong influence of the KMT, both as the Nationalist Party of mainland China and the governing power of Taiwan.

# CHAPTER 2
## THE TAIWANESE KUOMINTANG DYNASTY

IN THE PREVIOUS chapter, we outlined that part of the history of mainland China which gave rise to the Republic of China, otherwise known as Taiwan. While this book is not meant to be a history, political or otherwise, of Taiwan, Chapter 2 outlines a basic narration of recent events that will be useful to the reader.

Until the 1970s, the KMT's Republic of China was recognized as the sole legitimate government of mainland China by the United States and most Western nations, who refused to recognize the People's Republic of China because of the Cold War. The KMT continued to rule Taiwan under martial law, with the excuse of being vigilant against Communist infiltration and preparing to retake the mainland. They controlled the country under a one-party authoritarian state and political opposition wasn't tolerated. In 1971 the KMT government walked out of the United Nations (UN) when it recognized the PRC government in Beijing as the legitimate holder of China's UN seat. They'd been offered dual representation, but Chiang Kai-shek demanded a seat on the Security Council, which wasn't acceptable to the PRC. Chiang said 'the sky is not big enough for two suns' and the KMT was expelled from the UN and replaced by the PRC. In 1979 the United States switched recognition from Taipei to Beijing.

Chiang Kai-shek died in 1975 and was succeeded to the leadership of the KMT by his son, Chiang Ching-kuo, who opted to take the title of Chairman rather than his father's title of Director General. Chiang Ching-kuo was the head of the feared secret police, but under his administration there was a gradual loosening of political control and a transition toward democracy. Although opposition parties were still illegal, opponents of the KMT were no longer forbidden to hold meetings or publish papers. The Democratic Progressive Party (DPP) was formed at the end of 1986 and Chiang decided against dissolving the group or persecuting its leaders. In the following year Chaing ended martial law on the island of Taiwan and, after his death in 1988, his successor, Lee Teng-hui continued to democratize the government. Lee's reforms included printing banknotes from the Central Bank instead of the usual Provincial Bank of Taiwan, but he failed to crack down on the massive corruption that pervaded the government and many KMT loyalists felt that Lee was betraying the ROC by taking reforms too far, while the opposition felt he wasn't taking them far enough.

Lee ran as the incumbent in Taiwan's first direct presidential election in 1996, against DPP candidate Peng Min-ming, and won. During the later years of Lee's administration, he was involved in corruption controversies relating to government release of land and weapons purchases—although no legal proceedings were taken against him.

The 2000 presidential election marked the end of unbroken rule by the KMT. The DPP leader, Chen Shui-bian became ruler of Taiwan for the next eight years. On the day before victory in the 2004 election, Chen and vice-presidential candidate Annette Lu were shot at in a failed assassination attempt, orchestrated by the KMT. Two shots were fired, one bullet grazing the president's stomach after penetrating the windshield of a jeep and several layers of clothing. The second bullet also penetrated the windshield and hit a knee cast the vice president was wearing, due to an earlier injury. Their injuries weren't life threatening. Police said the most likely suspect was Chen Yi-hsiung, an unemployed person who blamed the president for his woes and who was later found dead. However, Annette Lu was convinced there were two shooters.

After 2000, the KMT began to divest itself of its assets to quell its financial difficulties. The transactions weren't disclosed and the whereabouts of the money earned from selling assets was unknown. During the DPP's presidency they proposed a law in the Legislative Yuan to recover illegally acquired party assets and return them to the government. However, due to the DPP's lack of control over the legislative chamber, the law never materialized. The KMT did acknowledge that some of its assets were acquired through 'extra-legal' means and they promised to 'retro-endow' them to the government. However, the amount of the assets deemed to be illegal was never established. The DPP claimed that it was much larger than was ever acknowledged and that the KMT were prepared to sell at below market rates rather than return the assets to the government. Details of those transactions were never publicly disclosed.

Domestic politics during the Chen administration were largely at a stalemate, as the KMT only held a slim majority in the legislature. Among the many items that made little progress due to the stalemate was banking reform legislation, which would have helped in the consolidation of the many banks in Taiwan. The constitution was amended in 2005 to create a two-vote electoral system, with single member plurality seats and proportional representative seats, and to abolish the National Assembly, transferring most of its former power to the Legislative Yuan, and leaving further amendment voting to public referendums.

Politics is an expensive game, and politicians need money and resources, especially when they've been in a love–hate relationship with the people for many decades. We've seen that the native Taiwanese, often thought of as "domesticated Taiwanese," were always the majority of people in Taiwan, whether indigenous or seafaring adventurers who settled. However, over the last 70 years, it has become obvious that a minority people had "invaded" Taiwan—the KMT who fled mainland China after their defeat by Mao Zedong's Communists in 1949. Ever since, Taiwan has undergone great political and economic experimentation and the greatest success of those experiments has been its system of direct elections. Taiwan's divisive political scene is complicated, due to the majority of voters being divided into ethnic groups. However, in only a few countries across the world do citizens elect their leaders in such a direct way.

In 2005 Ma Ying-jeou became KMT chairman and, in 2007, he was indicted by the Taiwan High Prosecutor's Office for allegedly embezzling US$340,000. But he was acquitted of all charges and immediately filed suit against the prosecutors. In 2006 the KMT sold its headquarters at 11 Zhongshan South Road in Taipei to Evergreen Group for US$96 million (almost half its market value) and moved into a smaller building on Bade Road, in the eastern part of the city.

In 2008 Ma Ying-jeou won the presidential election and jailed his predecessor, Chen Shui-bian of the DPP, after Chen and his wife were convicted on bribery charges. Chen spent six years in prison and his supporters insisted his trial was politically motivated retribution by the KMT for his eight years in power. When Ma Ying-jeou of the KMT became President of Taiwan in 2008 his wife, Christine Chow Ma (Madam Chow) became First Lady. Madam Chow was employed by Mega International Commercial Bank (Mega Bank) in Taiwan and her "employment" continued after her husband became president. She became Secretary of Mega International Foundation and former Mega Bank Chairman Lin Thon Yong became Chairman.

The power money has over the Taiwanese people is huge. Maintaining and sustaining a ruling party and local politicians requires a system, as well as money. Basic industries in Taiwan were almost all controlled by government money via banks and parastatal companies (e.g. Mega Bank, Taiwan Bank, Chang Hwa Bank, Hua Nan Bank, Taiwan Land Bank, Taiwan Co-op Bank, China Steel, Taiwan Power, China Petroleum Corp, Taiwan Sugar, Taiwan Beer, etc.). As the ruling party in Taiwan for many years, the KMT amassed this vast business empire of banks, investment companies, petrochemical firms, and television and radio stations. It became the world's richest political party, with assets once estimated to be between US$10 billion and US$50 billion (excluding long-term dividends and donations)—often referred to as black gold. They controlled the police and the Department of Justice and they became a dynasty, ruled by the same group, who used their financial power to control the country and the Taiwanese people—and in 2008 Madam Chow became the Empress of that dynasty.

There have been many ancient dynasties throughout the history of China—the Qing Dynasty, the Ming Dynasty, the Song Dynasty, and so on—as far back as history goes. Taiwan's modern political party system supports political dynasties in much the same way as the ancient dynasties were supported, only now it's done with votes, rather than despotism. The KMT Dynasty is a financial noblesse, not based on any aristocratic lineage, but on the pedigree of wealth. Politics is power, and money makes politics—a good example of money overruling moral conviction was the 2016 US presidential election. It leaves a bad taste in the mouth, as did the jailing of Chen Shui-bian by the KMT.

By 2010, this act of political revenge was beginning to haunt the KMT Dynasty. Fears of reprisal by the voters kept them awake at night—how were they going to keep their vast wealth if they lost power again? These fears became an obsession, even after Ma Ying-jeou won the presidential election in 2012. The DPP were gaining popularity once more and it was increasingly likely that they would win the 2016 election. In March and April 2014, students protesting against corruption and undemocratic methods used by the KMT, occupied the parliament building. In July 2014, the KMT reported total assets of US$892.4 million and interest earnings of NT$981.52 million, much of it suspected to be ill-gotten. Events like this were changing the mood of the electorate and the Taiwanese dynasty of Ma Ying-jeou and Madam Chow saw the writing on the wall. Just as Ma Ying-jeou had jailed

Chen Shui-bian and his wife, Madam Chow feared that the same revenge would be taken on her and her husband once they lost the protection of power.

The KMT Dynasty must have decided to get its money out of Taiwan, long before the inevitable happened. And let's not forget, Madam Chow was a lawyer at Mega Bank, Taiwan's largest bank, for over 25 years. She was a general counsel and had a comprehensive knowledge of banking transactions and legal procedures in Taiwan, in the United States, and in the jurisdictions of Taipei's diplomatic allies—such as Panama (a close ally where the ROC spent much money to maintain diplomatic relationships), mainland China, and the UK. Who better to ensure the financial survival of the KMT Dynasty? After carefully studying the global financial crisis of 2007–2009, it probably didn't take her long to figure out what to do. She could fully utilize her financial and legal expertise to ensure the survival of her family and the KMT.

The KMT were right to be worried. In January 2016 the DPP gained the presidential seat and a substantial victory in the Legislative Yuan, winning 68 of the 113 seats and an outright majority in parliament. The election marked the first time a non-KMT party had won a majority in the legislature. The DPP set up the Ill-Gotten Party Assets Settlement Committee to investigate KMT assets acquired during the martial law period and recover those that were determined to be illegally acquired.

But Madam Chow probably didn't wait until 2016 to plan the exodus of KMT funds from Taiwan—oh no, she probably began planning it as soon as she became Empress of the KMT Dynasty in 2008. That's when she and her accomplices began to see the "shipping" potential of my company, TMT Group.

## MA YING-JEOU'S BACKGROUND AND INTELLIGENCE SYSTEM

Let's talk about former President Ma Ying-jeou's heritage of political intelligence, which can be traced to his mother, Ms. Chin Hou-hsiu. In 1949 the Kuomintang lost the domestic war and Ms. Chin and her husband retreated to Hong Kong, where Ma Ying-jeou was born in 1950. In 1952, she followed her husband's family and came to Taiwan. She went directly to the Ministry of National Defense and worked as a statistician in the General Political Department (later renamed the General Political Warfare Bureau in 1963) of the Ministry of National Defense. Later, Ms. Chin served as the director of the Business Department of the Central Bank Foreign Exchange Bureau because of her statistical and commercial background. It seems to me that this was an excellent arrangement to give KMT access to the nation's treasury.

Chin Hou-hsiu (November 19, 1922–May 2, 2014), was born in Ninxiang, Hunan Province. She served as a Lieutenant Colonel of the Republic of China, was a civil servant, a member of the Chinese Kuomintang, a staff member of the Shihmen Reservoir Management Bureau of Taiwan and mother of the former President of the Republic of China, Ma Ying-jeou.

Chin's father Chin Cheng Zhi once served as the head of the third section of The National Bureau of Investigation and Statistics, responsible for spying, reactionaries, assassination, and so on. After retreating to Taiwan following the KMT, he was appointed as the chief secretary of the police radio station and the editor-in-chief of its magazine.

2.1 Oh, those were the glorious days

# CHAPTER 3
## THE FINANCIAL DYNASTY

THE KMT PARTY'S assets started with the Big Four Families in the ROC: Kong, Song, Chiang and Chen. Mr. Chen Boda had once said that, in the early ROC, when the Big Four Families were in power, they had accumulated over US$20 billion in assets and monopolized the lifeblood of China's economy. In 1949 China's GDP was about US$18 billion. In 1993 Victor W. Liu, General Manager of Central Investment Holding Co. Ltd., pointed out that over 40-plus years of operation the KMT party had accumulated a total of NT$963.9 billion. Since the KMT party's retreat to Taiwan in 1949, their investments had included industries that had received Japan's post-war assets and were specially licensed in a party-state system.

The investments can be divided into seven major holding companies, including Central Investment Holding Co. Ltd., Kuang-Hwa Investment Holding Co. Ltd., Chien Hwa Investment Co. Ltd., Hua Hsia Investment Holding Co., and so on. The number of specially licensed and non-licensed companies have been over 300. For simplicity, I've called this conglomerate of holding companies the China Investment Fund.

The following is from Wikipedia on Central Investment Holding Co. Ltd.

> Major reinvestment companies (finance, petrochemicals, general, overseas business, securities investment): Mega Bills Finance Co. Ltd., International Bills Finance Corp, Central Insurance Co. Ltd., Taiwan Styrene Monomer Corporation, CAPCO, Chung-Hsin Electric &

Machinery Mfg. Corp, Oriental Union Chemical Corp., CDIB Capital Group, Fuh Hwa Financial Holdings Co. Ltd. (now: Yuanta Commercial Bank), Kaohsiung Business Bank, CTCI Corp., Chien Tai Cement Co. Ltd., Hsing Ta Cement Co. Ltd., Asia Cement Holdings Corporation, Shin Natural Gas, Tait Marketing & Distribution Co. Ltd., ZyXEL, Far Eastern Air Transport, International Venture Investment, Singfor life Insurance Co. Ltd., Global Investment Holdings Co. Ltd., China Investment and Development Co. Ltd., Onyx Ta-ho Energy Recovery Co. Ltd., Feng Shui Construction Co. Ltd., Han Yang Construction Co. Ltd., Yong Chang Construction Co. Ltd., Hong Chi Construction Co. Ltd., Chi Siang Industrial Co. Ltd., Chong Hwei Construction Co. Ltd., Chin Tai Construction Co. Ltd., Kuang-Hwa Investment Holding Co. Ltd.

The main reinvestment companies (energy technology): Fuh Hwa Financial Holding Co. Ltd. (now: Yuanta Commercial Bank), Hsin Kao Gas Co. Ltd., Shin Hsiung Natural Gas Inc., Hsin Tai Gas Co. Ltd., Shin Nan Natural Gas Co. Ltd., Safwy Gas Co. Ltd., San Shing Fastech Corp., Shin Co. Ltd., Far Eastern Air Transport Corporation, United Microelectronic Corp., Twinhead International Corp. Hua Hsia Investment Holding Co. Ltd.

The main reinvestment companies (culture): China Television Company, Broadcasting Corporation of China, Central Motion Pictures Corporation, Central Daily, China Daily News, Cheng Chung Book Store, Shin Her, Chi Sheng Investment Co. Ltd., Chunghwa Picture Tubes Ltd., Central Motion Pictures Corporation.

The main reinvestment companies (construction): Feng Shui Construction Co. Ltd., Han Yang Construction Co. Ltd., Yong Chang Construction Co. Ltd., Hong Chi Construction Co. Ltd., Chi Siang Industrial Co. Ltd., Chong Hwei Construction Co. Ltd., Chin Tai Construction Co. Ltd., China Development Financial Holdings Co. Ltd. Chien Hwa Investment Co. Ltd.

The main reinvestment companies (finance): Bank SinoPac, China Development Financial Holdings Co. Ltd., CTBC Bank, Mega Bills Finance Co. Ltd., Kaohsiung Business Bank, CTCI Corp., Asia Pacific Holding Corp., Cathay Life Insurance Co. Ltd., China Development Financial Holdings Co. Ltd.

The main shipping and airline companies: Taiwan Navigation Corporation, China Airlines, Yan Ming Line, China Shipbuilding Corporation.

The main reinvestment companies (overseas investments): New Horizon, Asia Pacific Holding Corp., Liberia, Great Star Singapore, Chang Tai Investment Co. Ltd., Jing De Investment.

Others: Yu Hwa Development Co. Ltd., Shuang Yuan Investment Co. Ltd., Zhung Yuan Construction Co. Ltd., Feng Yuan Construction Co. Ltd., Chiloo Industries Inc, Yu Tai Industries Co. Ltd., Yu Tai Development Industries Co. Ltd., Sheng Chang Investment and Consultancy Co. Ltd., Palasia Hotel Palau, Japan Taiwan Trade Development Co., CIH(BV), KOPPEL, APH Investment and New Horizon. Natural gas suppliers include 12 companies, namely: Shin Lung, Shin, Shin Yun, Shin Chia, Shin Nan, Shin Ying, Hsin Kao (HK), Shin Hsiung, Shin Ping (SP), Hsin Tai, Shin Zee (SZ), Shin Chung.

## THE PRINCELINGS ACROSS THE STRAIT

The story begins with the Four Princes of the KMT in the 1970s and 1980s in Taiwan. The following shows the relations between the second generations of the KMT's prominent and influential senior officials in the financial system of China and Hong Kong:

Frederick Chien (Chien Foo). Representative to the United States, ROC (November 19, 1982—July 20, 1990). Minister of Foreign Affairs, ROC (May 30, 1990—June 8, 1996). Currently: Cathay Bank Director, Cathay Foundation Chairman.

His son, Carl Chien (born December 10, 1964). Education: MBA, Georgetown University. Vice President, Asset Management, Morgan Stanley (Wall Street) (1994–1997). Executive Director, Goldman Sachs (1997–2002). General Manager, Taiwan Region, JPMorgan Chase Bank, in charge of the "Cathay Bank Merger" in August 2002. President, Taiwan Region, JPMorgan Chase Bank (February 2004). Chairman, President, Asia-Pacific Region and Taiwan Region, JPMorgan Chase Bank (2017).

Lien Chan, Minister of Foreign Affairs, ROC (July 20, 1988–May 30, 1990). Governor, Taiwan Provincial Government, ROC (June 15, 1990–February 27, 1993). Premier, ROC (February 27, 1993–August 31, 1997). Vice President, ROC (May 20, 1996–May 20, 2000).

His son, Lien Sheng-Wu (born in 1974). Currently Chairman, Shin Capital; Executive Director, Toipo Capital Management; Executive Director, Toipo Equity Investment, Bank of China Tianjin Branch; Director, SinoPac Securities Corporation.

Other son, Lien Sheng-Wen (Sean Lien) (born in 1970). Executive Director, Asia Pacific Capital fund, GE Ventures. Vice President, Morgan Stanley. Director, Bank SinoPac (January 2011—June 2014).

Chen Li-an, Minister of Economic Affairs (July 20, 1998–June 1, 1990). Minister of National Defense (June 1, 1990 - February 1, 1993). President of the Control Yuan (February 1, 1993–September 23, 1995). Chairman, Fu Yu Venture Capital Fund (from 2002 to now).

Daughter, Chen Yu-hui (Yu-hwei Chen) (born in 1973). Currently working in ABN AMRO HK.

In addition to the above, former Vice President Vincent C. Siew's (Siew Wan-chang) son, Jhih-you Siew, currently serves as Chief Executive of Mainland Policy, Taiwan Industrial Bank. Former Vice President Wu Den-yih's son works in Hong Kong's financial circle. Chiang Pin-kung's children are currently doing business in China, so they are called the Princelings across the Strait.

Next, let's talk about the former KMT President Ma Ying-jeou, whose motto was 'gentle, kind, respectful, frugal, and courteous.' He seemed to be gentle and elegant, but actually he had an unquenchable thirst for power, which we can figure out from the asset-related and financial-related scandals exposed by the media during Ma's presidency, these include:

**1. Taipei Dome project:** Ma Ying-jeou hurriedly signed the Taipei Dome build-operate-transfer contract with Far Glory Group before leaving office. Prosecutors should investigate this project for potential illegal moves.

**2. Broadcasting Corporation of China (BCC) case:** Under Ma Ying-jeou's meticulous design, four short-term companies were established by Jaw Shaw-kong to conduct fake transactions with Hua Hsia Investment Holding Co. They acquired BCC without effort and the entire transaction process was under the table.

**3. Central Motion Pictures Corporation (CMPC) "dog-eat-dog" case:** The KMT party sold CMPC under the table, and its former president Alex Tsai (Tsai Cheng-yuan) and former vice president Chuang Wan-chun excused each other because 'dog eats dog.'

**4. China Television Company money-laundering case:** The KMT party sold the 3C companies, such as China Television Company, BCC, and CMPC, which were worth more than US$15.2 billion in total, at a price of US$4 billion to Rongli Investment Company. It was clearly indicated in the contract that the buyer would pay a certain amount of 'sharing profit,' that is, the final selling price would be decided based on the future actual price of these estates. It involved potential money laundering.

**5. National Development Research Institute Land-selling case:** Ma Ying-jeou sold the Institute's land to

Yuanli Construction at a price of US$4.25 billion. A proviso was added to the contract that the KMT would be responsible for completing the application for changing the urban plan and the purpose of the land to residential use before the transaction. "Mayor" Ma is suspected of profiting "Chairman" Ma.

**6. Taipei Bank:** over-lending to BCC case.

**7. Mega Bank New York:** money-laundering case.

**8. Ching Fu Shipbuilding:** bank fraud case.

Ma Ying-jeou, Minister of Justice, ROC (1993). Mayor of Taipei, ROC (1998). President, ROC (2008—2014).

Allen Tsai (son-in-law) worked at Deutsche Bank, currently working at JP Morgan Chase Hong Kong, and lives in Hong Kong.

Ma's wife, Christine Chow Ma (Chow Mei-ching) worked at the Mega International Commercial Bank in Taiwan in its legal department.

Therefore, at a critical moment when the world is paying close attention to money laundering and the international financial order, and if Taiwan cannot get rid of the party-state system, while the KMT has access to the nation's treasury the interests of financial groups will take precedence over the state's interests and any conflict with the interests of the renowned families and the KMT officials' second generations are avoided.

But exposure is always just one step away.

*3.1: KMT ill-gotten asset building in Taipei*

# CHAPTER 4
## THE BEGINNING OF THE SCAM

THE STORY OF me (Nobu Sue) converting A Whale, a supertanker of mine, to skim oil after the notorious British Petroleum (BP) spillage in the Macondo Well has not been told—at least not correctly. The Macondo Prospect was a BP-operated oil and gas well in the US Exclusive Economic Zone of the Gulf of Mexico. The Prospect was the site of the Deepwater Horizon drilling rig explosion in April 2010 that caused the largest oil spill in human history. To help clean up the spillage, I spent millions of dollars converting my A Whale tanker into the world's biggest skimming vessel, which could suck up oily seawater, use a Weir system to separate off the oil, and deposit the cleansed organic water back into the sea.

We had successfully collected one million barrels of oil and seawater mixture. However, the separation process didn't work because of a specific gravity difference (seawater is 1.025 and oil is less than 0.85) and separating the different gravities was impossible due to the secret injection of untold amounts of dispersant by BP, which broke the oil into small droplets. The design of the A Whale conversion had been based on dark and sticky oil samples without any dispersant. But it worked in principle and has been accepted as a success, albeit grudgingly, by technicians and engineers who know what they're talking about. I don't intend to delve too deeply into this story, but the event made such an impact that, even today, litigation continues in hundreds of BP legal disputes.

The US government issued a new law right after the Macondo spill which stated that nobody could collect oil within a certain distance from the Gulf Coast. This was told to me by Mr Frank Peeples in Savannah, Georgia, who had a huge business network in US coastal logistics, warehousing, and transportation. Consequently, my contact in America couldn't send me appropriate oil/dispersant samples and that affected the conversion process in the initial design—it would've taken a month to adapt the skimming system on A Whale. Notwithstanding, eight US Naval Institute specialists came aboard A Whale to freely gather information on how the skimming process worked in the world's largest coated tanker. It was only possible to skim oil with a coated tanker. A normal very large crude carrier (VLCC) has no coating so, after oil skimming, the vessel would no longer be suitable to carry oil. This is why my design for the world's largest oil-skimming tanker was an epoch-making challenge.

*4.1: Fully coated tanker, A Whale*

An A Whale patent was filed, but I decided to allow the world to use the technology in the event of future oil spills. Later on, in 2015, the US government and the American Bureau of Shipping quietly built, with our knowledge, two Aframax tankers for responding to oil spill disasters, capable of skimming, adapting the technology they acquired aboard A Whale to the US oil spill response program.

On June 20, 2010, when I was on board the A Whale navigation deck, my office called and told me that representatives of Mega International Commercial Bank had visited TMT's Taipei office and met with Green Huang, TMT Group's Chief Financial Officer. Mega Bank's International Department Deputy Head, Chan Tin-Hwa, and two young Chinatrust bankers were interested in building a financial relationship with TMT.

'Nobu is the Shining Star of Taiwan, as far as we're concerned. We want to lend him money.'

I answered from the A Whale's satellite telephone.

'This is great news.'

I told my office to ensure the documentation was in order and went ahead with a US$84 million loan for C Whale, the sister vessel of A Whale. We had just finished a US$25 million loan for A Duckling, a nine-year-old, cape size bulk carrier (Corporation in Panama, a Panamanian-flagged vessel). The A Duckling transaction was concluded in April 2010 with Mega Bank, the contract being signed after only three weeks negotiation, but the syndication of the C Whale loan by Mega Bank and Chinatrust began two months later.

It would be useful here to explain that each ship has its own corporation—in other words, a company is set up for each ship where that ship is registered. It's standard maritime procedure and is used for administrative purposes—to manage corporate taxation and other maritime regulations where that ship is registered, rather than where the ship is owned and operates. Consequently, A Duckling (ship) will have a corresponding A Duckling Corporation; C Whale (ship) will have a corresponding C Whale Corporation. In other words, the vessel itself is responsible for payment of liens or mortgages. When an owner encumbers a vessel with a ship's mortgage, it is the ship itself that guarantees payment, rather than the owner.

Mega Bank, which was Taiwan's largest bank in 2010, was 20% owned by the Taiwan government, 20% owned by Chinatrust Bank (controlled by the Jeffrey Koo family), and the other 60% was publicly owned. When I returned from the USA and visited them in Taipei in August 2010, the bankers were very welcoming and saluted me as a hero of Taiwan. They expressed full support for my business and wanted to finance my Whale ships and make TMT the number one shipping fleet in the region. The Chinatrust bankers were very aggressive in offering terms and no KYC (know your customer) processing was carried out. There were five conditions:

1) 7% cash deposit of the entire loan, payable in advance.

2) My personal guarantee.

3) Issue a corporate Taiwanese check.

4) Each ship owning company in Panama, Marshall Islands, and Liberia as borrower.

5) TMT corporate guarantees.

The banks would then meet TMT's future financing requirements with favorable terms. This was in complete contrast to the Western financial markets, where the banks had just been through the 2007–2009 crisis and a credit crunch was in operation.

The Chinatrust bankers drew up a prospectus for a syndicated Whale loan, which involved my unique design. There were several patents involved:

Oil pipes built in underneath the deck, for loading and discharging—on a standard ship, they're all exposed on deck.

Hybrid propulsion—not granted at that time, but already built in.

Hybrid discharging pump—not granted at that time, but already built in.

## THE BEGINNING OF THE SCAM

The syndication (a loan offered by a group of lenders) required by the banks was probably at the behest of Madam Chow (aka Christine Chow), wife of Taiwan President Ma Ying-jeou. I later heard some banking CEOs refer to her by the nickname 'Ta Chie,' which translates into English as Big Mama.

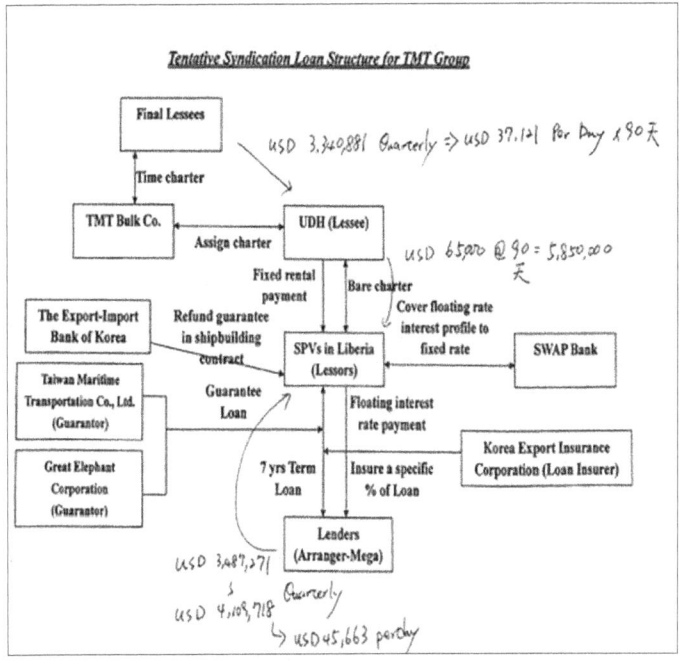

*4.2 Tentative syndication loan structure for TMT Group*

However, the loan documents didn't include a securities description, containing the usual details of a ship's particulars. Neither did they include the proper pledge documents, only the corporate finance paperwork as if it was a single corporation loan. Corporate finance is quite different to the normal ship asset-based finance. This made TMT Group a target in the event of a default—the target of the Panamanian Corporation. In other words, the ship's corporation, registered in Panama, could pass on responsibility to TMT (Taiwan). A default with a corporate guarantee would also allow the lenders to do whatever they wanted in the creation of subsidiary companies. Shares could be sold to parties in Panama, the banks could take over TMT and its guarantor in the Panamanian Corporation and change the chairman and directors, and even bring an Article of Incorporation to open the accounts, if it had such intentions.

The most suspicious thing was that the name of the small law firm, Ding & Ding, appeared on the front page of the A Duckling loan documents. Ding & Ding was the law firm that handled most of the legal cases for President Ma Ying-jeou and his family dynasty, rather than the larger law firm of Lee & Li, which had offices in the headquarters of Formosa Plastics Corp. on Dung Hwa North Road. A later analysis of the A Duckling loan documents, produced by the Mayer Brown law firm in Hong Kong, concluded that these were not normal ship finance documents. They were supposed to be professional corporate loan documents, beyond the normal remit of Ding & Ding (just for information, their email address was dingandding@gmail.com, it seems very odd for a "major" legal firm to have a gmail address?). We believed it to be a US$40 million ship value with a US$25 million loan—in actual fact, it was designed to trigger the default clause and initiate the Article of Incorporation.

This is where it gets a little complicated. In 2008 TMT had sold a cape size vessel called A Duckling, registered under a Panama flag, to Star Bulk Carriers (SBLK on Nasdaq). Petros Pappas and I were co-chairmen of Star Bulk at the time and the ship was sold as a Pappas-controlled vessel (with the uniquely named Vinyl Corporation as intermediary). In 2009, TMT bought a younger cape size ship, also called A Duckling and used the same A Duckling Corporation. The old A Duckling was sold to a Pappas private company after I'd left the board of Star Bulk, and there's some mystery surrounding the transaction, which was handled by the Panama law firm of Quijano & Associates and others.

The A Duckling finance of US$25 million was paid to TMT Panama S.A.—so then Mega Bank knew of the existence of TMT Panama S.A. and could use Mayer Brown LLP to create TMT Panama S.A. as secondary creditor, with Ugly Duckling Panama (we gave shares to Mega) as English guarantor. Considering Mega Bank's huge influence and freedom to do what it liked in Panama—Taiwan maintained great diplomatic relations with Panama, which had Mega's largest overseas banking unit outside Taiwan—it is highly possible that Mega Bank's lawyers and Pappas' lawyers made contact with each other in the Panama registry to figure out how to delete the old A Duckling name and use the same name for the new vessel. When the first A Duckling mortgage (loan) was registered for US$25 million, there must have been back and forth communication between Mega Bank and Petros Pappas, directly or indirectly through the lawyers.

Let me explain. The Mega Bank/Pappas connection was in the two A Duckling ships. TMT sold the old A Duckling, built in 1991, to Star Bulk in 2007. A few years later, Petros Pappas sold it on to his subsidiaries after it had been renamed, but it maintained the Panama flag. The A Duckling deal involved the A Duckling Corporation, which was retained by TMT when we bought the new ship in 2009. The new ship was then given the similar name of A Duckling under the A Duckling Corporation. When Pappas tried to delete the A Duckling name from the old ship, several lawyers in Panama must have contacted A Duckling Corporation—since A Duckling Corporation's entire shares were already pledged to Mega Bank, under the terms of the loan. This sounds really convoluted, doesn't it? However, it's pretty standard stuff to aficionados of maritime finance and procedure.

And so, we became vulnerable to Mega creating many corporate accounts in Panama and London. My question is, what happened to the A Duckling Corporation shares and registry and the articles of incorporation of Ugly Duckling? Are they with the Panama Canal lawyers? Someone must know.

I don't know the full extent of the connection and collusion between Pappas and Mega Bank, but I do know that many law firms were involved at the time, all dealing with the matter in one way or another: Quijano & Associates, Aries Law, Morgan & Morgan PA, the Panama Canal lawyers and others.

Another strange occurrence involved my C Whale ship. As I've said, while I was in Macondo, this vessel (which cost US$155 million to build) concluded a US$84 million loan arranged by Mega Bank and Chinatrust Bank. Chan Tin-Hwa of Mega and two Chinatrust bankers wrote the prospectus, including the underdeck piping, and they knew it was a very good investment. However, two weeks later, while I was still on board the A Whale and busy oil skimming, some rather suspect extra documents were required by the banks. I got a telephone call from Green Huang, my CFO, and I had no alternative but to accept an addendum on the loan agreement—had I been in Taiwan I might not have agreed. What happened was that strange additional documents were inserted into the derivative agreement, which were never discussed and which were never agreed to in the contract. Three pages were added, allowing seven banks to trade in derivatives. Is this not evidence that proves the TMT loan was money sourced from the "China Investment Fund" (which is what I call the KMT conglomerate of holding companies), to be used by Mega Bank a few days before the loan was arranged for C Whale?

To me, at least, it proves that the loan was arranged to move money overseas from Taiwan for the China Investment Fund. It looks very like they were using loans made to my TMT company to get their cash out of Taiwan without anyone knowing.

Why the China Investment Fund?

Because the China Investment Fund refers to the ROC, which is the official KMT title for Taiwan. Also, because it controls all the KMT cash and investments and it functions, like the old feudal system of the Chinese emperors, on three levels:

1) The Lords—the KMT elite

# THE BEGINNING OF THE SCAM

2) The Vassals—those who support the lords in exchange for privileges

3) The Serfs—the general workforce who produce the wealth by their work.

Wealth flows to 1) in the form of taxes, some of which is given to 2) as a reward for their control of 3). It's a simple formula that has worked in China for 5,000 years and which is still in operation today.

So, you can see what was probably happening. If the money being loaned to TMT by Mega Bank to build or purchase ships, actually belonged to the KMT in Taiwan, when that money was paid back with interest, or retrieved by forcing TMT into default and selling its ships, it was not returned to Taiwan, but was deposited abroad in China Investment Fund (KMT) accounts. This is money laundering and it is very likely how the KMT "shipped" (if you'll pardon the pun) its allegedly ill-gotten liquified assets out of Taiwan, without anyone suspecting what was going on.

*4.3: Petros Pappas*

# CHAPTER 5
## BIG MAMA'S INVISIBLE HAND

THERE WERE 46 banks licensed by the Ministry of Finance in Taiwan—syndicate finance went to over 20 banks, almost half of all Taiwanese banks. They strictly followed the, so-called, guidelines of the Ministry, part of which was the nomination of their CEOs. The person who decided who those CEOs would be was controlled by President Ma Ying-jeou and the First Lady, Madam Chow—aka Big Mama. Consequently, it was common knowledge that Big Mama's invisible hand worked throughout the top management of those banks, either through the Ministry of Finance guidelines or through a discreet sharing of business practices and culture. The banking industry was heavily regulated, and the nomination of CEOs only came with the government's blessing, so CEOs were under government control. In fact, the regulators' offices were next to the banks in Kaohsiung, Taichung, and other major cities—it was a revolving door scenario. Small government-controlled banks, from the Bank of Kaohsiung to Taichung Commercial Bank, always did loan syndication to cover their risks.

As I said, the syndicated A Duckling loan went to over 20 of those banks. Looking at it today, it's obvious there was something strange about the whole TMT ship financing process. All the documents were initially set up as financing A Duckling Panama Corporation, but they were signed and drawn down at the end of 2011 for A Whale, and signed and drawn down at the end of 2010 for B Whale. The lawyers concerned were all connected, just like the banks—firms such as Mayer Brown LLP, Johnson Stokes & Master LLP, Ding & Ding, and Formosa Translational Attorneys at Law were all involved in one loan process. Normally, one law firm handles the entire loan, but in TMT cases, Mega Bank had requested several banks' involvement. Highly suspect—I mean, you can't have this level of intrigue within banks without the collaboration of associated services, such as accountants and lawyers. Can you?

Big Mama had tremendous power in the financial world. She nominated or changed the heads of many banks and one such nomination was McKinney Tsai. Tsai was Vice President of Mega Bank from 2006, assisting the merger of Chiao Tung Bank into Mega International Commercial Bank. He visited New York many times, either alone or with Madam Chow, to finalize the set up of Mega Bank's New York branch, which had the same address as the Central Bank of China, Taipei. A special license, called Regulation K, was even given by the Bush administration to several Taiwan banks, including Mega Bank, Chinatrust, Shanghai Commercial Savings Bank, and Cathay United Bank. It offered guidelines for bank holding companies engaged in international transactions.

I was introduced to McKinney Tsai by Chan Tin-Hwa of Mega Bank in August 2010, after I came back from the Deepwater Horizon oil spill. Tsai had been made CEO of Mega Bank in April 2010 (the same time as the first A Duckling deal with Mega Bank), as a reward for his diligence and loyalty to the dynasty. They sent a person who loved golf to a man who also loved golf. Was this a coincidence? I think not, they obviously knew my story and believed they could make use of me. McKinney Tsai visited my offices and I gave him a tour for about 30 minutes.

'Do you play golf, Nobu?'

'Of course.'

It was well known in Taiwan that I played golf. A few days later, I was invited to Mega Bank's offices to meet him again.

His manner was friendly and we amicably discussed how the bank worked.

'You borrow money from the bank, the bank charges interest. You pay the bank's profit margin plus the agreed interest, then we lend you the money to finance your ships, as many as you like. Simple.'

I was impressed by his brainpower, quick wit, charisma, and charm. We kept in close contact after that and, if I had any issues, I could see him again, even at short notice, in the chairman's office.

The Sue–Tsai relationship was well known within the bank. He and his wife were invited to Whale ship-naming ceremonies and he even gave speeches on occasion. His right-hand lady, Ms Chen, was invited several times to Hyundai Heavy Industries in Ulsan, Korea. McKinney Tsai and I played golf more than 80 times over a two-year period and I became his golf tutor, teaching him the finer aspects of the game. I was curious about his non-compliance business culture. At international meetings and dinner parties, general managers and branch managers tried to obtain preapproval for lending activities. It was a whispering culture to which he never committed himself and I wondered just how much power he really had.

One day, I asked him why he hadn't made a move to merge with other banks and create a truly global institution, big enough to compete with Wall Street or the City of London. He told me it was Madam Chow's and the government's decision, not his.

'With my small salary, Nobu, I don't want to do it.'

I was surprised by his faux humility.

'I grew up in a small town in the south, this is enough achievement for me.'

There was a hint of cynicism in his smile.

Despite his tongue-in-cheek self-abasement, I respected McKinney Tsai's achievements. Taiwan's global banking network was very fragile, as the country didn't have official diplomatic relations with many nations, despite being in the top 20 as far as GDP was concerned. The conversion of New Taiwan dollars into US dollars, euros, yen, pounds, and so on, required skill and diplomacy because many banks needed the protection of a political relationship, which they didn't have. McKinney Tsai walked a skilful tightrope through the global financial jungle and Mega Bank's New York branch was approved to be an intermediary bank for clearing US dollars and for opening investment banks under its umbrella. No mean feat for someone who 'grew up in a small town in the south.'

*5.1: McKinney Tsai (© Liberty Times)*

As well as appointing CEOs, Big Mama was able to distribute power to her family. In 2012, her eldest daughter, Lesley Ma, married Allen Pei-Jan Tsai, a Taiwanese-American fashion model who also had extensive connections in the banking community. From 2006 to 2008, he worked in Hong Kong for RREEF, a real estate affiliate of Deutsche Bank, with people such as Soo Cheon Lee, of SC Lowy, and other young bankers. After his marriage to Lesley Ma, Allen Tsai moved to JPMorgan Chase (JPMC) in Hong Kong and was involved in major financial deals. It's said that he didn't even have to come into JPMC's office, he was allowed to 'work from home.' It was commonplace in Hong Kong for firms to hire the sons or daughters of top officials from mainland China and Taiwan, to develop business in the Greater China area. This was one of the reasons JPMC was fined US$264 million for Office of Foreign Assets Control (OFAC) violations in the summer of 2016.

But we'll cover that later.

The case of Chinatrust Bank, owned by the Koo family, was even more blatant. Jeffery Koo Sr., former Chairman of Chinatrust Bank, which owned 20% of Mega Bank, had had strong ties to Taiwan's political insiders ever since the Japanese colonial era. His son, Jeffery Koo Jr., was a big player in the Taiwan economy: he purchased China Development Bank at a very low price; purchased Tokyo Star (Japan) Bank from a New York hedge fund; purchased 18% of shares in the Mega International Bank merger with Chiao Tung Bank; purchased a securities company; and created the KGI group (The Koos Group), including KGI Bank. The Koos Group is a Pan-Asian business group involved in a vast range of industries, including banking, manufacturing, petrochemicals, electronics, leasing, cement, financial services, hospitality, real estate, private equity, and investment banking. Reporting on insider dealings was taboo for journalists in Taiwan, as the media moguls they worked for were part of the same circle. If people had dug into awkward issues, they would've opened a Pandora's box and exposed many scandals.

Some would argue that it's only possible to engage in amicable business on a small island like Taiwan with the blessing and involvement of political insiders, and it's probably true that McKinney Tsai knew he could only make deals with the blessing of Big Mama's invisible hand. To counteract that argument, I would say that cabalism doesn't happen only in

Taiwan, but that it is widespread throughout the world—and that's financially unhealthy.

The mortgage to TMT was initially a 100% loan from two banks—Chinatrust and Mega International Commercial Bank. Then, within two weeks of drawdown, it was split into a number of syndications, without informing TMT. The other banks involved in the syndication were First Bank, Shanghai Commercial Savings Bank, Bank SinoPac, Cathay United Bank, and a few more government-controlled banks. This is very suspicious in itself, that a loan from two main banks could then be owned by a number of minor banks controlled by the China Investment Fund—which, as I've said, was simply the umbrella term for KMT assets.

It's my firm belief that Big Mama's invisible hand was always involved in the plan to finance TMT Group's ships—right from the beginning, when I was originally contacted on the navigation deck of A Whale and offered finance to expand my business. It's not difficult to find out information about a company's situation, experience, and networks in the domestic and global shipping industry. The final piece of the plan was put into place at the end of 2011, to complete Cathay United Bank's financing of one of the world's largest and fastest RO-RO/PCTC (roll-on/roll-off—pure car and truck carrier) vessels, called A Ladybug. Most likely, Big Mama had already instructed her CEOs to lend money to specific vessels that TMT was building at Hyundai Heavy Industries, the world's largest shipyard in Korea.

When you think about it, this is a unique way to launder money—in fact, default would be a quicker method than repayment for the China Investment Fund to get its money safely deposited outside of Taiwan. For that purpose, six important actions were needed:

1) Create strict default terms (sudden death with no mitigation time whatsoever), so that, when default occurs, the loan can be controlled.

2) Request the borrower to pay his own cash to retention accounts before drawdown of the loan. This means a fund could be set up to receive money from other sources, or the fund could be used as the bank's own money to borrow through the credit creation system. So, the entire loan is not maintained in the bank's own balance sheet. This is possible because of the power of the political party involved.

3) Then don't inform the borrower of the retention accounts' daily and monthly statements, so the borrower believes it's an untouchable cash deposit in the form of a pledge. No interest is earned and no financial statement needs to be given to auditors or the borrower, so it can be designed to be used easily as the bank's own money under the borrower's account(s).

4) Make sure the loan period for new shipbuilding is seven years and not 15 years, so the chance of default is very high. Using this structure, the bank can use the borrower's balance sheet and not its own.

5) The bank should not do KYC procedure before lending the money.

6) Make sure many banks are involved in the syndication—spread it all around the Taiwan banking system so that channels to move money open up.

Major Taiwanese banks then quickly became involved in syndicated loans for 16 of TMT Group's ships.

For example, Shanghai Commercial Savings Bank had followed the KMT to Taiwan in the 1940s, even though it had been established for 90 years in Shanghai. The bank never did KYC but started to lend TMT US$50 million exposures for three small bulk carriers and one Panamax ship called B Max, a mid-sized cargo ship capable of passing through the lock chambers of the Panama Canal. TMT had built a total of nine of the largest Panamax ships in the world. The bank had been involved in many ship loans and never did any KYC, nor did it create a cash flow model to repay the loan over 12–15 years of normal shipping finance.

Another example is Bank SinoPac, which, on December 31, 2011, just before the end of the bank's fiscal year, signed a contract with TMT for a US$90 million loan—a 100% loan by a single bank. They, oddly, requested the operator (Blue Whale Corporation) to open an account at Bank SinoPac's Hong Kong branch and not the Taiwan branch. It's like this, if you open an account and lend money in Taiwan, then request payment back to Hong Kong, you can theoretically move money from Taiwan to Hong Kong. Bank SinoPac was connected to Lien Chan, who was Vice President of Taiwan and the number two figure in the KMT.

The same thing happened with a First Bank loan—First Bank was the second largest government-owned bank after Taiwan Bank. The loan was also executed at the end of the fiscal year and the loan documents also created by the law firm Ding & Ding.

As the nomination of the CEOs of the top 20 banks only came with the KMT's blessing, it's not surprising that Madam Chow had tremendous control and power in the financial world. CEO's were very likely under her control through shareholding schemes and the regulatory revolving door—the feudal system again. McKinney Tsai was one of those people. He was Vice President of Mega Bank in 2006 and became CEO in 2011, in appreciation for his hard work—was part of that work playing golf with me and lulling me into a false sense of credulity?

## CHRISTINE MA'S (MADAM CHOW) AND CLOSE FRIENDS' LOAN AGENDA

2010: Closing December 29 in Taiwan, Bank SinoPac 100%, asked to open a Hong Kong account on first day of drawdown.

2011: Closing December 29 in Taiwan, First Bank 100%, must close before end of year—equity needed.

2012: Q3, July 1, request other securities for 2011 unsecured loan.

2012: Q4, loan of US$250 million from Chinatrust Commercial Bank, Mega Bank syndications given to Macquarie Bank.

2012: November 22, Macquarie Bank used the money provided by Chinatrust and Mega Bank to buy A Ladybug loans—approved POA (power of attorney) issued in Sydney.

2013: February, refinanced in the Mega Bank Tung Nan branch office—Mayer Brown LLP translated addendum into English, but the draft only with Mayer Brown. This is the same technique used for the B Whale loan, the lawyer's name was there, but no final documents were provided.

*5.2: Madam Chow*

# CHAPTER 6
## PLAN X: EXECUTION STARTED

THE 2012 PRESIDENTIAL election was the KMT's last hurrah. Even though Ma Ying-jeou won with 74% of the vote, the writing was on the wall for the dynasty. Aging immigrant voters from mainland China would pass away and young Taiwanese, who were already demonstrating about the social unfairness of wealth distribution, would vote against the KMT. Many people were returning to cities in China (today there are over a million Taiwanese living in Shanghai) and the populism that spread through the younger generations all over the world in the wake of the 2007–2009 financial crisis, also affected Taiwan. The result would be defeat in the 2016 elections, not only for President Ma and Madam Chow, but also for the parliamentary party.

The KMT would become a minority party.

The fears of President Ma, Madam Chow (Big Mama), and other top KMT political leaders must have resulted in a state of panic. What were they going to do? How would they be able to protect their wealth? Once the DPP took over again, they'd be sure to try and find the KMT assets that had, allegedly, been illegally accumulated over the years in power. They'd been protected by a parliamentary majority during the first DPP presidency, but that wouldn't be the case after 2016. As I've said, it began with an asset stripping exercise. The sale of the KMT party headquarters, at almost half-price, to the chairman of Evergreen Marine Corporation was indicative of this. Selling off those assets at below-value prices was one thing, but the money would still have to be laundered.

Shipping companies such as Evergreen, Wan Hai, Yang Ming, U-Ming Shipping, Taiwan Navigation, Ta-Ho Maritime, and Formosa Shipping were all clients of Mega Bank. It wouldn't have been difficult for Madam Chow to plan for the dynasty's financial survival, with her knowledge of all the lawyers in Taiwan and her experience as Mega Bank's former general counsel.

Plan X.

I'd played golf with and entertained Mega Bank's Chairman, McKinney Tsai, for a long time, ever since my first visit to his office in 2010. He'd invited me to the Ladies Professional Golf Association in Taiwan with him in 2011 and 2012. We'd played together over 80 times in two years and had once taken a private jet to Kota Kinabalu in Malaysia for 18 holes at the Sutera Harbour Golf and Country Club with former Mega Chairman Lin Tsong Yun.

The following narration of how a TMT unsecured loan was manipulated by Mega Bank is complicated and difficult to understand, but please bear with me and I'll do my best to explain. In 2012 Tsai invited me to visit his office at Mega Bank on Chi Lin Road. It was an amicable meeting and he told me he was prepared to give me an unsecured loan to purchase a bunker to fuel my ships. It had a 180-day revolving LOC (letter of credit). I believed this NT$600 million loan was a favor to me due to our friendship over the past two years, and because I had already been paying his original loan for the same length of time, down 30% without any default. It seemed like a good deal to cement our relationship—a kind of US$25 million present, if you like.

A few months later this amount was used up and Tsai granted me another US$15 million extension to the existing US$25 million loan, to bring the total to US$40 million. The agreement documents were prepared by the Tung Nan branch of Mega Bank—the general manager's assistant, Chen Su Min, who played golf with McKinney Tsai's wife, offered many services to TMT, including a free safety deposit box, which I didn't require.

After the BP Macondo Well oil-skimming episode in 2010, TMT fleets had been blacklisted and boycotted by the major players in the oil market, including Exxon Mobil, Shell, BP, and Total—and by BHP Billiton, Rio Tinto, and Vale in the iron ore market. TMT had to pay back the loan at US$40,000 per day, while its fleet was earning less than US$10,000 per day and was idle, due to the boycott. As well as that, the Greek shipping magnate, Petros Pappas, disclosed TMT's corporate veil in South Africa, as a result of legal cases (Oceanbulk vs TMT) in the Star Bulk corporate dispute involving the ship called Vinyl Corporation, which I've already mentioned. He then began to arrest TMT vessels all over the world. The lawsuits continued with several Greek shipowners and English maritime lawyers.

Some TMT vessels had been arrested in 2008 and, since then, other TMT vessels had been arrested by Cathay United Bank, coordinated by an English lawyer called George Panagopolus, for Evangelos Marinakis, another Greek shipowner, and Capital Maritime & Trading Corp. (clients of Reed Smith LLP).

The C Ladybug was arrested by Active Tankers. The dispute was for only US$0.25 million, in a London arbitration of the sale and purchase of a ship valued at US$1 million, bought from Marinakis in 2004. The arbitration continued for eight years and made a few maritime lawyers very rich. When arbitration began, TMT was very busy with other cases and didn't remit a court fee. The shrewd lawyer, George Panagopolus of Reed Smith LLP, used this as an excuse for Marinakis to arrest C Ladybug. This was not acceptable as a maritime claim and TMT is preparing to take action in the future to sue Marinakis and his legal representative. C Ladybug was arrested in February 2012 in Antwerp by reason of not paying legal costs. The costs in question arose on a ship sale owned by Maranakis and unrelated to TMT. The legal fee wasn't even due for another three months. Furthermore, legal cost is not a maritime lien (a maritime lien is a privileged claim upon sea-connected property, such as a ship, for services rendered to, or injuries caused by, that property). So, lawyer's fees could not be a legal reason for arrest, but that's what happened in a UK court when the lawyer applied in Antwerp.

On top of that, Cathay United Bank requested payment of US$70 million, which was way above the real outstanding debt. There was coordination between Maranakis' lawyer, George Panagopolus, and an unknown English lawyer who worked with him. This is another mystery that needs to be exposed by future discoveries.

I was also involved in a lawsuit with Vantage Drilling Corporation (VTG)—today called Vantage Drilling International—this resulted in the E Whale ship being arrested by NewLead Holdings Ltd. for Michael Zolotas, another Greek shipowner (see how the Greeks had it in for me) and I was sentenced, in absentia, to 18 months in prison by an English court. I hired an English QC to solve the mistakes made in the English court. He said, if I attended the court and apologized they would reduce the sentence to zero, but if I didn't apologize the court would uphold a sentence of six months because I didn't send my lawyer to the first hearing. As far as I was concerned this was a joke because the court was relying on an eighteenth-century precedent set when Britain invaded some South Sea island. It was recorded that the island chief didn't have a QC to attend a court hearing, which was considered contempt of the British legal system, so the island was forfeited to Britain. I'm not sure if there's been another case like that. This hasn't happened anywhere else, not even when Timothy Geithner (former US Secretary of the Treasury) missed court in America after the 2008 financial crisis.

I did not go to prison and, in February 2013, TMT settled the NewLead dispute at Zurich airport, in the presence of Michael Zolotas, George Panagopoulos, Alan Donnelly, TMT's financial advisor at the time, and myself. Later, in

## PLAN X: EXECUTION STARTED

2015, Michael Zolotas cheated public investors. I discovered he'd actually created a fake business in a Bahrain deal and was eventually jailed in Cyprus. The arrest of E Whale was designed to prevent TMT from discovering his money flow. It was karma. Michael Zolotas sold four ships to a public company called Aries in 2009, when he was having problems. He didn't change the accounts and continued to request high cost payments to his private account from TMT. I was too busy to sue him in a criminal case—so far.

In the summer of 2012, McKinney Tsai told me that Mega Bank would have a new person in charge from New York and we could restructure the problem loan. In July 2012 he asked me to visit him at the Mega Bank head office in Taipei. The attendees were Tsai himself, his secretary Chen Su Min, TMT's CFO Green Huang, and me. During the meeting, he was a little nervous about asking me for some securities to cover an unsecured loan of US$45 million exposure, even though TMT's credit drawdown was just over US$40 million. I wasn't sure what it meant, since trust had already been built between us during our two-year relationship. I told him I didn't have a ship to fit this specific amount, but I could give him A Ladybug to use as collateral, which was worth almost US$100 million. He smiled in an astonished kind of way. He must have thought 'this guy is stupid.' TMT's CFO Green Huang told me it just meant giving security without receiving any money, which would have been nearly US$60 million in cash. I replied that it was okay since Tsai told me this would help my company and we were good friends.

Hyundai Heavy Industries (HHI) had agreed to deliver A Ladybug free of mortgage and TMT concurred with my decision to use that vessel as security for the previously unsecured US$40 million loan. The transaction was created in the Tung Nan branch of Mega International Commercial Bank. This was common practice because many Taiwan banks give loans through branches, not head offices. At that time I had no idea they would use A Ladybug Panamanian flagship as a vehicle for what I can only describe as a scam.

Our orders with Hyundai were for 32 ships (including A Ladybug) worth US$2.6 billion, which were being built. McKinney Tsai didn't offer financing for the other ships under construction, nor even mention them, nor show any interest whatsoever. If I'd thought about it carefully, I'd have realized something was very odd—Tsai never asked me about the business of TMT. He never asked how TMT would finance the other ships at HHI in Korea. He never asked about the TMT lawsuits being reported in news media, such as TradeWinds and Reuters. He wasn't interested in all that. Of course, I had no idea at the time that the plan was probably already under way and that the money being loaned was probably from the China Investment Fund and the KMT, which wouldn't be exposed until several years later.

On the golf course, during a private game in September 2012, Tsai told me he'd be reorganizing Mega Bank. The Head of the International Department, Chan Tin Hua, would be replaced with a new Deputy General Manager and my account would be handled by a new replacement from overseas. I just listened and continued playing. The bank was completely reorganized by early 2013 and the new replacement was a lady lawyer called Priscilla Hsing. She appeared to be very experienced in international deals and I didn't give it a second thought.

As a result of the oil and mining boycott and all the problems with the Greeks, which were affecting business, TMT decided to hire a firm called AlixPartners, who were specialists in turnaround management, or corporate renewal. They were recommended by Alan Donnelly, who ran a consulting firm in London called Sovereign Strategy. He said AlixPartners were famous for restructuring General Motors and other high-profile companies and they could help TMT solve its problems. I traveled to AlixPartners' New York office, where I had an eight-hour meeting with their Lisa Donahue and Esben Christensen and explained TMT's business to them.

## PLAN X: EXECUTION STARTED

Lisa Donahue referred me to her shipping expert, Albert Stein in London, who had been connected to the law firm Bracewell & Giuliana LLP from Houston, Texas. An early restructuring plan was prepared by AlixPartners by the end of February, then Albert Stein flew to Taipei to present it to the banks in March. I missed the flight and arrived one day later.

TMT had a modern fleet of 16 ships, with an average age of two years. I believed the restructuring of the loans shouldn't be too difficult, considering my close professional and personal relationships with the top people at Mega Bank. What I didn't expect was that McKinney Tsai might be inviting me to play golf on the one hand, while working hard behind my back to seize TMT's assets on the other.

The AlixPartners presentation was boycotted. I heard this from Green Huang when I arrived the next day, jet lagged. I immediately took Albert Stein to Mega Bank's head office, where we met the bank's Deputy Senior Vice President (International Department), who McKinney Tsai had told me about. It was my first meeting with her. Priscilla Hsing was smiling and welcomed us in. She listened to what we had to say but said very little in reply. It was clear that she wasn't taking us seriously, even though she kept on smiling. When we went back to the car, after the 45-minute meeting, Albert Stein told me it looked like the Taiwanese banks wouldn't be interested in restructuring my debts nor be willing to discuss them with us.

He was right. After that first morning meeting, we went to the Tung Nang office of Chinatrust Bank to meet the two smart bankers who had written TMT's prospectus for the syndication of the C Whale loan. They were aggressive and uncooperative, seeming confused and confrontational, and the meeting only lasted a few minutes. The same thing happened when we visited Cathay United Bank in the afternoon—they weren't interested in talking to us. It seemed that there was some type of order from the top to those bankers. Taiwan's banking system is an organic system where the big boss decides everything. They were refusing to work with us. All was in vain. No restructuring and no interest. The bankers wouldn't lend us their umbrellas when it rained. That's the real story.

But why?

Because, at a secret meeting held on the third floor of Mega Bank's headquarters on March 8, 2013, Mega Bank, First Commercial Bank, and Chinatrust had already decided to take legal action and sell TMT's ships. In fact, I believe several buyers had already been contacted by Mega Bank and Chinatrust. It was very likely a concerted action to sell TMT's assets, on the pretext that TMT wasn't performing in a viable manner. How did we find out? Details of that secret meeting emerged from a Petros Pappas E Whale disclosure in South Africa, which was found in 2015. It clearly showed that Pappas and Mega Bank had been colluding for some time and that Mega Bank had forced TMT to accept new secured-term loans so that the bank could get A Ladybug for free. This information wasn't disclosed to the court in Houston after I filed for Chapter 11 bankruptcy. I believe the Taiwanese banks submitted faked documents and made minimum disclosure to the court, which amounts to contempt of the US legal system.

But more about Chapter 11 later.

The boycott of the AlixPartners plan also proved that Priscilla Hsing had her own restructuring plan to take over TMT assets and use them to move out the KMT billions. You see, McKinney Tsai knew me and knew I hired financial advisors when I needed them. They couldn't leave anything to chance, in case the Dynasty's escape plan, which I've called Plan X, was destroyed. So, the order obviously came down to McKinney Tsai—which had all started with an unsecured loan, now A Ladybug, along with personal and corporate guarantees, "secured" that loan. They probably explained to him how they needed to make sure that an irregular loan could be tied in and become part of the overall Taiwanese bank loans for 16 ships, not recorded at the bank's head office in Chi Lin Road, but at the Dong Hwa branch.

## PLAN X: EXECUTION STARTED

I'm sure he did what he was told—I never saw McKinney Tsai again.

On March 14, 2013, the chairman of Cathay United Bank ordered the arrest of C Ladybug in Antwerp, Belgium. Other banks followed suit. Chinatrust even spread rumors among the syndication banks that selling TMT ships would make them good money. The C Handy was arrested and F Elephant was going to be auctioned off by BHP Billiton in mainland China. They weren't concerned about the situation at all because the order that probably went out from the KMT was that no bank should negotiate with me regarding restructuring. They should all act in concert—Madam Chow would have needed to control the loans and not allow them to go the way of TMT's AlixPartners restructuring plan.

It had to go her way!

On April 1, 2013, Priscilla Hsing requested me to sell off some assets. But I couldn't help thinking that Hsing was very reticent for a Deputy General Manager of Mega Bank. She had an air of stealth about her, like a spider waiting to spring a trap on an unsuspecting fly. It was April Fool's Day, so I didn't really take her seriously. I had faith in Chairman McKinney Tsai, with whom I played golf nearly every week over the previous year, and whose wife and sons I knew. Furthermore, TMT had provided sufficient securities, such as A Ladybug, to satisfy Mega Bank's demands. TMT's balance sheet was also very strong. Then she asked me if I knew of this famous UK shipping fund company that was looking for good assets to buy cheaply. I'd heard of the company, but I pretended I didn't because I'd never used it myself. It's obvious to me now that she must have had many clandestine buyers who were looking for private deals to purchase TMT's assets at distressed prices.

This indicated that Mega Bank was already in the execution stage of Plan X.

Later the same month, on April 15, Mega Bank finally gave TMT a body blow. The bank suddenly used a promissory note in an attempt to default a repayment installment, within the 90-day period, and only allowed about 75 minutes for that payment to be made. Mega Bank sent me an email at 1:45pm, right before the bank's 3:00pm closing time, to request an immediate payment of US$1.7 million. If not paid, the result would be the default of TMT's entire outstanding loan. The funny thing was, it was Mayer Brown, as Mega Bank's lawyers, who served the notice, but the email came from Mr. Lee and Ms. Chen at Mega Bank's head office and the Tung Nan branch respectively. A strange kind of hierarchy, wasn't it? It was impossible to make that payment so, at this stage, I started to consider pre-Chapter 11 bankruptcy procedures, under which TMT might be able to reorganize its business as it attempted to offload debt and return to profitability.

In the meantime, myself and TMT (Taipei) tried to ask for government help as a small/medium enterprise (SME), but the size of the company excluded it as an SME, so that drafting a restructuring plan that way failed. Green Huang and I tried to propose a restructuring plan that would be acceptable to everybody. In May 2013, we were invited to Mega Bank's head office to meet Mr Lin, the then Head of the bank's International Department—neither Priscilla Hsing or any of her team participated, which was very odd. He requested a payment of US$20 million as a cash injection to restructure all TMT's financing in Taiwanese banks—much the same as Priscilla Hsing had suggested the previous month. I felt very strange about the repeated offer and considered it a violation of Taiwanese law, so I didn't concur.

I traveled to AlixPartners' London office to try and save my company. Albert Stein, who had been connected to the law firm Bracewell & Giuliana LLP in New York, said it was a good idea to file under Chapter 11, and they could file using US entities in Bracewell. It was a persuasive proposal, considering that everything else had failed and the banks didn't seem prepared to listen to reason. That day, between London and New York, I was introduced over the phone to Evan Flaschen from Bracewell & Giuliani LLP. I decided to fly to New York to meet him. During the meeting, when I asked who would manage the bankruptcy case, there was silence. Flaschen did not say clearly if it would be he, or me.

On June 17, 2013, Green Huang approached me when I arrived at TMT's offices in Taipei.

'Priscilla Hsing is here.'

I was tired from traveling, but I agreed to see her. It was to be our final meeting. She asked me again to accept Mega Bank's terms. I said nothing. At the end of the meeting she asked whether or not TMT would file for bankruptcy under Chapter 11. I remained silent. I can clearly remember her face at that moment, it was full of fury. I'd never seen her that angry before. What probably worried Priscilla Hsing most was the prospect of Plan X being derailed and this final meeting angered her so much because I wouldn't comment on whether or not I was going to file for bankruptcy under Chapter 11.

Chapter 11 bankruptcy is special because it gives the company filing for bankruptcy a chance to stay alive. A case filed under Chapter 11 of the United States Bankruptcy Code is frequently referred to as a reorganization bankruptcy. Chapter 11 provides for such reorganization, which is what TMT and AlixPartners proposed to the banks. A Chapter 11 debtor proposes a plan of reorganization to keep the business alive and pay creditors over time. It gave me hope for TMT—little did I know that hope would be in vain, due to secret collaborations and the manipulation of the court on an unprecedented scale. The tentacles of the KMT were even able to reach into the US legal system.

Because I refused to comply with Priscilla Hsing's requirements, more ships were arrested in various jurisdictions. This is how it seems to me now, looking back at it all—TMT ships were unwittingly carrying KMT money, as well as cargo, and the evidence was already disappearing, even before filing for Chapter 11.

I'm hoping it will all be disclosed by the banks in future litigation.

# DYNASTY ESCAPE

*Figure 6.1a: Mega Bank New York branch, built in 1902 as the Chamber of Commerce*

*6.1b: Mega Bank New York branch sign*

# CHAPTER 7
## FILING UNDER CHAPTER 11 ON JUNE 20, 2013

EVAN FLASCHEN FROM Bracewell & Giuliani in New York felt good about the case. During our meeting, we decided to allocate US$15,000 to set up TMT Procurement USA. Flaschen suggested we file under Chapter 11 in Houston, Texas.

'Why Houston?'

'Business in the Houston courts has fallen off since 2008 and they need cases.'

Also, Jason Cohen of Bracewell was assistant to Judge Isgur, who was a US bankruptcy judge in the Southern District of Texas.

On June 20, 2013, TMT Procurement filed for Chapter 11 bankruptcy at a court in Houston, Texas, just as recommended by Bracewell LLP's Evan Flaschen. Incidentally, Kim Pu-tsung, the ROC's (Taiwan) ambassador to the USA, visited Houston at the same time, from New York.

Was this a coincidence?

Because, shortly after the Chapter 11 filing, the Taiwan banks took very strange and swift actions. On July 7, 2013, Taiwan's government ordered the Ministry of Finance (MOF) and the Financial Supervisory Commission (FSC) to cut the outstanding loans by half. Some of the banks weren't happy with this drastic measure. It was very unusual that the government didn't seek an independent third-party opinion and analysis for proper valuations and use of assets to recover the loss. I mean, if the ships could have sailed, they could have made money—nevertheless, that's what the government ordered. The A Duckling loan was US$25 million and was cut to US$12.5 million. As I said before, A Ladybug was a newly built RO-RO/PCTC vessel worth nearly US$100 million—it had US$40.3 million outstanding, which was cut to US$20.15 million.

Actually, the halving of the loans is a very interesting story. I believe it was done to make sure no bank lost money on the TMT case—they lost money from former profits they had made in accounting, but actually the money lent was almost certainly from the investment side (the China Investment Fund), given to the commercial side (Mega International Commercial Bank) and loaned to TMT. If so, many banks didn't actually lose money in their balance sheets, financial statements, and audit analyses, except for Chinatrust Bank, which didn't want to be seen to be involved in the scam or wasn't willing to commit itself. This also seemed to confirm that the TMT loans weren't using the banks' money, but China Investment Fund money, supplied from the very first loan drawdown.

The big question is, who had the power to order that cut? Who could send such an order to the head of the MOF? Madam Chow?

It's such a coincidence that there was that order from the MOF to cut TMT debts by half on July 7, 2013—when you consider that the person in charge of the China Investment Fund (collective) was also a board member of Mega Holdings, and he was appointed to the board on behalf of the MOF. It's all well covered up and although they are not affiliates, legally, Mega Holdings and the China Investment Fund share the same personnel, who are connected to the KMT and the MOF. As I said, it was an incestuous ball of worms and very difficult to untangle. But I'm determined to do just that and further revelations will be made in my third book, which I will be writing after this one is completed.

Then came the second strange occurrence.

The Panama registry showed that the A Ladybug guaranteed loan was sold to Macquarie Bank at the end of

2012, without notifying TMT, which was almost certainly a criminal act. The registry entry needed to be deleted but wasn't, and there were some strange arrangements of US$20 million second mortgages being backdated. The second mortgages were found in a Panama registry and the documents provided to Chapter 11's Judge Isgur. This was completely off the wall and even more shocking was the fact that so many prestigious law firms without POA letters in Panama were involved—including Quijano & Associates, Morgan & Morgan PA, Aries Law, and Torrijos & Associates.

Going back to Priscilla Hsing for a moment. I believe she knew the money was financed by the KMT from day one and her job was to keep me from finding out. She was concerned about the ongoing Mega Bank revelations regarding the A Ladybug loan Macquarie Bank already owned. The strange documentation was first revealed by Mr Lee, who worked under Priscilla Hsing—the email notice and other documents didn't follow any banking compliance properly. Hand delivery after 5:00pm on December 31, 2013? It's not legally binding in Taiwan to hand deliver without the recipient signing—and TMT was closed after 5:00pm on December 31. Interestingly, it was only later I discovered that the Panamanian lawyers who were involved never submitted POA letters to alter the mortgage documents. There were other issues that came to light much later, like the selling of the three Ladybugs—A, B, and D—at private Malta sales, which had been involved in second mortgage issues from February 2014. I realize this is all quite confusing and it's a story that involves the ships, and the Malta government, and its legal system, of which I will write more in my next book.

So stay tuned.

However, for the purpose of simplicity, in my opinion there were two phases to the plan. First, to sell the TMT ship loans to third parties, thus breaking the direct link to Mega Bank, Chinatrust Bank, and so on, and, as a consequence, the China Investment Fund. Second, the sale of the physical ships after arrests in a variety of countries, so the money retrieved would not come back to Taiwan but would be deposited in prearranged KMT accounts overseas.

As can be seen from the preceding paragraphs, the paper trail, or in many cases, the computer data trail, was deliberately obscured, over and over again. For instance, on December 30, 2013, I believe Mega Bank faked a transfer for the purpose of cleaning up its balance sheet. It wasn't signed by Macquarie Bank, but it cut and pasted a Macquarie signature. This raised suspicions that A Ladybug was used to raise US$54 million and was either sold to Macquarie as a first mortgage, or became the first anti-money laundering (AML) case to be later uncovered by the NYDFS (New York State Department of Financial Services).

But we'll discuss Mega Bank's exposed money laundering in a later chapter.

Mega Bank chose New York-based Oaktree Capital Management (listed on the NY Stock Exchange), instead of the British fund Priscilla Hsing asked me about, to do its money laundering and pay Taiwan bankers. Oaktree was paid through a designated account, but was never disclosed as the counterparty that bought TMT loans. Instead they structured the sales with JPMorgan Chase N.A. (North America) as the buyer. The loans were sold at almost scrap value, plus extra equity for two-year-old ships—which was unheard of. It was a clear plan to sell TMT's ships to the banks' closely associated business partners and the loans were packaged just how the banks wanted. Furthermore, my current law firm, HooverSlovacek LLP, discovered a US$100 million loan at a very low interest rate to Oaktree Capital Management from Taishin International Bank in November 2013.

The first loan was transferred to OCM Formosa Strait Holdings, which was disclosed in Taiwan on November 7, 2013. However, under Chapter 11, it was disclosed on January 21, 2014, as the sale of a Chinatrust Bank loan. The relevant information should have been entered in the disclosure, but it wasn't. This is also related to a disclosure made by Seward & Kissel LLP (acting for the Unsecured Credit Committee, UCC, led by HHI) that equity from the purchase of six Whale ships went to Taishin Bank from a subsidiary of Shing Kwan Financial Holdings in a secret deal.

Incidentally, the TMT VLCC B Elephant was detained by the Egyptian navy for allegedly damaging an underwater cable in Egyptian waters off Alexandria on March 22, 2013. The Egyptian Navy and Telecom were seeking US$40 million in compensation from TMT, meanwhile keeping the vessel and crew in detention. Initially there were 17 crew on board, then two engineers were allowed to leave the vessel, the rest were held hostage for many months. The compensation demanded by the Egyptian Navy and Telecom was obviously too exorbitant to be taken seriously and it was just another case of a state-backed act of piracy against TMT.

In the end, Peter Evensen, the CEO of Teekay Tankers (Canada) paid a P&I (protection and indemnity) premium related amount of US$10 million in what can only be called a collusion with Lloyd's of London. After that, Teekay Tankers owned B Elephant. They got a ship worth in excess of US$60 million, for just US$10 million. Nice profit, if you can get it. My question is, why didn't the Britannia Club and insurers settle the matter before TMT filed for bankruptcy? Because, as soon as TMT filed for Chapter 11 bankruptcy in June 2013, the vultures started gathering.

So far, TMT has found that Marshall Islands and Panama-flagged ships involved in the Chapter 11 case were registered for backdated second mortgages of US$20 million each on June 20, 2013. Liberian flag records were destroyed when all Liberia-registered ships were transferred to Greek flags in July 2014. TMT also suspected that all Liberia-flagged Whale ships had US$20 million second mortgages. Let me explain—it was big news when US$320 million disappeared from the KMT flagship fund in Mega International Commercial Bank. The opposition party complained strongly and campaigned in the media for the bank to be sued. If you look at this in parallel to TMT's Chapter 11—US$20 million second mortgages on 16 ships is equal to a total of US$320 million, that is, the Mega/China Investment Fund scandal derived from US$320 million second mortgages on TMT ships. You don't have to be a genius to make the connection.

In addition, a total of US$376 million disappeared from TMT's Chapter 11 case after analyzing the monthly operating reports. This was done by a big data analysis and the story was brought to court. It must be that the US$320 million of China Investment Fund money was used for the US$20 million second mortgages for each of the 16 ships I've already mentioned. After it was removed from the lien, the money went to a JPMC investment run by JPMC Taiwan CEO, Ms Shi. Next, Oaktree paid money to the designated accounts, but never disclosed which accounts it went to. There were three branches of JPMC involved and it's not clear how the money was moved between them. Of course, the difference of US$56 million is related to A Ladybug—more details in the next book.

JPMorgan Chase New York CEO, Jamie Dimon, reacted furiously and fired the CEO of JPMC Taiwan, Shi, and her team of ten at the end of June 2017. No bank with US$100 billion of funds would announce that a CEO had internally violated the law—in any case, it wasn't an internal violation of law, but an external violation of law—you don't fire people who violate internal compliance and the real reason was never explained to the Securities and Exchange Commission (SEC) or the public in Taiwan. JPMC had paid for this kind of violation before. In September 2016 JPMC paid a big fine to the US Department of Justice to settle a mainland Chinese daughter-and-son hiring program that violated the Foreign Corrupt Practices Act (FCPA).

Mega Bank was under a two-year moratorium for supervision by the NYDFS, and the first inspection from the USA was in July 2017. There was also a US$29 million fine by the Federal Reserve Board (FRB) in Washington DC against the US operations of Mega Bank for AML violations. The FRB told Mega it needed to improve its AML oversight and controls, saying its branches in New York, Chicago, and Silicon Valley didn't maintain an effective program to comply with the US Bank Secrecy Act (BSA) and AML laws. The board said that examinations conducted by the Federal Reserve Banks of New York, Chicago, and San Francisco, between June and December 2016, disclosed significant deficiencies relating to the branches' risk management and compliance with the requirements of the BSA and AML laws.

Getting back to Chapter 11, the creditor lawyer who represented Mega Bank and Chinatrust was Mayer Brown LLP. In my opinion, there was a significant conflict of interest, as Mayer Brown was formerly known as Johnson Stokes & Master, who were the lawyers for all the Whale ships back in 2010. Nobody seemed to care about that and Charles Kelley, the creditor lawyer from Mayer Brown, would not agree to the restructuring plan set out in Chapter 11. In fact, everything that went on pre-Chapter 11, from 2010 to 2013, was never offered in evidence to the court, even though it was relevant and highly significant and might have affected decisions made by the judge.

You can see how convoluted and complicated the Chapter 11 case was turning out to be. It was almost impossible to understand what was going on at the time, unless you were a qualified bankruptcy lawyer, which I was not. It will also be quite difficult for people reading this book to follow, but I will try to simplify what went on in the court in subsequent chapters. For now, suffice to say there was a lot of stuff going on behind the scenes that neither myself nor TMT were aware of.

The overall KMT plan was working—the restructuring of TMT was being blocked by complicated, litigious double-dealing.

*7.1 Nobu Sue in the Chapter 11 Court*

# CHAPTER 8

## THE HIJACKED LOANS

TMT WAS TARGETED and its loans were hijacked—there's no doubt in my mind about that. TMT was used as a vehicle to move funds from Taiwan banks to overseas destinations—there's no doubt in my mind about that either. There are answers to the questions these facts throw up. Those answers must be found. For Plan X to succeed, the following conditions had to apply:

It had to be manageable.

It had to be spreadable.

It had to be confidential.

It had to be untraceable via money remittance.

It had to be run by a few people, dividing up the work.

It had to be run by outsiders hired specifically for the job, who could then move on after their role in the plan was over.

It had to be spread among many banks, to make it invisible.

It had to involve middlemen from foreign banks, whom the Taiwan authorities couldn't reach.

It had to be set up so that it would not be easy to apply jurisdiction in the future.

It had to be easy to delete the evidence in a way that wouldn't seem criminal.

The TMT case met all the above conditions.

Mega Bank's boss, McKinney Tsai obviously followed instructions from Madam Chow, who was most likely supported by President Ma. I have no doubt that McKinney Tsai did not act alone in making sure the money was transferred from Taiwan to overseas destinations without leaving any evidence behind—I believe he followed orders from the First Lady, with the President's blessing. I've spent the last ten years investigating and analyzing how banks move money around using client loans or, in more sophisticated cases, using Collateralized Debt Obligations (CDOs) and CDSs and other, newer financial products. I can safely conclude that it's beyond the ability of financial supervisors and regulators to detect these unlawful activities if they're planned with sophisticated partners. It's impossible to carry out effective AML checks with knowledge of only one party—it requires details of the middlemen and the third parties whose accounts are being hijacked.

The final part of the plan was instigated by Chinatrust and Oaktree. They had an investment company called Oaktree Huntington (Cayman) 6CTB—confirmed by Oaktree lawyers, Paul Weiss Rifkind Wharton & Garrison LLP, under oath in a Chapter 11 court hearing in New York on July 14, 2014. The explanation given by Oaktree's lawyer was quite amazing and based on Oaktree Huntington (Cayman) 6CTB fund being renamed as OCM Formosa Strait Holdings before January 1, 2014. Consequently, the trial balance on December 31, 2013 had lots of hidden stories to tell. It seems the KMT had injected a total of US$320 million into OCM Formosa Strait Holdings, formerly Oaktree Huntington (Cayman) 6CTB fund. I will write more on this in my next book.

There's also evidence showing that, on January 21, 2014, OCM Formosa Strait Holdings bought a US$13.5 million loan from Mega Bank, arranged to JPMorgan Chase N.A., with the authorizing signature of Vice President Stephen Clark. However, the original initials were those of Chris Craig, but were crossed out and overwritten with the signature of Stephen Clark. Stephen Clark was based in JPMC's New York head office, while Chris Craig was based in the credit risk department in London. Contrarily, all the declarations made by the banks in Taiwan were reported to the Financial Conduct Authority and SEC of Taiwan, with JPMorgan Chase N.A. as the buyer of the loans. Very mysterious. Was it New York or London?

More in my next book.

Once Chinatrust Bank started to sell its part of the US$18 million loan of the TMT portfolio, Macquarie Bank simultaneously became the official debtor-in-possession (DIP) lender. In fact, two months before, Macquarie Bank had contacted Lisa Donahue, Chief Financial Advisor (to debtors) at AlixPartners, saying they were willing to provide US$20 million as a DIP lender. The DIP lender plays a significant role and has the final say in a restructuring plan's approval.

I think a further explanation of DIP lending is required here, for clarity.

In the right situation a Chapter 11 bankruptcy can provide certain options to facilitate financing. If a company needs money, but lenders are unwilling to finance that company because of concern over legal challenges, the bankruptcy code offers a way to guarantee a potential loan won't be challenged. When a company files for Chapter 11 bankruptcy, the company's management and board of directors remain in possession of the business. For that reason, the company is called the DIP. When the debtor company secures a lender, it files a motion seeking bankruptcy court approval of the DIP financing. The company will need the existing lenders' lien position to be protected (they won't be worse off) if the DIP loan is approved. An existing lender may be willing to make a DIP loan, even if it has refused to make further loans outside of bankruptcy.

Unlike a loan outside of bankruptcy, if the court approves a DIP loan, that loan will not be subject to legal challenge—DIP loans are usually made by insiders, or a "stalking horse" purchaser, looking to buy the company's assets. It isn't easy but, in the right circumstances, a distressed company may be able to use Chapter 11 DIP financing to get the liquidity it needs to finance a formal Chapter 11 restructuring. DIP loans are expensive and can be highly lucrative for the DIP lender.

Of course, Macquarie didn't use their own money for the DIP loan. No, Mega Bank gave them the US$20 million and they used the free money and charged only 1%. So, the US$20 million became US$20.20 million. Charles Schreiber was fronting things from New York and he visited Houston, but the boss was a man called Black, who was based in Washington DC and was connected to Kim Pu-tsung, the Taiwan Ambassador from 2012 to 2014. During the course of the Chapter 11 bankruptcy hearings, the DIP lender (Macquarie Bank) never agreed on anything positive for the restructuring plan.

The good standing of companies involved in the debt sales became very dubious. The company names kept changing, until there was no way to identify a company's legitimate registration in the Chapter 11 process.

The two consecutive sales of ships from January 21–23, 2014, by Chinatrust and Ta Chong Bank (part of the Formosa Plastics Group) were completed and signed between JPMC's Stephen Clark and Mega Bank. Incidentally, Formosa Plastics Group was responsible for a serious discharge of toxic pollution from one of its steel complexes. The release resulted in an estimated 115 tons of dead fish washing ashore in Vietnam. The environmental pollution negatively affected the livelihood of 200,000 people, including local fishers. In July 2016, Formosa Plastics Group pledged to pay compensation to Vietnamese impacted by the environmentally toxic discharge in the amount of $500 million.

As far as I'm concerned, part of the funds, ranging from US$55 million to US$61.5 million per ship went into money laundering—the C Whale was sold at a total price of US$51.5 million to Chris Craig on January 28, 2014, as a new lender. The public website for the Taichung Bank (part of the Shin Kwan Group) and Cathay Bank transfers announced that JPMorgan Chase N.A. sold the debt to JPMorgan Chase N.A.—in other words, they sold it to themselves. But the dates of receipt of the money were all wrong—I mean it's impossible to pay money a day before you receive it—on January 27, 2014. Taishin Bank was the only bank that didn't sell its E Whale debt—and this was to produce a future whistle-blower as to how all the seemingly unlawful transactions were undertaken. However, as already stated, it had arranged a US$100 million favorable term loan to Oaktree Capital that started in September and closed the first week of November 2013. Taishin Bank continued to be the creditor in D Whale, and this loan of US$100 million was never disclosed in Chapter 11, even though Taishin Bank was part of the Chapter 11 case—in other words, they didn't declare the true picture to the bankruptcy court.

There were more interesting matters discovered on the last day of filing particulars of claims on November 13, 2013. True accounts of all the claims and debts were not properly filed in a fitting way to the US Chapter 11 bankruptcy court. The information that was supposed to be presented to the court was never complete.

More details of these discrepancies in my next book.

I was told by the CEO of ORIX, Taiwan (a subsidiary of ORIX Corporation, the Japanese financial services firm), that the sales of Mega Bank debt had involved JPMC as a go-between and that the transactions were unusual because there was an assignment clause from JPMC, which made the Taiwan banks not directly involved parties. I tried to get more details, but the auction process in the Taiwan prospectus specifically requested potential participants, who weren't qualified, to destroy the invitation documents. The conditions prevented Japanese companies from participating in the auction from a compliance aspect. So, it seems to me that the loans were predetermined to sell to Oaktree and Monarch Capital (the largest shareholder in Star Bulk Carriers) in New York, by the banking regulators in Taiwan—that is, the Dynasty.

Plan X was completed.

Here's what I believe was the sequence of events:

Mega Bank, Chinatrust, and Ta Chong Bank were told by the KMT government and Madam Chow to get involved (clandestinely) in a US$320 million unsecured loan, which was sold to JPMorgan Chase N.A. in New York in November 2013—this was not disclosed to the Chapter 11 court in Houston.

Chinatrust did the first trade simultaneously as Taishin Bank gave a US$100 million loan to Oaktree Capital—in November 2013.

Kaohsiung Bank sold a small amount of the loan to SC Lowy Financial (HK) for US$3.06 million on December 17, 2013. In effect, the entire ships' loans were divided into many bits—almost like a CDS. At the same time, the DIP loan in Chapter 11 was given to TMT by Macquarie Bank, quietly, without disclosure.

Mega Bank's top management, with a wkc3@megabank.co.tw group email, could internally control everything that was happening—it's suspicious that there are three same names within the bank.

On December 25, 2013, Priscilla Hsing sent an email to Nobu Sue saying that, in a month's time, she won't be responsible for signing documents—this was to cover her footprint in the matter.

# THE HIJACKED LOANS

The KMT fund (the China Investment Fund) invested in this crime, so that the debts of five ships were fully covered by the end of 2013 as profit for the banks.

On January 15, 2014, the first loan transfer to a KMT related bank—Shanghai Commercial Savings Bank transferred to Macquarie Bank and Deutsche Bank. But the documents were printed on "error paper." In fact, it was all printed on error paper. Strange?

On January 21, 2014, Chinatrust finally sold the loan balance to JPMC, so that the money could be retrieved in a proper way. This transaction was reported to the Chapter 11 court. Once the money was received by JPMC, it was paid back to Chinatrust in Taiwan so it would look like a clean deal.

On January 23, 2014, the same thing happened for US$3.5 million under the signature of Stephen Clark.

On January 27, 2014, the entire syndicated balance was paid to nine banks. All Taiwan banks involved received payment by January 28. Chris Craig signed the transfer documents in London.

On January 28, 2014, the first bank deal on A Whale with SC Lowy and Monarch Capital (second largest shareholder in Star Bulk Carriers) was done in one day. This was the only ship deal done in one day with Barclays Bank (NY) and a Singapore SWIFT code payment—which is impossible to execute. It was faked and never happened.

On January 29, 2014, Mega Bank, Oaktree, and JPMorgan Chase N.A. were all involved in New York, but signed two separate contracts. Mega Bank and JPMC signed the agreement in London—it was signed by Chris Craig, who worked in the JPMC's credit risk department.

The agreement between Oaktree and JPMorgan Chase N.A. was only duly signed by Oaktree representing OCM Formosa Strait Holdings.

Why the separate funds?

The answer is that Oaktree (OCM Formosa Strait Holdings) remitted to a Mega Bank nominated account, not to JPMC. It was supposed to be KMT funds for JPMC. If it was the latter, JPMorgan Chase N.A. had to keep it as the final owner of the funds or remit the money to the nominated account—either Mega International Commercial Bank New York Agency (SWIFT Code ICBCUS33—ICBC is International Commercial Bank of China and 33 is for New York), or possibly to KMT funds.

E Whale was arrested by Mega Bank in South Africa in early 2013, so it needed to go to public auction, the US court ruling couldn't be applied. So why wasn't the E Whale loan money paid back to the Chapter 11 estate? The first deal was between the small Kaohsiung Bank and SC Lowy Financial (HK), but it changed name in the transaction to SC Lowy Primary Investment, in Tung Hwa—North Road 214, Floor 7, Ms Jennifer Atkinson, telephone 02-5588-1798. Was this real? I found out this was the address of law firm Lee & Li, who were connected to the Formosa Plastics Group bank, Ta Chong Bank (they recently sold Ta Chong Bank, to distance themselves from the scam). The money was supposed to come back to the Chapter 11 estate, instead of coming back in the monthly operational report. There are a few more details that need to be confirmed, but TMT Chapter 11 and I can provide detailed evidence of the above,

The filing under Chapter 11 needs to be analyzed from different angles. Keep in mind that First Bank, Chung Hwa Bank, Mega Bank, Hua Nan Bank, CBT Bank, Taichung Bank, Kaohsiung Bank, Taiwan Bank, Land Bank, and Cooperative Bank were all government shareholder banks whose CEOs were nominated by Big Mama, Madam Chow.

# THE HIJACKED LOANS

Here are some interesting questions for you to ponder:

Why did Macquarie Bank offer US$20 million cash as an investment bank interested in Chapter 11 (which could be called a conflict of interest, as loan holders)?

Why was a small fund like SC Lowy involved—as an ex-colleague of Deutsche Bank, on the inside? SC Lowy's office in Hong Kong is next to Shanghai Commercial Bank Hong Kong, the headquarters of Shanghai Commercial Savings Bank in Taipei.

Why did Shanghai Commercial Savings Bank, as a private bank, loan so much and then immediately sell all the debt to Macquarie Bank?

Why was paid commission recirculating around Macquarie? (Macquarie Bank Taiwan is only 30 meters away from the KMT head office).

On December 31, 2013, it's highly likely that the banks received funds from the KMT in the form of US$20 million second mortgages, so they didn't need to write off the debt in their financial statements. On January 27, 2014, they were all repaid with KMT funds. Taiwan banks were told, and believed, that the debt was sold to JPMorgan Chase N.A. But, actually, JPMC paid the money on January 29 in New York, receiving the funds from OCM Formosa, but not knowing the account details. There were several loans related to Chinatrust, Ta Chong Bank, and Shanghai Commercial Savings Bank sold to JPMC in November and to Macquarie in December. These transactions are positively scandalous—the dates don't match and the banks clearly demonstrated collusion. Why did they tell JPMC to camouflage the transactions? Why did JPMC, one of the world's largest fortress banks, need to do that? The highest Taiwanese banker in the JPMC hierarchy was Carl Chien, head of JPMorgan Chase (Asia). He represented the whole of Asia for JPMC, reporting directly to Jamie Dimon and the heads of the European, investment banking, and commercial banking divisions. He was also the son of Chien Foo, who was Foreign Minister of Taiwan from 1990 to 1996.

Keeping corruption "within the family"?

Intermediary banks needed to have clear contracts disclosed in Chapter 11. Questions were raised. JPMC's vice president in New York denied that Chris Craig in London had the authority to sign. Chris Craig's signatures were created in a Chinatrust–Ta Chong Bank transaction and the date of transfer was five days later. This was scandalous and related documents were not disclosed in Chapter 11. JPMC's lawyer declared in front of Judge Isgur that JPMC's role in Chapter 11 was that of broker. Nevertheless, it was proved that JPMC wasn't the broker, as they had held Chinatrust's US$40 million loan and Ta Chong Bank's US$30 million loan for over two months. We have the statements from JPMC as evidence for both.

Suddenly, former Mega Bank CEO, McKinney Tsai, was appointed a board director at Cathay United Bank in February 2016. This was a very significant move, even to people outside financial circles. The NYDFS investigation into Mega Bank money laundering had already started at the end of 2014, right after TMT's 16 ships were sold. This coincided with the story of Oaktree trying to settle with TMT in Chicago in 2014. Nevertheless, by the beginning of 2016 it got very serious and McKinney Tsai was subsequently indicted.

On August 21, 2016, the NYDFS, judged by many to be the most effective AML enforcement regulator in the USA, concluded a Consent Order (a legal document that provides information about an agreement mutually reached by people involved in a legal case) with Mega Bank, which had major branches in New York and the Republic of Panama. This agreement, which included a US$180 million fine for massive AML deficiencies, along with the bank's mandatory institution of major remedial measures across the board on compliance, should be required reading for all compliance officers. The deficiencies were so widespread that the readers are encouraged to review the complete text. Just as important, especially for compliance officers at banks located in North America, are the details surrounding the AML failures at the bank's two Panama offices—one in Panama City and the other in the Colon Free Trade Zone. The NYDFS Order, which specifically refers to Panama as a 'high-risk jurisdiction for money laundering,' describes a shopping list of AML defects (see further details about this in Chapter 18—The Samson Wu Story: Fake News?).

One of the most unusual violations listed was the pattern of 'debit authorizations' (payment reversals) whereby, often months after a wire transfer was effectuated it was reversed and the funds returned. Of particular note was the fact that the bank allowed this transfer even after the customer had closed his account in Panama. Some of these transfers were to and from the same customer. The utility of a bank permitting such a technique to facilitate money laundering is painfully obvious.

Neither the Panama City nor the Colon branch had been subject to any action by Panamanian banking regulators, according to public records. Compliance officers should immediately check their recent wire transfer records to determine whether or not their banks have engaged in any transactions with Mega Bank. They should immediately open an investigation into the circumstances surrounding those transfers, the parties involved, and the underlying business relationships shown by those transfers.

Taiwan's banks openly handled renminbi (RMB—the official currency of the PRC) business, starting from 2012. This coincided with the KMT's capital outflow. There was much capital outflow from 2012 to 2014 because of Taiwan's banks lending to mainland China. Banks could make a 6% interest return compared to a 2% Taiwan loan interest return. One example is a Chinatrust–CITIC joint venture that started in 2014. The intention was to move money between Taiwan and China. However, alliance talks were cancelled immediately after the US$180 million AML case, led by the NYDFS, started. This was a case of an AML violation affecting relationships across Taiwan. Chinatrust CEO Jeffery Koo Jr. was arrested by Taiwanese authorities and later released on a bail of US$3 million. Taiwan MOF is looking into his suspected involvement in illegal transactions. He is now facing charges of violating the Banking Act and the Securities and Exchange Act, which may put him in jail for 12 years. It seems that the authorities are making sure that he will not tell the true story of the AML case related to the 2012–2014 banking scandals.

*8.1: McKinney Tsai arrest*

*8.2: Jeffery Koo Jr. investigated*

# CHAPTER 9
## CHAPTER 11 BANKRUPTCY: PART II

LET'S TAKE A step back.

The Chapter 11 bankruptcy case was a traumatic event for Priscilla Hsing, the Deputy Vice President of Mega Bank. I believe she'd had direct instructions from the very top of the government and the KMT Party to handle the China Investment Fund scamming of TMT loans. Because of Chapter 11, it must have become clear to her that the entire Plan X now needed to be concealed and she probably contacted Mayer Brown LLP, who were Mega International Commercial Bank's lawyers—there was a lot of internal communication between the Hong Kong, New York, and Houston offices. As I said previously, Ambassador Kim Pu-tsung was visiting Texas at the same time and I can imagine him listening to the trembling voice of Priscilla Hsing on the phone from Taipei, telling him that TMT had filed for bankruptcy under Chapter 11. From then, Mayer Brown's Charles Kelley and Michael Lloite in New York were appointed to handle the matter. See Mayer Brown LLP's letter on page 184, where TMT Panama S.A. is cited as second lender. However, in this context TMT is a borrower, not a lender. Surprisingly, this was from the deed set up for the C Whale. An amazing finding, and an indication that it was planned from the beginning, in 2010.

So much skulduggery!

What was the big problem? Well, to start with, the registry of the A Ladybug needed to be filed properly. Surprisingly, ten days after TMT filed for Chapter 11, the Taiwan FSC instructed a cut of the Taiwan banks' exposure in half, so there would be no loss situations in the audited financial statements at the end of 2013. This fact would also need to be explained in court—but it never was. The fact that the money for the loans had already been sourced from within the banking system, through the China Investment Fund, meant that the entire scam would need to be concealed from the court. Also, it seems Mayer Brown was ordered not to disclose the A Ladybug loan that was sold to Macquarie Bank—this could only have been meant to buy time.

Mayer Brown contacted Bracewell & Giuliana LLP, who were supposed to be helping present TMT's Chapter 11 restructuring plan, to try to buy that time. They created something called 'Good Faith or Bad Faith Chapter 11.' Basically, it was an argument to oppose the proposed restructuring of TMT. This begs the question, why would they oppose the restructuring of a company with such solid assets and a young, modern fleet, only two years old? This was not just uncommon, it was highly unusual, to say the least. What was also highly unusual was the fact that AlixPartners' Head of Shipping, Lisa Donahue, kept telling me that the Taiwan banks were not willing to talk to me. All I could do was wait for the loans to be sold to New York hedge funds and then I could start talking about restructuring.

Things didn't really change until September 2013, with a phone call from Lisa Donahue. She said Macquarie Bank was willing to offer money to help with Chapter 11, but the terms were tough, and they wanted the second mortgages and 9% interest. The devil was in the detail, in this case the terms and conditions, but I had no choice but to accept. Those terms and conditions became very extraordinary and Macquarie Bank's Ann Chen, along with two other ladies, came to Bracewell LLP's Rockefeller Center offices 'to say hello.' I clearly remember the meeting. None of those ladies had any idea about what they were doing in shipping and wouldn't know the bow from the stern of a TMT vessel. How could these three young Chinese women decide to give US$20 million second mortgage loans on all 16 ships to the Chapter 11 DIP? Of course, they could not—the decision had already been made elsewhere and they were simply rubber-stamping it, or signing without knowing what POA were in Macquarie Bank compliances. The meeting was very short, but to me it was a gift from heaven, giving me the money to move my ships and generate income.

Macquarie Bank had other ideas.

In November 2013, the court approved the US$20 million DIP loan from Macquarie, which was paid to Whitney Bank (Online Banking) in two tranches. All the money was swallowed up for fees and services and none of it went to the ships. As well as that, Mayer Brown LLP was still buying time with their good-faith/bad-faith plan and no ship was able to move, also consuming TMT's US$58 million retention fund. Seward & Kissel LLP represented the UCC, the body trying to recover money for the parties led by HHI, Hyundai Samho Heavy Industries, and others. However, they remained silent. TMT had ordered US$2.6 billion in ships from Korea's number one shipyard and Hyundai were the only ones who understood how good those ships were and their true value— yet they were unwilling to come to court to support TMT and give evidence as to the true value of the ships. I didn't find out the reason why until January 2018.

But it seemed to me they must have been under instruction from Seward & Kissel LLP, their legal counsel in New York, who were also legal counsel for Star Bulk Carriers. Oaktree (who owned more than 50% of Star Bulk shares) and Monarch had already agreed to buy, or were in negotiations to buy, TMT debts at steep discounts. They couldn't use Seward & Kissel, so they hired Paul Weiss LLP and Willkie Farr LLP, both prestigious law firms.

The Chapter 11 case moved on in December 2013 when the court heard that the Taiwan banks had started to sell the loans to JPMC, and Oaktree, and Monarch (who two major shareholders of Petros Pappas' Star Bulk Carriers. I was, at one time, co-chairman of Star Bulk with Pappas, when he took

30% of shares during a conspiracy in 2008—detailed in my book *The Gold Man from the East*).

Time went by and people got replaced—Lisa Donahue from AlixPartners and lawyers from Bracewell & Giuliani disappeared from the scene—and it was interesting to see how the game continued. Taiwanese lawyers sat on the floor from June 20, 2013, to January 31, 2014. One thing didn't change, and it struck me as odd—a Chinese man with receding hair sat in the center of the court. He never missed a session. He always looked straight at the judge, eight hours a day. He never moved. He listened to what was happening in the court every minute of the day. It was as if he had a secret microphone concealed somewhere and was recording everything and reporting back to make sure the true story would never come out.

A spy? I once stood behind him in the toilet and, even then he never said a word. A silent KMT spy in the court for over 200 days?

The Chapter 11 bankruptcy court case was like a movie. Chris Declare, Vantage Drilling's Chief Administration Officer, and Paul Bragg, Vantage CEO, hired lawyers Vidal Martinez LLP to buy the share pledge of US$50 million. Martinez lived in Houston and had been an attorney there for over 40 years. He'd previously worked for Paul Bragg and John O'Reilly, Vantage directors, on OFAC and FCPA issues. Then, in 2014, he was back in the Vantage saddle, coming to the fourth-floor courtroom, and exchanging information on a daily basis. Martinez showed up from September onward to buy out the terms. Just let me say this, I considered Chris Declare to be incompetent, but he had the loyalty of Paul Bragg, who was eventually fired after Vantage violated SEC regulations. He decided to look for revenge on F3 Capital, the largest shareholders, who owned 70% at one time, but that's another story.

Let's talk about Vidal Martinez for a moment. He was hired by Vantage Drilling for several reasons, one was to handle a FPCA Pakistan Compliance issue for one of its first drilling rigs, the other, I believe, was to destroy Nobu Sue. Mayer Brown requested additional securities to sustain good faith and eventually I agreed to pledge 50 million Vantage shares to the court. The CEO of Vantage came to the stand under oath and declared he wanted to buy the shares whatever way he could. In America, the CEO of a company coming to a Texas court to buy shares without board approval is unheard of. Vantage hired Vidal Martinez to frustrate the Chapter 11 process by contacting most of the lawyers involved. It was a potential crime and violated SEC regulations and US corporate law.

So many lawyers and so much legal wrangling—DIP lawyers, Shanghai Bank lawyers, UCC Lawyers, Hyundai lawyers, TMT lawyers; and financial advisors—Mayer Brown's Charles Kelley, Bracewell & Giuliani's Evan Flaschen, Winston & Strawn's Charles Schreiber—who played a significant role in the Chapter 11 case, stopping all the ships from moving and generating money. So many experts showing up who knew absolutely nothing about the shipping industry, such as what a VLCC or a VLOO are. None of these, so-called, experts had any knowledge of what was happening in the shipping world. Every day it was like litigious musical chairs, and all of them charging a fortune. The Stanford MBA judge, Marvin Isgur, asked questions if the numbers didn't add up, but the lawyers tried to make grand orations in their efforts to secure the assets for whoever was hiring them, waxing lyrical rather than producing accurate facts and figures.

Nobody asked the key questions, such as, what was the root cause of the company's problems? The questions hinged more around abstract issues about what was good Chapter 11 practice and what wasn't. In the meantime, TMT ships remained idle, with full crews, consuming oil and other resources, and generating no income. One day a crew member died in Singapore and I had to fly out there to deal with the matter. None of the lawyers reported this to the court. The ship management company from Norway hid it, AlixPartners hid it—they all hid it from Judge Isgur. I wanted to voice it, but Evan Flaschen wouldn't allow me to. In reality, by not allowing the ships to move, they indirectly killed an engineer in Singapore, but failed to report this to the judge. It was just before Christmas, when they were all looking forward to going to their expensive homes for a nice holiday

Later on, the plan was to give a five-year favorable loan to Oaktree Capital Management, who seemingly collaborated in the scam to pay the purchase money to Mega-nominated banks. These could be in New York, London, Hong Kong, Sydney, Panama, or anywhere else. It wouldn't be possible to find out where. The deal was made so attractive that I believe Oaktree couldn't refuse to help with the money-laundering evidence. The crooked enterprise involved a huge amount of money to be moved, hidden, and the evidence deleted. It's not easy to keep billions of dollars in small banks and be able to hide the footprint. That's why this book, *Dynasty Escape*, is interesting, because it shines a light behind the scenes—into the dark corners of corruption.

On November 7, 2013, two major things happened. Oaktree and Taishin Bank entered into a five-year, US$100 million loan agreement, with 'favorable terms.' It seems some ships were mortgaged to Taishin Bank, but this is a breach of Taiwan law, which states that a bank cannot benefit and make money from asset sales. Taishin Bank later bought Fortuna Elephant at 15%, at the time of the 2016 mediation. This is also connected to Cathay United Bank's chairman being involved in the scandal of the one-dollar sale to Cortland Capital, when the chairman benefited to the tune of US$20 million.

Then a strange thing emerged.

November 13, 2013, was the last day for filing particulars of claims, to confirm how much each of the parties were owed. The Hyundai Group hired a different law firm, called Clifford Chance LLP, but their filings were, in my opinion, fraudulent. The first three pages were fine, but the rest of the 100-page-plus supporting document was "modified" by Clifford Chance

LLP and hand delivered to EPIC in Minnesota. EPIC is the key 24/7 information center for receiving computerized filing services. Why hand delivered? America is a huge country.

This is very odd indeed.

At the same time, TMT particulars of claim had other issues—there are other discrepancies regarding documents send by Fedex. AlixPartners presented, under oath, in a 2017 deposition, that the date stamp on those documents was changed. The details can be confirmed, and Fedex records will confirm, what looks like fraud in the filing. It was most likely a SWAP in New York, filed electronically by AlixPartners. This means that the TMT filing amount and the HHI filing amount in Chapter 11 are not compatible. What if the entire Chapter 11 became compromised as early as November 2013, when it's very likely the collusion and theatricals were first set up?

Chapter 11 action began in earnest on December 15, 2013, eight months after Mega Bank first sent the default notice at 1:45pm on April 15, 2013. A Ladybug officially created the cross default. The notice was sent from two offices—one from Mega Bank's head office and another from the Tung Nan branch. Mayer Brown LLP drew up the documents in draft form only. It was not official and the documents were kept at the Tung Nan branch. That's the reason default notices came from two offices.

It's obvious to me that TMT was cheated—the loan was originally unsecured on a LOC and was signed at Mega head office in July 2012. As I've already outlined, A Ladybug was then requested as collateral for the increased loan, which was subsequently sold to Macquarie bank in December 2013. Macquarie head office in Sydney had authorized the deal on November 22, 2012 (which, of course, is an incorrect date, used to confuse people), utilizing part of a loan of US$25 million from Mega Bank to purchase the A Ladybug loan at an agreed price which was paid in New York. This was probably the first clear case of money laundering.

I contend that TMT was totally defrauded by parallel documents that were drawn up later by Mayer Brown LLP and Winston & Strawn LLP for the DIP creditor, to cover up the process. Because of this misrepresentation, a clear picture wasn't presented to the Chapter 11 court and the, so-called, good faith/bad faith concept was created. On the surface, Chapter 11 was just a showcase because, behind the scenes, the big meetings involving the entire Taiwan banking system—and possibly New York, London, Hong Kong, Panama, Washington DC, and Taipei—were in full swing.

By the end of December 2013, the Panama Embassy in Taiwan was also in full swing and the final modifications for cooking the evidence were created in A Ladybug. The plan then became how to destroy the restructure plan submitted to the US court, prepared by TMT and AlixPartners and, of course, Evan Flaschen. But the news came back from Houston that the restructure proposal had failed and the judge authorized the selling of the ships.

Overall, the January 8, 2014, Chapter 11 hearings were disastrous, but I was in Taiwan and couldn't attend. When the automatic stay expired, the ships began to be sold. I've already mentioned that unsecured creditors formed the UCC—HHI and Hyundai Samho Industries, China Shipping, oil companies, Blystad Shipping (a Norwegian company I once helped when they were in trouble)—they were all there, like vultures round a carcass. As I said, I couldn't understand why Hyundai didn't want to come to Chapter 11 with Seward & Kissel LLP, who represented the UCC. Conflictingly, they hired Clifford Chance to file proof of claim—the total amount was US$187 million. The documents, in my opinion, were entered fraudulently, as the amount was cooked up and altered from Korea to New York, and again from New York to Houston. The filing was also suspicious because the Korean courier to New York, then to Houston, seems to have swapped documents along the way.

## CHAPTER 11 BANKRUPTCY: PART II

After Chapter 11, over three years, evidence of the scam needed to be cleaned up in such a way that neither the Chapter 11 court nor anyone else would be able to find out about it. We've already identified banks—such as Shanghai Commercial Saving Bank, Bank SinoPac, China Trust Bank, Taishin Bank, Cathay United Bank, and so on—who benefited in this business, most likely with the blessing of Big Mama. But it also required the involvement of middlemen such as JPMC, SC Lowy, and Macquarie Bank to sort out the mess. Once the demise of the KMT as the dynastic rulers of Taiwan became a reality, Madam Chow had to start executing Plan X to send as much funds as possible overseas. This needed to involve many international banks in Taiwan, such as Goldman Sachs, HSBC, Barclays, Standard Chartered Bank, ANZ Bank, CitiBank, Bank of America, UBS, Credit Swiss, Deutsche Bank, BNP Paribas, and Bank of New York Mellon.

Taiwan already had close relationships with four British banks, such as ANZ Bank (former RBS Taipei), HSBC, Standard Chartered, and Barclays. They were involved in the trading of CDSs and CDOs scandal in the USA and UK, and the subsequent Asian clean-up, between 2009 and 2011. Although it looks like there were many people involved—and you're thinking, 'how could they all be part of such a conspiracy?'—the truth is, only a small insider group could have had access to the complete plan. The rest could only know bits and pieces, not enough to connect up all the dots.

That was left to me to do!

To help me with that, as I mentioned already, I met with the CEO of ORIX in Taiwan and he told me that, as Japan's number one leasing company, they had received an invitation, but they found the sales to be highly unusual—not normal at all, utilizing a triangular affiliation, especially an assignment from JPMC to third buyers—in other words, Mega Bank didn't transact on a one-to-one basis, JPMC was in between. I requested a copy of the invitation prospectus but, as I think I told you, there was a condition that those who were unsuccessful had to destroy all documents and certainly not show them to outside parties. This clause alone violates the financial regulations of every Financial Services Commission and Securities and Exchange Commission in the world.

If that's not suspicious, what is?

*9.1: Bankruptcy Court insignia and Room 404*

# CHAPTER 10
## TMT VS MEGA BANK

THE TMT VS Mega Bank Chapter 11 case had many "unique" features:

1) Nobody asked what had happened in 2010 and why TMT filed for Chapter 11.

2) Nobody cared about MOR (management of risk), whether the figures were right or not.

3) Star Bulk shareholders and HHI were all using the same lawyers (Seward & Kissel), but they shared the work out to other lawyers to avoid multiple occasions of conflict of interest—51% of Star Bulk shareholders used Paul Weiss LLP and 20% of Star Bulk shareholders used Willkie Farr LLP. So, at least 51% of shareholders can be treated as affiliates. This was a serious legal conflict issue from day one.

4) Mayer Brown LLP were also TMT's lawyers for its subsidiary, F3 Capital, in Vantage Drilling, between 2009 and 2013. Bracewell & Giuliani LLP then became Vantage Drilling's lawyers and they were also involved in Chapter 11 for the debtors. More details will emerge surrounding ex-JPMC bankers and New York hedge funds.

5) Then there's Shanghai Commercial Bank in New York, Cathay United Bank in several US cities, First Bank in New York, Bank SinoPac in California, Chinatrust Bank in many US cities—all involved in one way or another.

Literally hundreds of lawyers around the world were involved in the TMT vs Mega Bank Chapter 11 case. This included lawyers in Singapore, China, UAE, South Africa, Liberia, the Marshall Islands, Panama, Malta, Belgium, America, and Britain. Each overseas ship arrest involved at least two law firms. In the case of Belgium, it involved nine law firms in Antwerp. The physical ships and real (not loan) sales involved Hong Kong, Greece, Germany, USA, and other countries.

The Chapter 11 courts involved venues in Austin, Dallas, Houston, Miami, Washington DC, Hartford Connecticut, New York, and other cities in the USA. It involved many law firms, paralegals, and associated professions. In fact, it became so big that there are now legal societies and institutions using the case of TMT in Chapter 11 as a source of study for their members.

We already know what the objectives of the KMT and bankers in Taiwan were—we already know their intentions. The DPP, the opposition parties, and Taiwan citizens were chasing the ill-gotten gains, accrued over the past 65 years, as per the DPP's public manifesto. The objective was to move the money without fingerprints. The answer was SWAP. This was the same thing that had happened during the 2008 Western financial crisis and is covered in detail in my book *The Gold Man from the East*. It happened in Hong Kong, Singapore, Tokyo, London, Sydney, New York, Panama, China, and many other places.

On December 15, 2013, at the same time as the Chapter 11 bankruptcy case got under way, the sale of all TMT loans began among 26 Taiwanese banks, led by Mega Bank, Shanghai Commercial and Savings Bank, Bank SinoPac, First Bank, Cathay United Bank, Chinatrust Bank, and Ta Chong Bank. It was a carbon copy of the big CDO sale in the Western financial crisis. Back in 2008 the big Western banks sold their toxic assets to governments in exchange for bailout funding. Now, Taiwan banks were selling TMT ship mortgages in exchange for KMT favors. Both were SWAPs of the worst kind—the kind that had been perfected on Wall

Street. Now the Taiwan bankers hired those same Wall Street "experts" to help them with their potential scam.

A ship is a single asset and normal procedure is to syndicate a ship's mortgage between a couple of banks. In TMT's case, the loans were divided into small sections to ensure that nobody saw or understood the big picture. They knew exactly what levels would be lawful and what would be unlawful. They knew how to avoid legal action by moving around different jurisdictions. They worked with the registration offices in Panama, Liberia, and the Marshall Islands, and their offices in New York, Panama, Greece, and London. They used bi-time accounting and law firms. The exceptions were Cathay United Bank's sale of Fortuna Elephant and the sale of C Ladybug and D Ladybug—otherwise, the rest were all divided up.

The most difficult were A Ladybug and A Duckling, which were 100% single loans from Mega Bank to the new buyers. A Duckling was sold to SC Lowy in Hong Kong, who benefited greatly from finance given by Mega Bank for acting as front buyers of ten other ship loans. I visited them in Hong Kong in February/March 2014 and discovered they did the deal through relationships with ex-colleagues in Deutsche Bank and Solus Asset Management in New York—one ex-colleague now runs a hedge fund from 410 Park Avenue. You see, the A Duckling loan agreement needed to be hidden, so it went to SC Lowy. In other words, SC Lowy got A Duckling for free.

Let's talk about SC Lowy for a moment. They began in 2009, right after the financial crisis, as a team of distressed debt traders who resigned from Deutsche Bank and set up their own boutique investment bank in Hong Kong. SC Lowy dealt exclusively in distressed and illiquid investments across Asia, an asset class that became increasingly fashionable among banks and hedge funds after the financial crisis. Michel Lowy founded the company, alongside Soo Cheon Lee. Lee estimated that the total size of the distressed market in Asia-Pacific, excluding Japan, was as high as US$100 billion. Lowy and Lee previously led Deutsche Bank's Asian distressed products group and cut their teeth at Cargill (the agribusiness giant who I'll mention later in connection with the B Max ship), trading distressed and illiquid investments in the aftermath of the 1997 Asian financial crisis.

Lowy caused a stir when he resigned from Deutsche Bank, having founded its Asian distressed debt operation in 1999. Under his leadership the group was regarded as the region's leading force in distressed debt trading and investing. While the opaque nature of trading in the loans and bonds of troubled companies makes industry data hard to come by, market participants said that investment banks and hedge funds had been aggressively moving into the Asian market in the hunt for under-priced debt. Half of the new bank's 14 employees followed Lowy from Deutsche Bank, including Chetan Baxi, Chief Operating Officer, and Robert Lepsoe, Head of Origination and Special Situations. Nine of the employees were also shareholders. They initially focused on leveraged buyout debt in Australia, which they sold on to banks and hedge funds. They also invested in portfolios of non-performing bank loans in Japan and traded in distressed assets across Asia-Pacific as opportunities appeared. So, you can see the caliber of vulture that was involved in TMT's Chapter 11.

Esben Christensen and Evan Flaschen were both working with Clarksons' Andy Case and Clarksons in Hong Kong. One week before the sale of A Duckling, MOL (Mitsui O.S.K. Lines) of Japan had sold a similar ship for US$28 million. I had a bidder who overbid Korea Line (SC Lowy's "client") by US$1 million, but Even Flaschen declined the higher bid at the request of his friends at SC Lowy. Just one example of what was, in my opinion, a conflict of interest. Similarly, Seward & Kissel had been the Star Bulk general counsel since 2008. They were also lawyers for HHI, Hyundai Samho, and Hyundai Mipo Shipyard. These apparent conflicts of interest became serious, so the filing of Particulars of Claim for the

Hyundai Group was done by Clifford Chance in New York, in my opinion to disguise such conflicts of interest. You can see what a web of intrigue and deceit was being spun to confuse and confound.

Moving on, the biggest risk to the plan was if the judge allowed the ships to move and work, and so generate revenue—so the US$20 million DIP loan was mostly paid in legal fees to AlixPartners and Bracewell & Giuliani, and the new money was never used to move vessels or generate cargoes, as it was meant to, except for one single voyage. The second difficulty was to make sure the ships were kept from me, Nobu Sue, as designee. Let me explain, the debtor designee should manage the Chapter 11 under the debtor lawyer, because the debtor lawyer would not have sufficient experience of the business to run the operation. However, in TMT's Chapter 11, Evan Flaschen of Bracewell & Giuliani decided to do it all by himself. I mean, I could work the ships and, if income was generated, the whole plan might be exposed. So the key was to take control of TMT away from me.

To help with that, I believe Petros Pappas, Seward & Kissel LLP, and others exaggerated a story that was circulated by the Greeks, who had been moving against me since 2008, and was reported in TradeWinds and other shipping publications in November 2013.

What they reported was an "Iranian incident": The US Department of the Treasury's OFAC issued a Finding of Violation against B Whale for breaking US trade sanctions against Iran at the time (but subsequently lifted). B Whale was part of the Chapter 11 bankruptcy proceedings in Houston and that put it under US jurisdiction when the sanctions violation was supposed to have occurred, between August and September 2013 (nobody was sure exactly when). The sanctions in force at the time prohibited dealings with the National Iranian Tanker Company (NITC). OFAC found that B Whale conducted a ship-to-ship transfer and received barrels of condensate crude oil (note that condensate is not crude oil) from the NITC VLCC vessel Nainital. They also alleged that B Whale tried to conceal evidence of the transaction. In fact, A Whale and B Whale were in a twelve-month moratorium, by bilateral agreement, from May 2013.

When what I believe was fake news came out, Evan Flaschen requested me to come to the Lancaster Hotel in Houston that weekend. He threatened me and said I should give up control of the entire TMT fleet, to prevent me going to prison. I was in the USA at the time and fairly confused by everything that was going on in Chapter 11. I honestly believed he had my best interests at heart and was genuinely trying to keep me out of jail—so I did what he asked. I didn't know at the time that both he and Bracewell & Giuliani had already received a money transfer from Mega Bank USA (ICBC LA and ICBC NYC). I didn't find that out until mediation in 2016. So, when I tried to get involved after that, the judge wouldn't allow it.

'Nobu, you're out!'

And they carried on with their secret meetings, to which I had no access.

In the end, as B Whale's assets had been liquidated in the Chapter 11, OFAC ruled that a Finding of Violation was appropriate, rather than a financial penalty or any charges against myself. So there was no danger of me going to prison and Evan Flaschen must have been lying to get me to relinquish control. Evan Flaschen, Charles Kelley, lawyers called Charles Schreiber and Mr Black (who I've already mentioned—both worked for Winston & Strawn LLP, the DIP lender's legal firm, in New York and Washington DC) seemed always to be working together. It was a drama that would have been well received on Broadway or London's Theatreland.

It was a totally crazy story, and it was just the tip of an orchestrated iceberg.

It was insane!

The "Iranian incident" was just one example of the conspiracy I believe Mega Bank and Star Bulk had engineered against me. The entire legal team, along with the Vantage team, under their Chief Administration Officer Chris Declare, worked with Vidal Martinez LLP in the Chapter 11 case on the fourth floor of the Southern District of Houston's Bankruptcy Court. They all worked together—even AlixPartners seemed to sell me out. Lisa Donahue began to use the 'privileged information' excuse not to copy emails to me, even though she was the original financial advisor I had hired. Lawyers came and went—disappeared somewhere and were replaced by others. It was a litigious revolving door, with everyone charging big bucks to get in on the act of destroying Nobu Sue and TMT. It was like a musical concert, where they were all playing in tune with each other, but being conducted from somewhere outside.

The Taiwan banks sold most of the loans in October 2013. The closing conditions were that everything would be completed between December 2013 and January 2014. The banks were acting in concert, to clean up the financial paper/computer-trail and hide the real profits or losses. It's like this, when there's an orchestral performance, there also has to be a conductor. Who?

The accountants at the Big Four banks in Taiwan must have been very busy. They had to work with the audited statements of over 40 banks. But the Shanghai Commercial & Savings Bank (SCSB) was private and had a history of over 100 years of collaboration with the KMT and Taiwan-China investment funds, which had created a special system. The New York office is situated on 55th Street, between Park Avenue and Lexington, only 100 meters from Solus Capital Management and Deutsche Bank's Distressed Products Group. They were of great assistance, as the Hong Kong office was used to handling huge amounts of money between Taiwan, China, and New York, for its best client, the China Investment Fund.

So, Mega Bank and the KMT did their job well—or at least they hired enough people to do that job for them. Those they didn't hire, they must have bribed or threatened, but they used all the international power at their disposal, power they had accumulated over the years the Dynasty was in control of Taiwan, usurping my country's resources.

*10.1: JPMorgan Chase building in central Hong Kong*

# CHAPTER II

## REVERSE ENGINEERING IN CHAPTER II

THE CHAINS OF instruction in the Chapter 11 case seem to have disappeared. This is why I say "reverse engineering," I mean without the head of the Dynasty beast, the rest fades away into a forest, a smoke-screen, a diversion. Chapter 11 happened in the first place because I wasn't willing to be treated again the way I had been by the RBS and JPMC in the 2008 financial crisis conspiracy (detailed in my book *The Gold Man from the East*). I also wondered why I should be paying US$20 million to Priscilla Hsing to rescue TMT from Mega Bank and the KMT—so I initiated Chapter 11 instead.

I believe OCM Formosa Strait Holdings, SC Lowy, Deutsche Bank, Macquarie Bank, et al. were all involved in a "triangular" fronting relationship. Conspiracies today involve digital crimes and how to avoid computer footprints. The KMT conspiracy had a similar pattern and method of involvement. I mean, it couldn't have happened simply by bilateral connections, it had to have that triangular (or even more complex) context to it, with time lapses and documents provided over several stages.

Let me try to be clearer. The patterns and footprints left by the conspirators were supposed to have been camouflaged, with all the relationships and collusions covered up. However, as time goes on, gaps appear in the smoke-screen, cracks appear in the bamboo curtain of concealment. They say 'chickens always come home to roost' and wrongdoing will be found out in time. It's the same as those many unpunished past crimes now being solved with the discovery of DNA. Similarly, I'm making new discoveries every day and I will expose the whole thing—the crime and the cover-up!

Let's look at what we know. The plan was to hide the outflow of money from Taiwan to overseas destinations. We don't know *exactly* how this was done, but there are three ways it could be accomplished:

1) The outflow occurred in the normal course of business transactions but, once the money was out, it was used in illegal ways.

2) The outflow didn't occur in a normal way and the money just suddenly showed up in overseas accounts in a normal way.

3) Neither the outflow nor the appearance of the money overseas were normal—both were abnormal and suspicious.

In the case of Mega Bank, option 3) is how I believe it was done. The money went out by means of a SWAP, but then the source of the funds wasn't clear, so there must have been another SWAP between Panama and New York. Was that why the AML scandal was discovered by the NYDFS and the US$180 million fine imposed?

This is why the total amount of money became as big as it did—double counting. Suspicions are that the New York branch of Mega International Commercial Bank controlled things between 2012 and 2014. The Mega branch had the SWIFT code ICBCUS33, which was at the same address as the former Bank of China, Taiwan—the US dollar-clearing Central Bank of Taiwan in the building built in 1902 to house the Chamber of Commerce. So, the Central Bank of Taiwan may also be involved in this scandal. If so, then most definitely more banks must have been involved, such as Hua Nan Commercial Bank, First Commercial Bank, Chang Hua Commercial Bank, and Taiwan Land Bank—or maybe even all eight government-controlled banks in one way or another. Robert Seiden, the financial investigator, told me he'd never seen so many banks working in concert in one case in New York, the most sophisticated US dollar-clearing system.

But the peculiar pattern continues. In international transactions it's customary to close deals on the same day, even with twelve-hour time differences. Yet here we see that the transactions were not closed on the same day. Why did it need two and even three days to close them? It didn't make sense in the banks' books of assets and liabilities. Furthermore, no compliances of POA in either the seller or the buyer were involved. Most compliances favored either JPMC, or Macquarie Bank, or Deutsche Bank.

I collected information from a banking industry specialist, who told me clearly that over US$40 million of transactions in the JPMC bank needed audit and legal department involvement in order to hold positions. Yet I didn't see any of those documents—the sparse documentation there was didn't provide enough information to distinguish whether it was novation or assignment of the loans.

It was sad to see so many good ships being sold at 30% to 50% of their true worth. The shipyards didn't help, and the lawyers kept charging huge fees. More than 16 retention accounts were opened by the banks that I, as designee, had no way to access. They didn't care about the special features of my ship designs, nor that the ships could do so many things. What also surprised me was that Lloyd's Register, which knew the ships, were also unwilling to attest the valuations. TMT assisted the world in oil skimming, despite the problems with the dispersant in the Gulf of Mexico disaster. Only A Whale could do this and I allowed the world to use the technology I invented for free. But the A Whale story wasn't important to the people in Houston—they weren't interested in oil skimming, only in skimming up as much money as they could.

I was sad to see TMT being torn apart. I later discovered an email Vantage Drilling sent to their lawyer, Vidal Martinez, as early as November 2013, stating that the TMT empire was collapsing. How did they know this? That email is one of several sent from Martinez LLP and Steiner Thompson (Director of Vantage Drilling) to all the directors of Vantage, stating that Nobu Sue's empire was going to be destroyed soon. This showed that the KMT plan must have been ready by November 2013 and everyone must have known that the Chapter 11 bankruptcy wasn't going to restructure TMT, but destroy it. It showed the collusion of the lawyers behind the scenes. I have emails from Petros Pappas, Ken Leung, Andy Case and others, detailing how they all collaborated with Seward & Kissel LLP and Clarksons and I believe even the judge may have known something underhand was going on, because he tried to prevent me from seeing the emails.

So, by January 2014, all the forces were aligned:

1) Mayer Brown, representing Mega International Commercial Bank and Chinatrust Bank wanted to sell the ships and get out.

2) Shanghai Commercial Bank wanted to sell the ships and it needed to hide the money laundering that happened between 2011 and 2013 in Taiwan, Hong Kong and New York.

3) Vidal Martinez was communicating with all parties to try to buy out the Vantage US$50 million shares from the court, so he could destroy TMT in Chapter 11.

4) Evan Flaschen was the debtors counsel and he set up the benefits in Bracewell & Giuliani LLP.

5) Albert Stein and Lisa Donahue disappeared from AlixPartners.

6) Peter Evensen of Teekay Told the AMA that Evan Flaschen wouldn't be able to restructure. He'll sell you to the hedge funds, which is exactly what happened.

This Chapter 11 case was so strange. It wasn't really Oaktree or Monarch, it was Star Bulk coming to purchase the TMT ships. Their general counsel was Seward & Kissel.

Hyundai Group built all the ships and their general counsel was Seward & Kissel. The lawyer for the unsecured creditors was Seward & Kissel. The, so-called, vulture fund got together and used different names for the entire collusion. I believe they worked together with the lawyers for the Taiwan banks, all under the direction of Petros Pappas and Madam Chow.

The object was:

1) To make as much money as possible.

2) To hide the Dynasty's escape plan.

3) Vantage to take over TMT and force me out.

4) JPMC, Star Bulk, Clarksons, AlixPartners, HHI, Cathay, Cortland Capital, Shanghai Bank, SinoPac, Taichung Bank, and others to get rid of the evidence of collusion as soon as they could.

Now, as a lone wolf they thought I was defeated, as the ships began to be sold one by one. It was a victory for Petros Pappas, who had started the whole thing. However, I have since seen emails of Pappas' communications with Ken Leung of Oaktree, Jennifer Box of JPMC, and Randy Ray of the Onassis Foundation.

All potentially incriminating.

In February 2014 I damaged my back and couldn't travel. I'd commuted between Taipei and Houston more than ten times in six months and exhausted my body carrying too many heavy documents around the world. I ended up not being able to move, so I stayed in Hong Kong and worked with Deloitte Touche (HK), with a view to evaluating the Chapter 11 case and trying to prepare hedge funds to buy out the remaining ships.

There are shipping meetings held in New York and Connecticut every spring and autumn. I came into contact with a strange ex-banker of JPMorgan Chase Shipping at one such meeting, who worked with Peter Evensen and Randy Ray in Miami, and with Albert Stein and Lisa Donahue, as well as with AMA CEO Peter Lund. Those people were major presenters at conferences such as Capital Link, Connecticut Shipping, and the Marine Money Conference. The banker told me that the world of shipping finance was 'populated by a small circle of very greedy people.' I wish I'd known earlier.

Deloitte Touche (HK) tried its best to help, but all efforts were derailed by Evan Flaschen, who wouldn't cooperate. He did the job he was most likely paid to do by the Dynasty and wasn't willing to rescue the TMT fleet. Deloitte Touche (HK) introduced me to several Hong Kong hedge funds, most of them believed the TMT Chapter 11 case was strange. They found that the information from Chapter 11 was so sparse and so closed to outsiders, that it seemed to be designed to prevent any external offers or concerns.

Evan Flaschen signed as designee while I was laid up in Hong Kong and I wasn't informed about what he was doing. The biggest scam was the B Max transfer of debt with Shanghai Bank and B Max DIP, for unknown reasons. In the end, the B Max money was paid by CarVal Investors (a global alternative investment company) to a Chinese court—a very strange matter altogether—and there is more detail about the B Max case in the next chapter.

*11.1: Taiwan Embassy in New York; the national flag is inside the entrance, not outside*

# CHAPTER 12
## SELLING THE ENTIRE FLEET

IN APRIL 2014 a US$20 million loan was sold for just one dollar to Cortland Capital Market Services in Chicago by Cathay United Bank. Generally speaking, the selling price should be pro rata to the loan. This one for only a dollar didn't make sense. Additionally, the name of the chairman of Cathay United Bank was stamped on the loan document—in Taiwan, chairmen never stamp loan documents.

The chairman of Cathay United Bank was also a former chairman of the smaller United Bank in Taiwan. Unethical things like this happened—a small bank could buy a big bank and the chairman then became boss of the big bank. This particular 70-year-old chairman spoke Japanese, Taiwanese, Chinese, and English, just like me. He bought a power station and a golf course without paying for them—all covered by insolvency profits.

Fortuna Elephant was sold for US$88 million, but F Whale had the best computerized engine and it was sold for US$78 million to Onassis Holdings, way below its true value. The ship's loan was only US$68 million in total, so that meant there was US$10 million in equity. The skulduggery involved the sale and purchase of small funds before the ship sale and the US$20 million second mortgages in the Marshall Islands were never involved. Evan Flaschen's designee signed to register the US$20 million loan and discharged it before the ship was delivered to Onassis in July 2014.

The only 'outsider' interested in TMT ship loans was CarVal Investors, a subsidiary of Cargill of Minnesota USA, with an office in Singapore. The CarVal fund was called Wayzata Banking, Financial & Insurance and it had been involved in 2009 with the financing of Vantage Drilling's first jack-up rig, at a 23% interest rate. It bought the TMT debt from the Bank of Kaohsiung on December 15, 2016, for US$1.75 million per ship at 70 cents on the dollar for the loans, which was very attractive at that time. The board at the Bank of Kaohsiung were against the sale, but the chairman, who was nominated by Big Mama, forced it through for CarVal.

The assets were small handy-sized vessels—called A Handy, B Handy, and C Handy—and a larger Panamax bulk carrier—called B Max. The ships were originally syndicated by Shanghai Commercial Savings Bank and other Taiwan banks, who became scared of the Chapter 11 bankruptcy.

The real story was that Shanghai Commercial Savings Bank had been a private bank of the KMT party for over 90 years, since the early 1920s. It was a small bank, privately held by special banking licensing companies. Shanghai Commercial Savings Bank also participated in the sales of C Whale, D Whale, E Whale, and F Whale loans, right after the exposure of Mega International Commercial Bank's money-laundering scandal.

The Shanghai Commercial Savings Bank scandal began in June 2011, when they started moving massive amounts of money out of Taiwan to Deutsche Bank's Wall Street branch. I later found out that Shanghai Bank had intentionally reduced interest rate charges in order to modify the TMT loans and conduct money laundering. In particular, the bank used a sticker for signatures, but mainly it amended the contracts (to pay the beneficiary) to set up its own account in Deutsche Bank, utilizing TMT loans. The worst thing was the final amendment documents, where they printed their own bank account in the Deutsche Bank Trust as beneficiary. My book, *The Gold Man from the East*, outlines how the same tactics were used by the RBS and JPMC, utilizing TMT's FFA (Forward Freight Agreement) clearing house name, set up in a normal

US dollar savings accounts. Basically, it's hijacking a client's name to freely control the flow of money.

I investigated and found out that the Hong Kong branch of Shanghai Commercial Savings Bank had met with a top gun from New York, probably to discuss how to destroy evidence of money laundering in 2011–2012. The people involved were mainly from the Deutsche Bank Distressed Products Group in the USA, London, and Hong Kong, but they weren't able to hide the smoking gun well enough. Can you guess who these ex-Distressed Product Group people were? Yes, of course, our old friends SC Lowy again.

I didn't know all the facts I know now when the shipping newspaper TradeWinds headlined 'TMT And CarVal Enter Restructuring For Four TMT Ships.' I was in Taipei, preparing the plan for the four RO-RO/PCTC vessels, so I wasn't able to attend when TMT accepted a 50%/50% joint venture, with veto rights. Incidentally, the RO-RO/PCTC plan was perfect to make close to a US$100 million that could be fully repaid but, as I said previously, the judge rejected it and US$20 million second mortgages were allowed on 16 ships, except for C Whale, with some very strange terms. I mean, why was it allowed to be backdated to June 20, 2013? Why was it necessary to add US$20 million to each ship, totaling US$320 million on a US$20 million DIP loan? The judge never asked those questions.

The CarVal deal was approved by the court and this was epoch making, after the four RO-RO/PCTC super carrier deal was rejected on June 8, 2014, by Judge Isgur. However, the approval process started to make it look like CarVal were going to cheat on the agreement. Evan Flaschen, Charles Kelley, Lisa Donahue, Esben Christensen, and two CarVal general managers, with lawyers, met in the London offices of Cargill (CarVal's parent company). I believe they intentionally changed the terms presented to the Houston bankruptcy court to the effect that TMT was accepting 49%/51%, with no veto. I tried to explain this to Judge Isgur, but he was in no position to listen to my story because all the lawyers backed-up what seemed to me to be forgery. It was at this moment that I knew the legal firms, and maybe even the judge, may be being manipulated by outside influences.

Clearly, CarVal were able to see what was going on in the TMT Chapter 11 case and wanted some of the action. Their general shipping manager in Singapore was a good person and I had a short conversation with him after the RO-RO/PCTC plan was rejected by Judge Isgur. It was clear that he understood shipping and the true value of the TMT ships with their unique design. After failure in Chapter 11, I met him on the top floor of the Mandarin Hotel in Singapore. I was straight with him.

'Why did CarVal lie and change the terms for the court?'

He was silent for a while, then he made a strange offer.

'Can you sell your portions?'

I was shocked, but it was clear from the eyes of this blonde-haired, Western businessman that he was hiding something, and that he was under pressure to keep it hidden.

Later on, I found out that the Marshall Islands registry had only 85% for all four ships bought by CarVal. The owner of the other 15% couldn't be identified. The loan transfers went to Solus Limited and Ultra Master Fund Ltd., which all belonged to a former boss of Deutsche Bank Distressed Products Group, from Solus Capital, at 410 Park Avenue, near the offices of Shanghai Commercial Savings Bank in New York. How could 85% be in the Marshall Islands—and where was the other 15%? And how were the ex-stars of Deutsche Bank's Distressed Products Group involved?

The answer will come as we are in litigation at the time of writing this book.

# SELLING THE ENTIRE FLEET

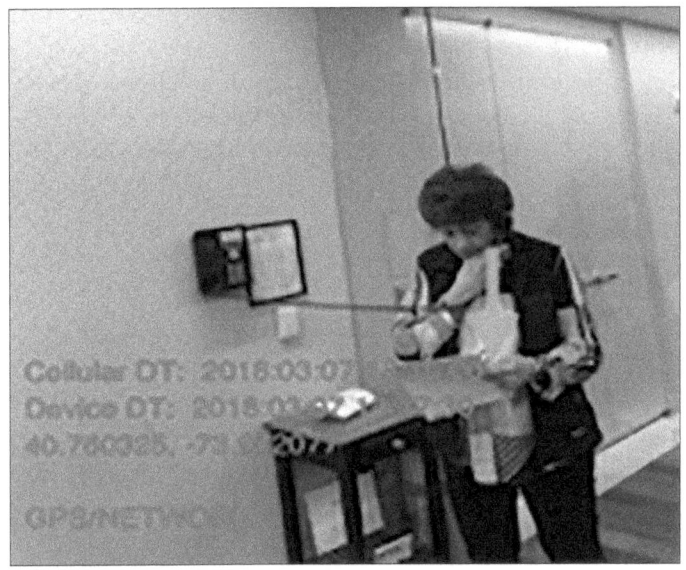

*12.1: Serving documents on Solus Capital in Manhattan, which they refused to accept*

As we've seen, Evan Flaschen of Bracewell & Giuliani LLP was in full flow, selling TMT assets at below market prices for such a modern fleet. The crazy accounting of the US$20 million second mortgage, that was multiplied by 16 to total US$320 million, was like something out of the Wild West days of Texas lawlessness. The DIP lender (Macquarie) had so much power and completely destroyed the Chapter 11 restructuring proposals to protect their own interests and the interests of others. Even Judge Isgur was, at best, hoodwinked into believing Charles Kelley of Mayer Brown LLP, who was representing the interests of Mega Bank and Chinatrust Bank, the chief instigators of Plan X for the KMT.

Evan Flaschen was supposed to be representing TMT's interests, but I believe he tricked me into relinquishing what control I had to exclude me from the decision-making process. In April 2014 Flaschen recommended that I hire new lawyers. He must have known that I suspected him of collusion with

Mega Bank—a serious conflict of interest in clandestinely representing other parties as well as myself. There was so much subterfuge—after the sales of B Max, three Handy, and the Whale ships, I saw emails that proved Andy Case of Clarkson and Petros Pappas were involved with Oaktree and Monarch, that's when I hired the Texas law firm of HooverSlovacek LLP.

Chapter 11 was like running a marathon. You never knew what was going to happen from day to day, or even hour to hour. The judge had a lot of power and the lawyers seemed to enjoy spending other people's money. TMT had already spent US$120 million to keep the ships and all the retention money was gone, and another US$50 million in Vantage shares, with a market value of US$70 million—plus the added US$20 million DIP loan. However, despite all this cash flying about, nobody did anything to facilitate an income or a future for TMT. All they did was laugh and suck the lifeblood out of my company.

HooverSlovacek raised the issue of my patents for the underdeck piping of ultra super tankers and ore carriers. A Whale skimmed oil in the Gulf of Mexico, with its unique design it was the only ship in the world equipped to do such a thing back in April 2010. Deirdre Brown of HooverSlovacek LLP, got up to speed with the Chapter 11 proceedings very quickly and soon came to the conclusion that there was a lot of irregularity, to put it mildly. The loans transferred to JPMC, SC Lowy, and Macquarie Bank weren't clear. JPMorgan Chase N.A. was declared in Taiwan, but no reference, address, telephone number, or signature could be matched properly in any of the loan transactions. Deirdre Brown informed the Houston bankruptcy court and Judge Isgur of this. The judge was uneasy about it because he was so close to the bankers' lawyers, and the DIP lender, and even Evan Flaschen.

The next firm of lawyers to exit the Chapter 11 scene was Seward & Kissel—only they didn't leave voluntarily, they were fired by the judge for leaking information and their legal fees were forfeit. It didn't surprise me. Many others should have been fired as well—maybe even sent to prison!

Then Charles Kelley of Mayer Brown LLP, who represented Mega Bank and Chinatrust Bank, just disappeared from the scene. He was so proud of his role in making millions of dollars in legal fees while protecting the Taiwan banks. Then he ran away. I enquired why he left and was told he'd made a filing mistake that couldn't be explained. It seemed to me that all the lawyers were jumping ship. There was no more money to be made and they were afraid their unlawful collusion would be found out.

Deirdre Brown turned out to be one of the best bankruptcy process lawyers in the USA. She did everything by the book and was exceptionally diligent. My opponents didn't like her, but so what? As long as she was doing her job lawfully, there was nothing they could do about it. She was the one who discovered that Bruce Paulson of Seward & Kissel LLP had leaked Chapter 11 information to outsiders. We knew that information went to Hamish Norton, the president of Star Bulk, then to Hill Dickinson LLP and Clifford Chance, who worked for the Busan law firms of HHI.

HHI had 10% of the world's shipbuilding capacity and the world's largest shipyards in Korea. They'd used Seward & Kissel for all 16 ships' loan agreements. They were totally silent and unwilling to come to court to explain the special designs and consequential value of TMT's Whale, Elephant, and Max ships. They were the largest UCC member and could wield power in the Chapter 11 case. They could have helped TMT. Instead, their law firm, Seward & Kissel, was found culpable of wrongdoing and penalized by the judge. HHI put B Ladybug up for auction in Malta and decided to keep their heads down until the typhoon passed. When you consider that TMT had given HHI ship orders valued in excess of US$2.6 billion between 2006 and 2013, why was it that nobody came?

The answer will be in my next book, which will expose the Korean story, and possibly the retention account story as well. Where and how was the money moved?

For the record, besides HHI's claim of US$187 million in Chapter 11 (the documents being hand delivered by Clifford Chance to the EPIC office in the mid-west at 5:00pm), there were only US$60 million in unsecured loans claimed against TMT itself. So, TMT hadn't a great deal of obligation to unsecured creditors and had paid most of the people before Chapter 11, which can be proven.

Credit bids (by Star Bulk shareholders) was a system of buying ships that favored the lenders rather than other potential buyers, who might have been prepared to pay more. The sales process appeared fair, but in the USA lenders could match the highest bidders, then take over the ship and only pay the amount of the loan—which was, in almost every case, less than the true value of the ship. The exceptions were E Whale's auction in South Africa and C Whale's auction in Singapore. All the other Whale ships were sold by credit bids.

The biggest scam was Petros Pappas' Product Shipping & Trading buying E Whale. Evan Flaschen extended the closing deadline by three days and wouldn't allow the ship to sell to the other highest bidders. Oaktree and Monarch bought all the Whale ships but hid the names of who they were buying for. The money went to Mega Bank, who didn't pay it into Chapter 11, but into KMT accounts in various parts of the world, including Panama and America. This was the mystery with the operating report, which was filed every month.

When all the ships were sold, the multitude of lawyers involved requested HooverSlovacek LLP to settle the case. They congregated outside the court. I saw Evan Flaschen, Charles Schreiber, Paul Weiss, Clifford Chance, and others—about 50 altogether.

'We'll forgive all his personal liabilities, if Nobu agrees not to sue anyone.'

Edward Rothberg, from HooverSlovacek, explained that I had legitimate issues I could fight and maybe win, but it would cost money to do so. I decided not to settle.

At first it seemed like a bad decision, but things began to change after a couple of years. In the summer of 2016, the MegaGate scandal emerged. Deirdre Brown called me and said she had big news. The AML fine of US$180 million against Mega Bank, the Samson Wu fake news, and other Mega Bank scandals were all appearing daily on Taiwan television, despite the propaganda of the state-controlled network. I slowly realized the rot wasn't confined to just one bank, but that it must pervade the entire Taiwan banking system. It took me until 2018 to discover that the details of the HHI claim were fraudulent.

Also, the US$20 million second mortgages had to be sorted out for the new buyers. The Liberia and Panama registries had US$20 million, but the way those mortgages were backdated in those countries was fraudulent. As I said previously, they were changed by several lawyers without a POA in hand.

Some issues are still in litigation and can't be written about here, but some of the things that happened in the world's worst Chapter 11 case need to be disclosed as a warning to any business contemplating going down that route. Learn from my mistakes!

There were so many questionable things going on—accounting fraud, collusion, secret manipulations, money being paid into accounts in Los Angeles and New York by the ICBCUS33 SWIFT code, and so on, and on. Some of those activities I have detailed in this book, but my investigations are ongoing and there will be more exposés in my next book.

I'm not going away!

*12.2: In 2017 Cargill were fined US$10 million for misleading prices in SWAP trades*

*12.3: Louis Dreyfus Commodities*

# CHAPTER 13

## B MAX: THE DRAMA

I'VE MENTIONED B Max in the previous chapter, and the B Max case was a drama worthy of a film script. So that's what I've done—written it as a film script. It's the only way I can think of to describe the huge orchestrated collusion involved. You will be familiar with the cast of characters, as most of them have already been mentioned in previous chapters. I don't have all the evidence to prove the level of collusion and the segments of conversation here are very sketchy and inconclusive but, in my opinion, incriminating enough to raise serious questions that need to be answered.

*13.1: Pure theatre (© stocksnapper/123RF)*

## SYNOPSIS

The Louis Dreyfus company is a global merchant, involved in agriculture, food processing, international shipping, and finance. It owns and manages hedge funds and ocean vessels, it operates real estate development, management, and ownership. It is one of the quartet of companies that dominate world agricultural commodity trading.

Dreyfus makes up about 10% of the world's agricultural product trade flows. They are also the world's largest cotton, rice, and sugar trader, and are expanding to become the world's third biggest trader of copper, zinc, and lead concentrate. Louis Dreyfus Holding BV has its headquarters in the World Trade Center, Amsterdam, and Louis Dreyfus companies have offices in more than 100 countries, the major ones located in New York, London, Beijing, Paris, Geneva, Buenos Aires, São Paulo, and Singapore.

Dreyfus and three major grain houses controlled 70% of the world's grain trades and were, along with Chinese traders, involved in a scheme to ship soya beans with toxic burn from a cargo fire, knowing this was a criminal offense. The plot involved the compliance of Lloyd's of London insurers and a private solution conspiracy of Chapter 11 lawyers to hide and then destroy the evidence.

The case was also connected to the AML case of 2012. The evidence was already deleted. The way ships were sold threw up questions about collusion between three major grain houses and international banks situated in New York.

Once you begin to lie, you have to continue to lie, to cover-up the original lie—even under oath in a US court.

This is a true story!

## BACKSTORY

A Max and B Max were the first two of nine ships built by the Hyundai Samho Shipyard during 2011—2013.

B Max—84000 deadweight tonnage—was the largest Panamax beam ship designed by Nobu Sue. It was very suitable for carrying grain, especially soya bean, from Brazil to China.

A Max was the first Chinese charter (Pacific Bulk in Singapore) to complete a second voyage. B Max was waiting for its maiden voyage for the same charterers anchored off the port of Santos in Brazil in June 2013.

When TMT filed for Chapter 11 bankruptcy in the USA, news spread quickly around the world and the CEO of Dreyfus soon heard about it. The news was music to his ears, as he'd lost money in a previous FFA deal with TMT. He saw the situation as an opportunity to target TMT for destruction.

Panamax are mid-sized cargo ships, capable of passing through the lock chambers of the Panama Canal. This is a story concerning one such ship, in the most complex and interesting Chapter 11 case ever, that included hundreds of lawyers all around the world.

## SCENE: TMT OFFICES TAIWAN
### January 2013

In January, six months before filing for Chapter 11, Tsan Ting Hwa and two Chinatrust people request a cash payment for IRS, for ships. This is a problem—commercial banks having an interest in Whale ship derivatives. They request payment before default notices—it's Mafia-like pressure.

TING HWA
If you pay, we'll help to restructure the loans.

NOBU
Why?

TING HWA
Because payment will enable the loans to be repurchased and provide another source of funds.

                    NOBU
Mr Tsan, we haven't defaulted on your loan or
the Chinatrust loan, so why? Or is it the only
  way to create new loan systems to hide the
  China Investment Trust involvement with TMT?
Tsan smiles—the Chinatrust people say nothing.
                    NOBU
   Please give me your agreement in writing.
They refuse.

Do they know the secret background of the
loans? They were the first bankers to approach
TMT in January 2010, to meet Green Huang.
**CUT TO**

## SCENE: FLOOR 8 OF TMT OFFICES IN TAIPEI
**June 17, 2013**

Priscilla Hsing, Deputy Manager of Mega
International Bank's foreign department, is
present with Nobu Sue. Ms Hsing has been asked
by her boss to check where Nobu has been for
the last month. She contacted TMT's accounting
department, knowing Mr Su visited the USA
quite often. It wasn't difficult to check the
VPBDU of his private jet, and Nobu's moves
in and out through Taiwan immigration. Now
there's silence and she looks very serious.
                    HSING
    Are you going to pay $20 million, as
       we suggested to you last month?
                    NOBU
  No, $20 million won't solve the problem.
                    HSING
           Are you going to file for
             Chapter 11 in the USA?
Nobu doesn't answer immediately. Instead, he
looks straight into her eyes. Her face twists
into a grimace. She's an elite and powerful

woman, used to getting her own way. The silence continues for a moment or two, before Nobu speaks.

NOBU

I won't answer that question. Why won't the bank rescue such very good assets?

Without another word, she turns furiously and leaves the office, dragging her subordinate, Mr Lee, with her.

**CUT TO**

## SCENE: T-GRÃO LOADING TERMINAL AT THE PORT OF SANTOS, BRAZIL

There is a fire at the terminal and a cargo of soya beans is damaged. The firefighting means that water spreads into the silo and it will cost a lot of money to separate out the damaged cargo in Brazil.

**CUT TO**

## SCENE: DREYFUS GENEVA OFFICE

The Dreyfus CEO and GM are present. They look happy.

CEO

Smile! This is a very happy moment for me. TMT is going under. Call our offices and find out where the TMT ships are located.

GM

There's a ship called A Max with our traders, carrying soya beans to China. They say the ship is a wonderful design and can load a maximum cargo from Brazil … and even Argentinian grain.

CEO

The B Max is waiting to load cargo, is it not?

GM

Yes, it's anchored off the port of Santos.

                              CEO
            C'est une bonne idée to shift the
            burn cargo in our terminal in Brazil
                  … load it onto the B Max.
                              GM
            Are you joking? That cargo is toxic.
                              CEO
                          Just do it!
                              GM
            Yes sir. But we'll have to be careful … B
            Max has cargo from two terminals, one is
            ours and the other is a joint venture. If
            anyone finds out … we're committing a crime.
                              CEO
                Don't worry, I'll talk to Cargill,
                   Bunge, and ADM … if I need to.
All three are agribusinesses and competitors
of Dreyfus. The GM has no choice. He instructs
the traders to sell the cargo to Cargill,
so Dreyfus can't be identified as the sole
perpetrator of the crime.

**CUT TO**

## SCENE: PRIVATE CLUB IN PARIS

A representative of Lloyd's of London is
having an expensive dinner. His cell-phone
rings. He answers the call.

                          LLOYD'S MAN
            Hi Philip. What can we do for you?
                          DREYFUS CEO
              We had a negligence fire case in
                  Brazil. Can you assist us?
                          LLOYD'S MAN
            This happens all the time. We're happy to
            insure your business. Your Indian warehouse
            acquisitions are great. Let's hope we can
                  do business for the next 100 years.

> DREYFUS CEO
> The burned cargo is about 5,900 tons.
> I've found a ship to take the load
> and how to get it sorted out, which
> will be good for both of us.
>
> LLOYD'S MAN
> Philip, you're a genius.
>
> DREYFUS CEO
> Just a matter of mixing cargoes—2% as usual?

After dinner in a private club in Paris, the man from Lloyd's takes the TGV from the Gare du Nord back to Charing Cross. It's a comfortable ride.

**CUT TO**

## SCENE: CARVAL OFFICE IN SINGAPORE

CarVal is a global alternative asset manager and are 100% Cargill's fund manager.

Nobu Sue knows about this company—they financed the first rig for Vantage Drilling. In 2009 they charged 22% interest on the entire $160 million finance package. Vantage didn't make a great deal of money as it was all income received for repayment to Wayzata (a CarVal subsidiary). Nobu Sue led TMT finance to complete the new rig construction with PPL Shipyard in Singapore, a subsidiary of Sembcorp Marine, specialists in the design and construction of offshore drilling rigs.

> CARVAL CEO
> What TMT ships can we buy?
>
> CARVAL LEGAL
> It will be a good idea to buy Nobu's fleet of B Max and three Handy Max larger bulk carriers in the Handy-size class.
>
> CARVAL CEO
> Can we use them?

CARVAL LEGAL
Sure. We've heard from traders that those
ships were the best Panamaxes ever built,
with modern computerized engines.

CARVAL CEO
OK, let's buy the loans.

CARVAL LEGAL
We can approach Kaohsiung Bank first. They hold
some of the loans in the syndication led by
the Shanghai Commercial Savings Bank Ltd. Only
70 cents on the dollar for brand new ships.

**CUT TO**

## SCENE: LE CHATEAU RESTAURANT IN GENEVA

The Dreyfus GM is having lunch with the Cargill GM.

DREYFUS GM
We need to sell you a cargo of Brazil
soya bean at a good price.

CARGILL GM
Bien sûr. What price?

DREYFUS GM
There's some burn damage to the cargo.
We need to mix it ... small amounts
at a time. We'll make a small loss,
but you'll make a big profit.

CARGILL GM
We can sell it to Chinese traders, they
always like an easy kickback. They'll use B
Max charters to handle it. We used A Max and
that ship had extra pockets of hidden space.

BOTH
Santé.

**CUT TO**

## SCENE: B MAX'S FIRST BERTH

The ship arrives—the Captain is Chinese and
has been drinking. He believes it's normal,

good, clean grain and he can load a maximum
cargo and go straight home. He's already been
waiting for three weeks in anchorage, watching
many other ships get loaded and sail past him.
He just wants to go home.

**CUT TO**

## SCENE: T-GRÃO LOADING TERMINAL AT THE PORT OF SANTOS, BRAZIL

The terminal president gets a call from the
Dreyfus CEO.

> TERMINAL GM
> Sir, are you saying we need to load as
> much cargo as possible on B Max?
> DREYFUS CEO
> That's what we've arranged. The
> ship is in a Chapter 11 case and we
> don't want to leave fingerprints.
> TERMINAL GM
> Yes sir.

Some cargo is kept outside the silo, so loading
the cargo is unusual, to say the least.

If the loading of the damaged cargo gets
discovered, it will draw world attention to
what was a significant fire. The only way to do
it is to load a little of the damaged cargo at
a time in the dark, changing the load line and
putting it on top of the conveyor system.

The terminal president immediately gives
orders to load at night.

> TERMINAL GM: Tell the agents it was
> raining, so we couldn't load during the
> day ... only at night, from sunset to
> sunrise. You know the allowance, right?

When cargo is mixed, there are up to 2%
allowances, which can be used by Chinese
traders as another insurance scam. They can

load old grain on top and claim for water damage. However, this process takes a long time and the color can turn black, and even into soya sauce and become toxic. So the operation has to be clandestine.

The local Brazilian workers are tired by the time darkness falls and do the loading without alerting SGS (inspection company) or intercargo surveyors. It's a secret mission, quietly done.

**CUT TO**

## SCENE: T-GRÃO LOADING TERMINAL

Normally, a grain load should only take four days. However, as the cargo is loaded at night, it takes ten days. There are no surveyors and the Chief Officer wonders why it's taking so long, but nobody on board the ship knows they're loading a damaged cargo mixture—intentionally ordered by the CEO of Dreyfus.

The Terminal GM's phone rings.

CARGILL GM
Our contract was to load 25,000 metric tons in two days. Why is it already taking ten days?
TERMINAL GM
It's raining. This is not abnormal, to load at night if it rains.
CARGILL GM
Nonsense! Stop loading and shift the cargo. We need to arrest both ship and cargo.

The ship is laid up at anchorage for one week.

**CUT TO**

## SCENE: LE CHATEAU RESTAURANT IN GENEVA

The Cargill and Dreyfus CEOs are meeting for dinner.

CARGILL CEO
We need to sort this out. You need a Brazilian court judgment, Cargill won't be criminalized by exporting your crap to China.

DREYFUS CEO
OK, we'll sort this dispute in a Santos court. But we need to give the cargo to somebody. Who? Let's sell it to Bunge [Bunge Limited—a global agribusiness] during the voyage. Assignment? Swapping? Novation? Camouflage? We need to explain to the Chinese trader, who is our friend. He must know exactly how much is contaminated.

CARGILL CEO
B Max is the largest ship of its kind, so it can take 66,000 metric tons plus additional cargo. We must make sure the first cargo is discharged from number one hold, which wasn't loaded in Brazil at the first loading terminal. That way, Bunge stays clean.

**CUT TO**

## SCENE: T-GRÃO LOADING TERMINAL

The ship goes back and loads the balance of the cargo in Santos and leaves port on July 14, about a month after TMT filed for Chapter 11 bankruptcy.

Total cargo loaded as per draft survey at T-Grão: 29,515 metric tons—with 20,315 normal.

Total cargo loaded as per draft survey at Export Corridor: 42,086 metric tons—no draft survey figure.

STRANGE?

Total cargo loaded as per draft survey terminal shore scale: 71,601 metric tons.

Exactly 5,000 metric tons over the normal 60,000 metric tons; 10% more-or-less standard shipment quantity.

Because of Nobu's super design of B Max, the ship could load 5,000 metric tons more.
**CUT TO**

## SCENE: SOUTH CHINESE PORT OF FANCHENG

The Chinese have been notified that 5,500 metric tons of good grain has been given for free and that 71,500 metric tons were loaded—66,000 metric tons of normal cargo + 5,500 metric tons of damaged cargo.

> CHINESE
> Thank you. We will take over the ship when it arrives at the Fancheng silo. We'll sell it as a full cargo of 71,500 metric tons to the crushing mill in China.

The Chinese traders sign a voyage charter with the Chinese operators, so all the risk is with the operators and owners (TMT B Max Corporation).
**CUT TO**

## SCENE: LAY-BY BERTH

B Max shifts from T-Grão to a lay-by berth on July 16 at 11:25 local time. This is because repairs need to be carried out on the terminal's warehouses/silos, as alleged by the T-Grão port operator. This is damning evidence. The only valid reason for this is that the two lines needed to load the bad cargo have to be reconnected for normal operations and they have to make the ship leave in order to do this.

The vessel is berthed at the lay-by from July 16, 12:08 local time, to August 5, 05:46 hours local time—20 days, confirmed by the T-Grão terminal account. Why does this happen? Because it takes 20 days for the cargoes to sit and mix together so there's no evidence of the deception—no evidence of the night-time loading of the two cargoes.

The T-Grão terminal is owned by the Dreyfus Group.

## SCENE: VESSEL'S ARREST

B Max is arrested. But both terminals don't sign the arrest statements—this is odd. The general counsel looks at the details—is the non-signing by witnesses at both terminals a criminal offense?

On August 3 the Harbor Master Authorities notify that MV B Max has been arrested. It's arrested in Automatic Stay, so TMT and their lawyers should know about it. The arrest action is taken by Cargill, acting as shippers of a partial cargo of 5,970.427 metric tons. They're claiming that T-Grão loaded that total only onto the vessel and, therefore, they demand the mate's receipt on account of it. On the contrary, the T-Grão terminal issue a mate's receipt for both Louis Dreyfus and Biosev (another Dreyfus company), which covers the total cargo on board. Upon completion of loading operations at Export Corridor, the vessel remains idle at the terminal until August 7, 20:50 hours local time.

The Master and Agent both sign—but T-Grão terminal and Wharf 38 Export Corridor don't sign.

**CUT TO**

## SCENE: CHAPTER II COURT IN HOUSTON, TEXAS

The bankruptcy judge is present, along with Nobu Sue and a variety of lawyers—including Evan Flaschen (Bracewell & Giuliano LLP), Charles Kelley (Mayer Brown LLP), a Shanghai

Bank lawyer, and Charles Schreiber (Winston & Strawn LLP).

> FLASCHEN
> B Max has been arrested. We need to use debtor-in-possession money to rescue the ship, but we don't have enough.
>
> CHARLES Kelley
> Shanghai Commercial and Savings Bank, Chang Hua Bank, and Hua Nan Bank are the largest creditors.
>
> SHANGHAI BANK LAWYER
> Silence!
>
> SCHREIBER
> The DIP lender has no problem. It is a pari passu.
>
> JUDGE
> What's the solution?
>
> FLASCHEN
> Shanghai and Macquarie Banks have already had a private discussion and they're willing to give additional DIP to release from the China court and sell privately.
>
> JUDGE
> That's brilliant.
>
> SCHREIBER
> Your Honor, we are willing to add a small DIP of $3 million, in two parts … $900,000 to release from the China court and an additional $2.1 million to clear the sales and sort it out.
>
> FLASCHEN
> Due to difficulty we stipulated in the B Max DIP last paragraph, this case is to be kept confidential in the C11 filing.

Nobu comes onto the stand. There is a silence in the court.

> NOBU
> She is a new ship on her maiden voyage. She has no cranes and has just received her

first cargo. AlixPartners are handling this
case for me as designee and I have no more
information. But an accident with leaked
water is impossible. She loaded 71,500 metric
tons with maximum draft, so water coming in
during the voyage couldn't happen. Are you
saying that a Hyundai built ship received
water damaged cargo on its first voyage and
was arrested in China? This is killing
Chinese people with imported toxic food. A
Max, her sister ship, has done two voyages
without any such issues. I've done more than
1,000 shipments in my life and probably
200 of those were grain transportation.
This has never happened before. Where
is Britannia insurance, AlixPartners,
Shanghai Commercial Savings Bank, Chang Hwa
Commercial Bank, Hua Nan Commercial Bank?
Later on, the Chinese surveyor stated that,
in over ten years as an inspector, he'd never
seen this kind of incident. It's impossible.
It's criminal!

JUDGE

We will give you permission to take up
this case privately, at your own expense.
Then report back to the court.

All agreed in the Chapter 11 court.

**CUT TO**

## SCENE: SOUTH CHINESE PORT OF FANCHENG

B Max is released from arrest in Brazil and
arrives in China, where she unloads her cargo
and is arrested again by a Chinese court.
CarVal pays US$750,000 to have the ship
released. However, this doesn't match the
missing 15% of the B Max loan amount. The
last paragraph of the B Max DIP exhibit (see
Figure Ap.10?) shows that this loan can't

be disclosed because it was involved in the Chinese court process.

This is a joke, because there are over 100 ships arrested on the Chinese coast between 2008—2016 and the entire Chinese maritime system is very transparent. It's clear that the B Max DIP lender is working with CarVal, Mayer Brown LLP, Bracewell & Giuliani LLP, and Winston & Strawn LLP to hide the secrets of the Shanghai Commercial Bank, Chang Hwa Commercial Bank, and Hua Nan Commercial Bank loans.

Why can that be alleged? Because the Marshall Islands registry is a US-led system. If you only own 85% of a ship, you can't sell it. Yet the Onassis Group bought B Max, B Whale, and five other Whale ships, along with one VLCC vessel. The key evidence here is that the only way it could have happened is that Onassis, Randy Ray, and JPMorgan Chase Shipping bankers were insiders and part of the huge scam being perpetrated by Dreyfus, Cargill, and the rest.

**CUT TO**

## SCENE: LONDON

Evan Flaschen and AlixPartners in attendance for an agreement with CarVal and TMT. It's a 50/50 agreement, but the Chapter 11 Judge is happy to have the first plan approved.

Then CarVal change the terms and all the lawyers need to delete the plan. Why? It's the faked documents found by CarVal lawyers, signed by all transfers for closing. The loans are signed on error paper by Shanghai Bank, sold to Deutsche Bank, and then sold to CarVal.

The investigation in New York proved that many bankers and lawyers worked during January,

February, and March 2014 on how to hide the facts and the criminal money laundering of Hua Nan Commercial Bank, with Solus Asset Management involvement. All related to Deutsche Bank and SC Lowy Financial (bond traders) ex-bosses and juniors in the group. Solus Asset Management have to make its Delaware and Cayman subsidiaries become buyers to clean up the mess.

After the agreement, the lawyers involved in the deal find the fraudulent transfer, before the ship sales to Deutsche Bank and SC Lowy—and the Cargill, Bunge, and Dreyfus collusion.

Nobu goes against the Chinese charters and eventually discovers the full extent of the scam involved in the case.

It's the loan documents and NT$10 billion of potential money laundering among Taiwan banks during 2011 to May 2012. Especially in January and February, B Max causes headaches for Shanghai Bank, Chang Hwa Bank, and Hua Nan Bank. In such small offices, bankers are mostly from Hong Kong and knowledge of what's going on can easily be remembered.

**CUT TO**

## SCENE: FOUR SEASONS HOTEL, NEW YORK.

The most interesting thing is the involvement of a Winston & Strawn lawyer in Washington DC. None of the Chapter 11 lawyers had any connection to the American Capital. This led the investigation to the Taiwan Ambassador to the USA, Mr Kim Pu-tsung—a descendant of the family of the last emperor of the Chinese Qing Dynasty. He studied in Texas for six years and had many connections in Washington DC. His nomination was from October 2012 to the end of February 2014. What a coincidence!

The Taiwan Ambassador, Kim Pu-tsung, is present, having a sumptuous meal with a Winston & Strawn LLP lawyer. Whale ship loans are being sold to JPMC, Ladybug loans are being sold to Macquarie Bank.

> MR KIM
> My friend, I need you to make sure B Max in Macquarie has no issues.

> W&S LAWYER
> Mega Bank loaned us DIP for back-to-back … so we have 16 ships with $20 million second mortgages at 9% interest with sufficient profit. It can't look like fronting, so we add a commission of 1%, then it looks like it was trading. Macquarie Bank made good money in other deals, plus we have Vantage shares. But make sure the C Whale secured loan is excluded from the DIP, I don't want to be asked in the future why C Whale is separate.

> MR KIM
> Make sure nothing comes out in Chapter 11 to show pre-Chapter 11 documents.

> W&S LAWYER: Yes sir. Our mission was to tell Schreiber in New York to make sure no ship was moved or sold at a lower price so there's no equity rights. That way, Nobu Sue has no comeback in the future to ask questions.

> MR KIM
> Well done.

> W&S LAWYER
> Thank you sir. Schreiber told me, along with Charles Kelley, Evan Flaschen, and the Shanghai lawyers, as well as Deutsche Bank, SC Lowy, and the Solus Capital Management CEO, at the Four Seasons Hotel on 57th Street in New York that they will find solutions.

> MR KIM
> I'd like to go back for the 2014 Chinese New Year, but I can't until the last transfers

of Chang Hwa Bank and Hua Nan Bank are
done, at the end of February. They now
have the solutions. I hope none of them
talk to Priscilla Hsing, she's very loyal
and still watching the entire process.
W&S LAWYER
The Schreiber report was sent by email.
The final plan is, Evan Flaschen promised
me he'll make sure none of the documents
are made public. Of course, it's an excuse,
but he'll use the Chinese FPCA case in
China's court to prevent release.

**CUT TO**

## SCENE: OFFICES OF SHANGHAI COMMERCIAL BANK, NEW YORK.

It's February 2014 and the weather in New York is cold. Shanghai Commercial Bank has branches on Park Avenue and 56th Street—only 150 meters from Solus Capital Management's 7th floor office at 430 Park Avenue and its subsidiary at 410 Park Avenue. A variety of banking representatives and lawyers are present at this secret meeting.

CarVal have decided to buy four TMT ship loans. CarVal Singapore make their unexpected highest bid to the Shanghai Commercial Bank. However, Shanghai Commercial Bank loans haven't defaulted and are performing well. Moreover, they've already used TMT loans in working with Chang Hwa Bank and Hua Nan Bank. The boss' son is very busy in Hong Kong—he's bought land in central Hong Kong and designed a 25-story building, with the top floor for his private use.

HONK KONG BANKER
We can't give you the full loan,
as it was sold and cleared.

CARVAL LAWYER
We need full loan documents.
DEUTSCHE BANKER
We sold you what we had.
CARVAL LAWYER
Where did Hua Nan Bank sell to? We need that remaining 15%, after checking the Marshall Islands registry.
SHANGHAI BANKER
That was done in May 2012 … two years ago.
DEUTSCHE BANKER
OK, we'll ask our ex-hedge fund colleague, the CEO of Solus Capital Management. Let him get involved.
SC LOWY LAWYER
He was my ex-boss in the USA. Lowy was in London, then moved to Hong Kong.
SHANGHAI BANKER
So, how do we draw up the transfer documents? If we put what we're doing on paper, we'll all become criminals.
CARVAL LAWYER
We need to sign it on error paper and all sign together. But no lawyers' names should show up in any documents.
HONG KONG BANKER
Won't the US judge see it?
SC LOWY LAWYER
I asked my contact to convey to Schreiber to add an additional $2.9 million DIP for B Max, so that will solve it for all of us.
SHANGHAI BANKER
So, how do we sell the ships? Pappas recommends Onassis, as the Onassis name can make it legitimate. Also, what prices?
CARVAL LAWYER
It has to be the same price as the first mortgage of $25 million, so Nobu won't have any rights to come and examine the details.

> **DEUTSCHE BANKER**
> Schreiber has to have additional money to fund it … Macquarie is strong, we can take money from the excess on the other ships … A Ladybug in Malta, to cover the losses. Also, we want to sell at $24.5 so that Nobu has no right to request the profit and any documents related to the sale of ships to Onassis.
>
> **SC LOWY LAWYER**
> Then we'll cause default for A Ladybug's $20 million and use that money to get Evan Flaschen to recirculate. When the $20 million is discharged in the Marshall Islands, we'll bring the money back to the estate.
>
> **CARVAL LAWYER**
> Let's work out the B Max document in Chapter 11 and make sure nobody finds out. The last paragraph will make sure of that.
>
> **SHANGHAI BANKER**
> Let's drink to it. CarVal must make sure the restructure plan with Nobu is destroyed.
>
> **SC LOWY LAWYER**
> Yes, order CarVal Singapore not to accept it. Change the terms so Nobu can't get approval. You know how crazy he can be.
>
> **CARVAL LAWYER**
> By the way, the Max in Taiwan also needs to be signed on error paper, so London, New York, Hong Kong, and Taiwan are all in the same boat … if you'll pardon the pun, hahaha.
>
> **SOLUS MASTER FUND LAWYER**
> Schreiber, you and I have worked together for a long time. I'll do this just for you and my friends at SC Lowy, as we're all in the distressed fund business. But you know this is criminal?
>
> **CARVAL LAWYER**
> Only if it's found out.

**CUT TO**

## SCENE: CARVAL OFFICE IN SINGAPORE

TMT loan sales are announced in the insolvency market and discussed among bankers like Goldman Sachs, JPMC, UBS, Deutsche Bank, and others. CarVal are within this financial circle and receive the latest information on a daily basis.

> CARVAL LEGAL
> We have successfully bought loans from Macquarie Bank and Deutsche Bank, but we can only buy 85%.
>
> CARVAL CEO
> Why not the other 15%?
>
> CARVAL LEGAL
> Our Taiwan offices can't confirm why not.
>
> CARVAL CEO
> Strange. Anyway, we have the majority and they're good deals. We have experience in shipping and Nobu's ships are very well designed.
>
> CARVAL LEGAL
> What if we have issues?
>
> CARVAL CEO
> We can contact Nobu and offer to buy out his loans through the banks. Or we can offer proposals for restructuring as minor partners. Worst case scenario, 50/50, but with control.
>
> CARVAL LEGAL
> Good. We're smart and shipping companies are stupid.

This evidence is found by Marshall Islands US$20 million second mortgage documents. They clearly state only 85% of first mortgage is in hand. Very strange?

**CUT TO**

## SCENE: OFFICES OF SHANGHAI COMMERCIAL BANK, NEW YORK

The evidence is already deleted. Money is in a Deutsche Bank Trust at 4 Wall Street.

Shanghai Commercial Bank specialists get together and discuss how to handle the case.

SHANGHAI BANKER
The sale was partly to Deutsche Bank at the end of February. Now we need to decide how to make SC Lowy involved and sell to CarVal? CarVal want to buy the balance of 15%. We can't give them the original loan documents—that's the condition.

CARVAL LAWYER
Let's meet with Nobu. It's the only way, to buy Nobu's percentage at a good price. He called me and is willing to meet at the Mandarin Hotel. This was after the plan to restructure. Now's the time, as the lawyer review shows we can't go ahead with this project. Minnesota head office said no deal, we can't get internal approval.

**CUT TO**

## SCENE: THE MANDARIN HOTEL, EXECUTIVE LOUNGE, SINGAPORE

Nobu Sue meets with a CarVal Singapore fund manager on the top floor of the Mandarin Hotel, after they'd agreed a restructure plan. The CarVal man smiles, but he isn't happy.

CARVAL LAWYER
Nobu, I feel sorry for what happened in Houston. We agreed a plan in London, but ... can we buy your 49%?

                          NOBU
        You told me to go joint venture in
        London and two weeks later you want
        to buy me out? Is this because of the
        TradeWinds article … has your head office
          in Minnesota asked you to cancel?
                          CARVAL
                            No.
                          NOBU
                   This isn't good.
They part company.
**CUT TO**

## SCENE: CLARKSON SECURITIES, HOUSTON

The Houston boss bought the Aston Martin
Company. He's related to Vantage's John
O'Reilly. John O'Reilly's son works in
Clarkson's Houston office from 2013 to 2014.
Amanda Galloway joined Clarkson from RBS
Shipping in December 2013. She moved right
after TMT filed for Chapter 11, becoming a
Clarkson representative.
                       ALIXPARTNERS
B Max can be sold for over $30 million, as the
largest Panamax, with a new engine. We need to
sell to Onassis, people won't doubt that name.
                         CLARKSON
          No, the Onassis offer is max $24.5
              million, less commission.
                       ALIXPARTNERS
           OK, no issues, as we recovered
                98% of the outstanding.
                         CLARKSON
You gave me all 15 ships' brokerage.
Brokers are to serve the principals.
Onassis is a big client, who we need to
do lots of business with in the future.

> ALIXPARTNERS
> I'll tell your front man to sell to Onassis.
>
> AMANDA GALLOWAY
> I am an ex-RBS shipping lawyer and I worked with Gerard Joynson and Andy Georgiou. We need to destroy any evidence that we worked with TMT on FFAs. Since TMT has filed for Chapter 11, we need those documents deleted now, for six years from 2008. I came to make sure Clarkson's are not required to disclose any RBS related documents.
>
> ALIXPARTNERS
> We're happy enough ... we have issues in the Lakatamia/Clarkson litigation and now handle TMT's Chapter 11 ship sale. Hill Dickenson and Seward & Kissel are presenting the case. Bruce Paulson is in charge of Uniform Commercial Code signatures.

**CUT TO**

## SCENE: ONASSIS SHIPPING GROUP OFFICES

Present are the CEO and Randy Ray, a shipping advisor and ex-JPMorgan Chase Shipping executive, working with Peter Evensen in Teekay Tankers.

> RANDY
> TMT ships are fantastic. We want to own them all, and we can, working with Ken Leung and Petros Pappas.
>
> CEO
> Yes, those ships have a great design. You make the deal for six Whales and one Elephant. I spoke to Peter Evensen the other day and, confirming through my Hong Kong banker and ex-JPMorgan Chase connection ... they said Nobu will sell the lot. He has no choice. He was stupid and spent so much money on them ... now we can get them all at a discount.

RANDY
I'll call Peter now. Listen.
EVENSEN
Hi Randy. We priced TMT non-Chapter 11 VLCC from DSME at $77 million. Randy, we can set the prices and get all TMT's ships at a discount. Nobu designed good ships. It's only 60% of the new building price per ship. The $77 million one was built in 2012, so it's younger. Then you can price the Whales at $60–$65 million. We're working as commercial managers but it's not easy to fix these ships, you know.
RANDY
Peter, you're getting A Elephant, B Elephant, and C Elephant at a steal. He loaned $60 million and took all the ships. Amazing. It happened that Nobu is out. He lost in a strange arrest in Egypt, by the Egyptian navy, because of an alleged scam to damaged internet cable.
EVENSEN
Teekay had to pay money to the Egyptians and they made $10 million. It was a difficult decision. We're a public company, so I can't disclose how the deal was settled. Now new Teekay Tankers partners have a great deal to start, at $10 million less than a similar ship Nobu built in Daewoo Shipbuilding & Marine Engineering.
RANDY
Peter, you made it again. The DSME ship was a standard engine, but Teekay Tankers made a windfall profit, by close to $100 million.
CEO
He's a smart banker … he was our colleague, hahaha. So, the normal Very Large Crude Carrier was sold at $77 million. How about the other deal for me for $100 million?

                          RANDY
    Wait. I consulted with Evan Flaschen and
    requested that the other similar Belgian
    ships were sold at $100 million per ship in
    the market. But that deal was sold with a
    cargo charter attached, so it went for higher
    prices. Evan will go to the judge and say
    the deal isn't relevant, if anyone asks.
                           CEO
    So, the $77 million is Elephant and $10
    million more-or-less will be the Whales'
    valuation. Randy, you're a great ex-banker
    and deal-maker, like John Wallem of Simpson
    Spence Young, Andy Case of Clarkson, and
        Alan of Braemar Shipping Services.
                          RANDY
       You know Pappas is in the background
          to educate the parties … right?
                           CEO
                           Yes.
CarVal sell privately to Onassis, after
teaming up with Mayer Brown International LLP,
Winston & Strawn, and Washington KMT Lawyers,
using maximum DIP to transfer the matter to
the Marshall Islands. Marshall Islands records
for $20 million show only 85% and no following
information. But they were clearly sold to
Onassis at $24.5 million, reported to Judge
Isgur.

## CONCLUSION: THE PERFECT CRIME

According to the evidence:

1) The Chinese trader buyers know about the 5,970 metric tons damaged cargo. (See Chinese arrest documents which exactly stated the amount of loss as 5,900 metric tons. How did they know?)

2) Shippers know about the 14 meter draft so the ship can load 71,000 metric tons with its stowage capacity and

draft. So the 5,900 metric tons is over the standard for ships in this size.

3) No fingerprints left behind—because of the 20 days sitting in the lay-by berth. During that time, the conveyors were repaired and brought back to normal after the first loading.

4) Stowage plan and No. 1 cargo hold plus, with less damaged cargo. We wondered why the stowage plan declared at the loading port was different to that at the discharging port. Especially when the Bunge name appeared—then the ship was arrested.

5) Sailing from Santos—no draft survey—why? Because they didn't want the surveyors to find out that some of the cargo was burned and blackened.

6) First load took so long—last cargo of 29,000 metric tons took two days loading. The Captain's statement at the discharging port said the cargo was loading quickly and he couldn't see any blackened soya bean. How could he see damaged cargo loading at full speed in the dark?

B Max DIP Insert shows six points of irregularity

1) Last paragraph, can they sell before reporting to the court?

2) Majority lenders

3) US$900,000 plus $2.5 million balance? (the final figure undisclosed in Chapter 11).

4) Pari passu.

5) Interest rates for penalties are not clear

6) November 23, 2013, Macquarie POA in New York? Why?

Nobu and Evan Flaschen had totally different views after November 2013. Evan ran the show and Nobu's voice was never heard by the judge. This was a case of the debtor lawyer not acting for the state and the recovery of assets. Contrarily, Lisa Donahue, leading the financial restructuring firm, changed course by keeping bilateral communications and not including Nobu in certain email exchanges. In Nobu's opinion, Flaschen could have been bought out. He was very serious and Nobu is convinced he was persuaded by someone to change his course.

Flaschen needed to move his operations to Teekay Shipping (large operator of medium-sized tankers). He changed management and took 100% control, in order to hide the money that came from the Mega Bank KMT accounts. This case will continue and will show the full story of the cover-up during 2014 and sales to Onassis Shipping for the precise outstanding amount of $25 million, so that nobody would be able to see the evidence afterwards.

However, Nobu has found more evidence in CarVal hands—including the B Max sales, B Max DIP, $20 million second mortgages, and the 85% of loans stipulated in the Marshall Islands registry.

Cargill, Bunge, and Dreyfus (global agribusinesses) amicably settled the Santos litigation in March 2014, without any announcement whatsoever. This was found by an investigation into Jewish networking.

Nobu was given a Portuguese language court order sent from the Santos Court in Brazil in Spring 2014. Why did they settle quietly in April 2014? In Chapter 11, $20 million was on all 16 ships by DIP order on January 8, 2014. It was secured repayment. But how Macquarie could declare and make additional profit within seven days is a mystery. Unknown. We need the links between Schreiber, Cargill, Gardena, Evan Flaschen, and AlixPartners—and Cargill conversations between the grain houses to show other untold stories.

During March 2014, Nobu was in Hong Kong due to a back injury. Nobu had already flown more than eight times back and forth to the USA and around the world in economy class seats and this damaged his back. Evan Flaschen and Lisa Donahue had an obligation to inform Nobu about what was happening, but they didn't. Donahue actually came to Hong Kong to see Nobu, but she didn't report anything important about how the Chapter 11 case was being conducted. Furthermore, in order to sell and transfer titles, the DIP of US$3 million was fraudulently created. The final clause said the DIP could be sold to third parties—the judge never read this.

There's more to be discovered, for instance:

• There are many emails in Chapter 11 which need to be disclosed.

• The Mega Bank, Pappas, Seward & Kissel, Paulson, UCC, HHI, Kelley Drye, Schreiber, Charles Kelley, Michael Lloite, and Vidal Martinez orchestration of Chapter 11.

• Panama, Liberia, and Marshall Islands registry scam—especially the double payment of fees in Liberia.

• But the money flow wasn't clean and Shanghai Commercial Savings Bank invited Chang Hwa Bank and Hua Nan Bank to agree to be used as camouflage. Why were the drawdown and syndication dates the same in the B Max loan? Strange. It's mostly misrepresenting loans with intention to do syndication at the drawdown date but only having contact with ONE bank. The majority lenders kept changing—it was like playing mah-jong with the same loan. The loan documents couldn't identify who had exactly what shares in the loan because the small loans kept being amended, with the loan holders not being specified, and with the parties continuously buying and selling the loans. This technique allowed the banks involved to freely move money overseas each year. During 2012–2016, they could stay under the radar of Section 165(d) of the Dodd-Frank regulations.

• Hamish Norton became president of Star Bulk in January 2013, which was to target TMT. Ex-Goldman

Sachs banker Peter Espig, hired by Nobu Sue and nominated as Star Bulk director, continued to serve as director until 2013 and was then fired.

There is a historical pattern of motivation. Nobu believes the people involved are the same people who were involved in the 2008 financial crisis plan, along with a few special accountants, Wall Street lawyers, and special consultants.

## PATTERN

### AML and Money Moved from Taiwan Bank

Create personal guarantor plus corporate guarantor:

1) Take corporate guarantor and company shares hostage.

2) Use Panamanian companies.

3) No mitigation period and sudden-death contract. Change amendment: insert where the loan could be sold to majority lenders; put Shanghai Bank OBU account on the last page; and type Deutsche Bank account number on the following page. This means the amendment becomes a party between Taiwan Bank and USA bank. This makes it possible to use the lender's account for the bank's secret operation. The clients believed it was their money but didn't receive daily statements for these operations accounts and retention accounts.

4) Big transaction at the end of year.

5) Money transfers didn't happen in the US clearing system, to avoid fingerprints, but the amounts were so big that eventually the NYDFS found them.

| To: Huatai Guangzhou | From: Josh Huang |
|---|---|
| Attn: Mr. Huang Xueming | O'Ref: B13HTBRT121 |
| Y'Ref: Please advise | Page: 5 |
| Date : 19 Sep, 2013 | |

If you do not receive completely, please call us immediately

*Re: M.V. "B Max" discharging 71,601.920MT Soybeans in bulk at Fangcheng port, China*

*Alleged cargo damage*

*Further to our report dated of 18 Sep, 2013:*

I. SURVEY FINDINGS

1. The discharging operation to the other cargo hold Nos. 1, 5, 6 and 7 continued and the cargo condition was found in normal condition. Refer to following photos:

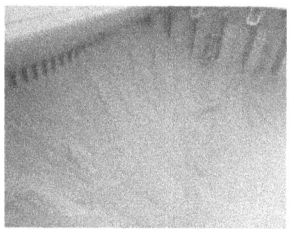

Cargo condition in hold No. 7

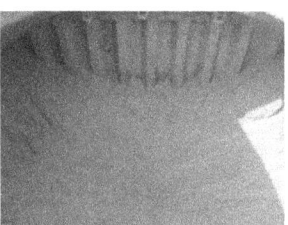

Cargo condition in hold No. 6

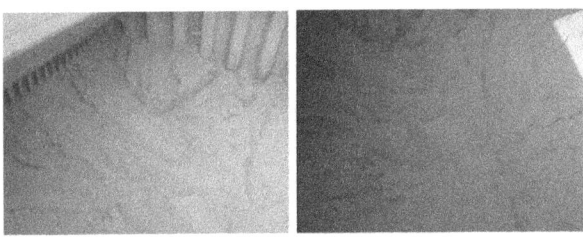

Cargo condition in hold No. 5

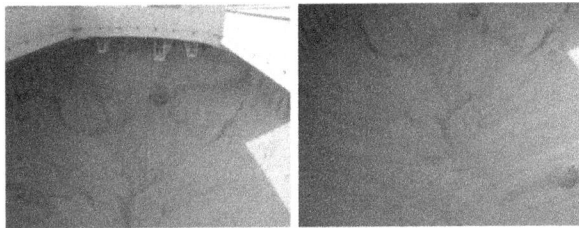

Cargo condition in hold No. 1

2. Some damaged cargo was found in cargo hold No. 2 during discharging on the afternoon of September 18, 2013, it was located at the mid and fore place with the length about one meter and the depth unknown. It was found zonal arrangement and the cargo above and below the damages cargo was found in normal condition, and the damaged cargo was serious discolor and moldy. We could not go into the hold for further inspection due to the discharging of the normal cargo in hold No. 2 was in progress. Refer to following photos:

Cargo condition in hold No. 2

3. At 1630 hours on September 18, 2013, our surveyor went into the cargo hold No. 4 together with the CCIC

surveyor for further inspection. The damaged cargo was found in two places, one was located at the mid and fore place with the length about eight meters and different depth, and another one was located at the after place and near the Australian ladder with the length about 1.5 meters and different depth. The damaged cargo also found zonal arrangement. The cargo above and below the damaged cargo was found in normal condition, and the damaged cargo was serious discolor and moldy, part of them was found black with bad odor. Representative samples had been taken by us. Refer to following photos:

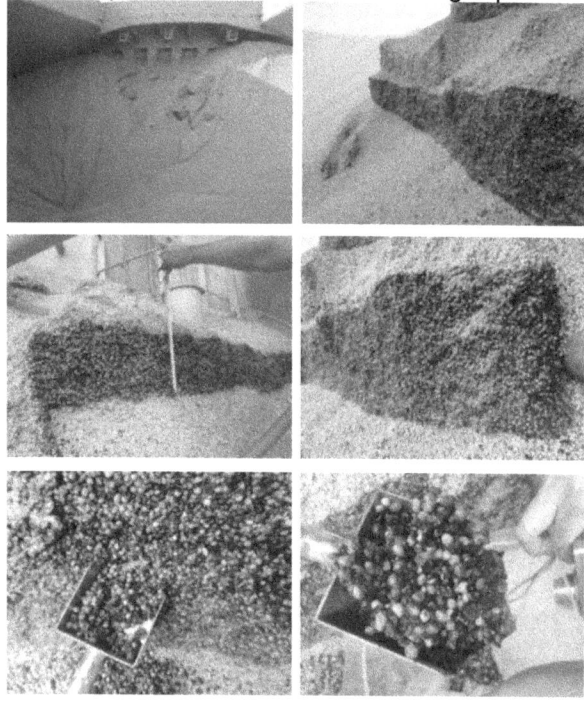

 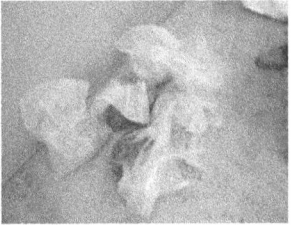

Cargo condition in hold No. 4

4. The condition of the rubber of the hatch covers and the manholes of cargo hold No. 2, No. 3, and No. 4 had been checked by us and found to be in normal and flexible condition. Refer to following photos:

Condition of rubber on hatch covers and manholes

5. According to the stevedore company, about 37,000 MT had been discharged till to 0800 hours on September 19, 2013.

We will keep you advised of further development

*13.2 Email from Balance Cargo Control and Survey Ltd. containing images of damage to cargo and cargo hold*

*13.3: B Max before sailing to Brazil*

# CHAPTER 14
## SHANGHAI COMMERCIAL & SAVINGS BANK LTD.

IT IS IMPORTANT to record that Mega Bank wasn't the only chief culprit in the Dynasty Escape story. I have included some exhibits here to illustrate how Shanghai Commercial & Savings Bank Ltd. (SCSB) was also a prime player and used four different law firms to hide their involvement.

SCSB had over 100 years of history and was known as the private bank of the KMT. It was involved in money laundering as a private bank and, although it was called the "Shanghai" Bank, the Shanghai office had been closed and the Taipei and Hong Kong offices became its flagship location. (SCSB in Hong Kong recently completed a new building next to Hong Kong Shanghai Banking Corporation's headquarters in central Hong Kong).

It all began on the day TMT was supposed to be guarantor, as the borrower's transfer agent, for a 15-year period, and documents were created by the bank without notifying TMT. Have you ever heard of a borrower handling the transfer of money?

Seward & Kissel lawyers were involved in HHI and Hyundai Samho Industries ship delivery and pre-delivery since the beginning of construction. It's curious that their Mr Dine flew to Ulsan in September 2011 to sign documents, because those documents have both right-handed and left-handed signatures. Was he ambidextrous? I don't think so.

## CONCLUSION

SCSB was involved in private money laundering. It was involved in the syndication of five Whale ships and was lead arranger in four other ships. Chang Hwa Bank and Hua Nan Bank were also involved in the financing.

After Mega Bank and First Bank, the KMT decided to move SCSB accounts overseas in 2011 and designated accounts were moved to Deutsche Bank—so the entire Overseas Banking Unit connecting Shanghai, Hong Kong, and Taiwan was transferred to Deutsche Bank Trust's New York account at 4 Wall Street.

This is related to Solus Capital at 430 Park Avenue and SC Lowy Hong Kong, Cayman Islands, and Deutsche Bank London—they are all connected.

The B Whale final drawdown was done on December 30, 2010 (100% financed by Bank Sinopac). Bankers told us they had orders from their "boss" to close at the end of year and never to go beyond at time of closing. I remember because I had to stay till late on the last day of the year.

A Whale was done on December 30, 2011 (100% financed by First Bank).

By the end of 2011, the KMT's entire funds had been moved out of Taiwan.

The Panama set up of Ugly Duckling Corporation, A Duckling, and A Ladybug was all done through 2010–2012. The NYDFS investigation made it clear that the AML was done between 2012–2014. The underground investigation against eight Taiwanese banks is still ongoing in New York (I've already shown that China Central Bank Taipei is located at the same address as Mega Bank's New York branch—60 Trinity Street).

The last movements were the A Ladybug unsecured loan and the Taichung Bank Ro-Ro Line unsecured US$20 million credit.

The most important evidence is Seward & Kissel's Mr Dine's left-handed signature for the retention account pledge agreement, dated June 7, 2011. Pledger C Handy to Pledgee SCSB—DBTMT 000472-000486. Tiffany Chang is the faked signature of the Dun Pai branch.

Furthermore, on June 17, 2011, the law firm Ding & Ding used the Greek attorneys Reeder & Simpson P.C.

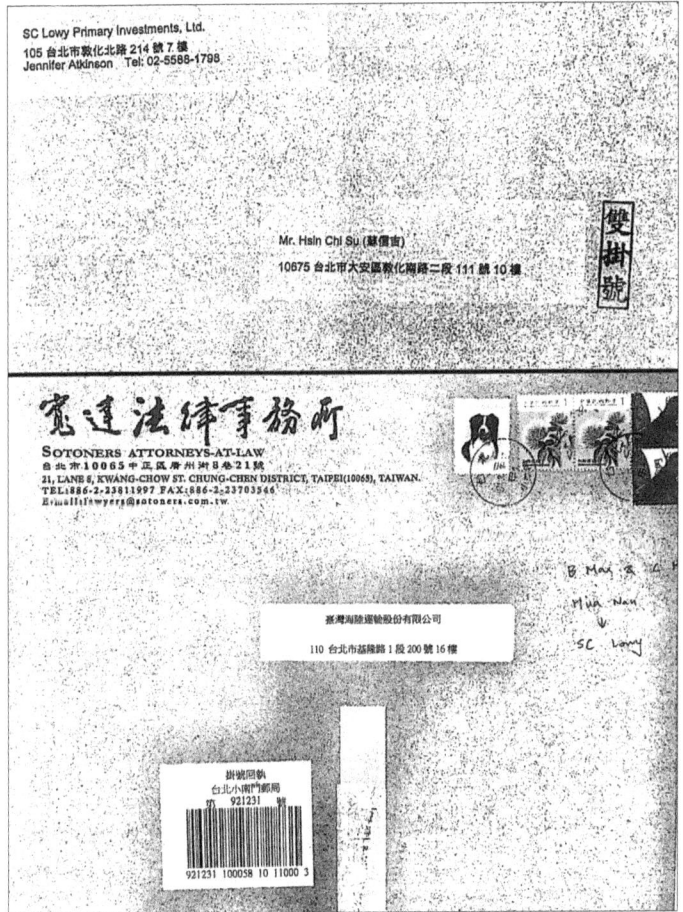

*14.1a–c: SCSB used four law firms to hide the story*

# SOTONERS
## ATTORNEYS-AT-LAW

台北市10065中正區廣州街8巷21號

TELEPHONE: 886-2-23811997
FACSIMILE: 886-2-23703546
E-mail: lawyers@sotoners.com.tw

21, LANE 8, KWANG-CHOW ST. CHUNG-CHEN DISTRICT, TAIPEI(10065), TAIWAN.

Your ref.: To Be Advised
Our ref: KW/223031

Date: 18 October 2013
Total: 1 page

To: Mr. Greene Hung, A Handy Corporation

12 F., No. 167, Fu Hsin N. Rd., Taipei, Taiwan, ROC

T: +886 8771 1663/ F: +886 2 8771 1523

RE: Assignment of Loan Agreement dated March 24 2011

Dear Sirs,

We are acting for and on behalf of The Shanghai Commercial & Savings Bank, Ltd. (hereinafter referred as SCSB) for the captioned matters.

SCSB decides to assign all of their rights, interests, benefits and obligations under the Loan Agreement with your esteemed company dated on March 24 2011 to the third party, Deutsche Bank AG London Branch. As per the Article 10.02 of the said Agreement, SCSB put you on a formal notice of the above. Without receiving your disagreement with reasonable grounds in three days (ie. by 22 October 2013), SCSB will complete the assignment with the third party, Deutsche Bank AG London Branch. Any further issues related to the Agreement, you may contact with them directly.

If you have any queries, please feel free to contact us.

Best regards,

Roger Wang
Sotoners Attorneys-At-Law

# SHANGHAI COMMERCIAL & SAVINGS BANK LTD.

**SOTONERS**
**ATTORNEYS-AT-LAW**

TELEPHONE: 886-2-23811997
FACSIMILE: 886-2-23703546
E-mail: lawyers@sotoners.com.tw

台北市10065中正區廣州街巷弄21號    21, LANE 8, KWANG-CHOW ST. CHUNG-CHEN DISTRICT, TAIPEI(10065), TAIWAN.

Your ref.: To Be Advised  
Our ref.: KW/223031

Date: 18 October 2013  
Total: 1 page

To: **Mr. Greene Hung, B Handy Corporation**

12 F., No. 167, Fu Hsin N. Rd., Taipei, Taiwan, ROC

T: +886 8771 1663/ F: +886 2 8771 1523

**RE: Assignment of Loan Agreement dated April 27 2011**

Dear Sirs,

We are acting for and on behalf of The Shanghai Commercial & Savings Bank, Ltd. (hereinafter referred as SCSB) for the captioned matters.

SCSB decides to assign all of their rights, interests, benefits and obligations under the Loan Agreement with your esteemed company dated on April 27 2011 to the third party, Deutsche Bank AG London Branch. As per the Article 10.02 of the said Agreement, SCSB put you on a formal notice of the above. Without receiving your disagreement with reasonable grounds in three days (ie. by 22 October 2013), SCSB will complete the assignment with the third party, Deutsche Bank AG London Branch. Any further issues related to the Agreement, you may contact with them directly.

If you have any queries, please feel free to contact us.

Best regards,

Roger Wang  
Sotoners Attorneys-At-Law

- Structure of KMT AML with SCSB and Mega Bank
- Undisclosed Wall Street consultants were hired to facilitate this
- Accounts were created in the Colon and Panama City branches of Mega Bank

- An English guarantor was involved in Mega Bank's London office

- The loans began in 2009, once the receiver accounts were structured

- The banks chosen to connect globally were SCSB and Taichung Bank, which had participated in five Whales led by Mega Bank syndications

- Of the eight major banks involved, four were government-owned and politically motivated—Mega Bank was the principle one, then SCSB, First Bank, and Bank Sinopac

- Far Eastern Bank and Taipei Fubon Bank avoided getting involved as they could smell the danger involved in joining the TMT scandal

- The Primary Dealer Credit Facility (PDCF) money, with the banks' own accounts being created as retention accounts, is very important because:

    o TMT paid a cash fund of about 7% of total borrowing amount as a retention account over the course of a month previous to the drawdown date

    o The banks could use that money to borrow more than 20 times the amount from the Taiwan Central Bank, so the loan amount could go to the banks' investment divisions

    o Then the money was sent to the banks' commercial divisions and used as ship loans to TMT

    o There was no board of directors nor was KYC done for the finance

    o After the loans were completed, syndication was formed within two weeks, money was paid into Deutsche Bank, JPMorgan Chase N.A., and Macquarie Bank accounts—and it disappeared

o So, basically, the entire TMT US$800 million-plus loans never damaged the banks balance sheets.

After that, in 2016, many senior bank managers left Taiwan and bought houses in California. Were the PDCF and the Central Bank of Taiwan involved?

Further discovery is ongoing.

The structural set up is huge, involving more than 30 Taiwanese banks. It became obvious that there were patterns of irregularity. So far, we have identified at least eight routes. It's too early to write out everything, but at least the SCSB story suggests that the Mega Bank scandal wasn't just Mega Bank, but also involved many Taiwanese and Hong Kong banks and, indeed, the global banking system as it exists today.

These are the eight routes:

1. Taichung Bank gave Ro-Ro Line's US$20 million unsecured loans plus new flagship land sales to Bank of America at a hugely discounted price

2. Cathay United Bank's chairman was involved in selling US$20 million to Cortland Capital for one dollar. Chairman Chen's stamp was found on the sale documents beside the corporate seal—which is unheard of in Taiwanese banking practice

3. Chinatrust Bank sold to JPMorgan Chase in November 2013, but JPMorgan Chase N.A. denied this in their Asia Pacific representative's declaration

4. Bank Sinopac involved Hong Kong and Macau for B Whale sales to the Greek Onassis Group

5. First Commercial Bank sold A Whale in one day through SC Lowy to Monarch Capital New York

6. SCSB in Taiwan, Hong Kong, and Macau ended up going to Deutsche Bank's global connections

7. Mega Bank in Taiwan was a route for the many faked signatures of Priscilla Hsing related to Macquarie Bank

and then JPMorgan Chase N.A. Ended up with Oaktree Capital, who owned 51% of Star Bulk Carriers

8. Taishin Bank route—Taishin Bank was the only bank that didn't sell the loan but bought more loans. It had financed US$100 million to Oaktree during Chapter 11, but never disclosed this to the court.

Some of these eight routes are already in litigation in some jurisdictions. They will expose the entire AML scandal (the largest since the Panama Papers), which is related to that investigated by the NYDFS in 2012–2014.

This chapter is ongoing—further revelations in my book: *The Gold Man from the East.*

*14.2: Shangai Commercial Bank*

# CHAPTER 15
## KMT MONEY LAUNDERING AND THE CHINA INVESTMENT FUND

THE FULL NAME of the Dodd-Frank Act is the Dodd-Frank Wall Street Reform and Consumer Protection Act, but it's more generally referred to as just Dodd-Frank. In simple terms, it's an American law that places regulations on the financial industry. It grew out of the financial crisis of 2008 with the intention of preventing another collapse of major financial institutions like Lehman Brothers. It was also meant to protect people from abusive lending practices by banks. It became law in 2010 and was named after Senator Christopher Dodd and US representative Barney Frank, who sponsored it. The bill contained 16 major areas of reform across hundreds of pages, but not all the provisions were put in place and the Trump administration is aiming to water it down.

One of the main aims of Dodd-Frank was to have banks subjected to a number of regulations, along with the possibility of being broken up if they were considered 'too big to fail.' To do that, the act created the Financial Stability Oversight Council, chaired by the Treasury Secretary and with nine members, including the Federal Reserve, the Securities and Exchange Commission and the Consumer Financial Protection Bureau. The Council was set up to protect people from 'unscrupulous business practices' by banks, such as risky lending. It also oversees non-bank financial firms, such as hedge funds.

The Volcker Rule is part of Dodd-Frank and prohibits banks from owning, investing in, or sponsoring hedge funds, private equity funds, or any proprietary trading operations for their own profit. However, banks can keep funds that are less than 3% of revenue. The Volcker Rule does allow some trading when it's necessary for a bank to run its business (e.g. banks can engage in currency trading to offset their own holdings in a foreign currency). Dodd-Frank requires that the riskiest derivatives, like CDSs (that old SWAP word again), be regulated by the SEC or the Commodity Futures Trading Commission. To help fight corruption and insider trading, Dodd-Frank contains a whistle-blower provision. Someone with information about corruption can report it for a reward.

To many Wall Street banks, Dodd-Frank was seen as an overreaction to the crash of 2008 that would stop economic growth. On the other hand, some people said the regulations didn't go far enough to reign in out-of-control banks from taking risks and being bailed out by public money. In 2018 the Trump administration blocked and rescinded several Dodd-Frank rules, withdrew hundreds of other regulations, and signed 15 Congressional Review Act resolutions. It seems that the current American president is all in favor of the big banks getting back to where they were pre-2008 and causing another global financial crisis.

But what has this got to do with Mega Bank and the KMT?

Well, Section 165(d) of Dodd-Frank requires banks with non-banking assets in excess of US$50 billion to draft a plan that would allow regulators to step in and either sell things off or shut them down in as minimally disruptive a way as possible, similar to how a business would be dissolved in bankruptcy.

What if all the documents were intentionally destroyed and that's why they weren't available? The key issue became Dodd-Frank Section 165(d)—the main reporting system for testing undisclosed items for all Taiwanese banks in New York from 2013 to 2016. The first chapter for JPMC, G5, and Deutsche Bank should consist of 150–200 pages—even if there weren't many transactions there still should be about 50 pages or so, but there were only 8–12 pages for most Taiwanese banks operating in New York, apart from Chinatrust Bank. Only Chinatrust Bank accepted consumer banking regulations.

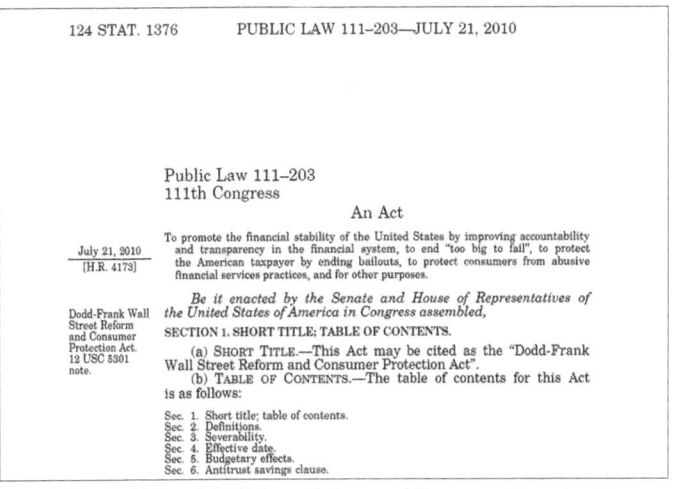

*15.1: Dodd-Frank Wall Street Reform and Consumer Protection Act*

Taiwanese banks were not reporting correctly under the terms of Section 165(d) of Dodd-Frank. There were standard processes established for Mega Bank, Hua Nan Bank, Chang Hwa Bank, First Bank, Shanghai Commercial Bank, Chinatrust Bank, Cathay United Bank, and others, but those processes had already been violated by 2013 and continued to be violated. There is another story of how Panamaian diplomatic relations with Taiwan suddenly ended and shifted to mainland China. I need to write about this in my next book.

As I've said throughout *Dynasty Escape*, I plan to dig more deeply and write a further book. My investigations will expose the political and economic systems of Taiwan and even, to some extent, Chinese culture itself. China's 5,000 years of history was based on dynasty, with no democracy, which all has a bearing on the case of TMT and of Nobu Sue.

You remember I told you about when McKinney Tsai invited me to Mega Bank's head office in July 2012 and asked for a ship to cover the unsecured loans of US$40 million? I gave him A Ladybug, which was worth almost US$100 million, and I trusted him with the difference of nearly US$60 million because we were close friends and played golf together. Remember I said it was all transacted at the Tung Nan branch of Mega International Commercial Bank, which was common practice? I believe without a doubt that McKinney Tsai sold the loan at a low price to Macquarie Bank on November 22, 2012, and the money was paid in New York or Sydney. A NYDFS press release clearly stated that AML cases occurred from 2012 to 2014, and this case was within that time period. The date suggests Mega's involvement in AML in 2012. So, this might be the first AML-related transaction, together or not together with other deals, which we can only speculate upon until further evidence comes to light. I mean, there must have been an undisclosed deal between Macquarie Bank and Mega Bank on November 22, 2012, with the POA being signed in Sydney head office. Macquarie Bank is Australia's number one investment bank, located only 30 miles from KMT's Taipei head office.

I will discuss the Mega Bank AML case in conjunction with the Samson Wu story in Chapter 17, but here is a report by Liang-Sa Loh and J.R. Wu for the international news agency, Reuters:

> TAIPEI, August 23, 2016 (Reuters)—Taiwan is investigating if Mega Financial Holding Co and its banking unit broke local criminal laws in a case that led to U.S. authorities fining the state-controlled group $180 million for anti-money laundering violations.
>
> New York authorities on Friday slapped Mega International Commercial Bank with the fine for violations that included lax attention to risk exposure

in Panama, the first time in a decade that a Taiwan-based financial institution has been penalized by U.S. authorities.

The fine is a major embarrassment for the Taiwan government because Mega Financial, whose management has close ties to key government officials, is an industry pillar in the island's financial system.

The disciplinary action comes as anti-money laundering (AML) controls at banks in Greater China are under intense scrutiny abroad, following a series of high-profile judicial investigations and regulatory probes in the United States and Europe.

Taiwan authorities are examining documents from Mega Financial and its banking unit as part of the investigation, Chang Chieh-chin, deputy head prosecutor with the Taipei District Public Prosecutors Office, told Reuters by telephone.

The former chairman of Mega Financial Tsai Yeou-tsair is a defendant in the case and has been banned from traveling outside of Taiwan, Chang said, adding that current Chairman Shiu Kuang-si was asked into the prosecutor's office late on Tuesday to assist with the investigation.

Tsai has quit as a board director of Cathay Financial Holding Co, another Taiwanese firm, due to personal reasons, Cathay said in a statement Tuesday.

Prosecutors also are reviewing information from the island's finance ministry and Financial Supervisory Commission regarding the matter.

'We are gathering information and will review it to see if there has been any violation of criminal law in Taiwan,' Chang said.

The New York State Department of Financial Services (NYDFS) said Mega's U.S. compliance program was a 'hollow shell' with insufficient transaction monitoring and reporting controls and inconsistent compliance policies.

The bank's compliance staff also lacked familiarity with U.S. AML regulations while several were also conflicted because they held multiple roles, the DFS said in a court document.

The DFS found that nearly $11.5 billion of credit transactions took place between Mega's New York and Panama branches in 2013 and 2014.'The bank's head office was indifferent toward risks associated with transactions involving Panama,' despite the fact it was recognized as a high-risk jurisdiction, the DFS said in a statement.

Mega Financial chairman Shiu defended the bank's conduct, saying it did not help customers launder money overseas. Mega International Commercial's New York branch failed to report a 'suspect transaction' to U.S. authorities, as required by law, he told Reuters.

Mega's branch in Colon, Panama, had closed an account by a customer from Central or South America because it was deemed a suspicious account, he said.

When money was remitted to the shuttered account, the branch rejected and returned the funds to the originating bank, he said. However, under U.S. rules, remittances involving suspicious accounts must be declared to New York financial authorities, which Mega failed to do, he said.

Mega Financial said in a statement that about 200 corporate customers are mentioned in the Panama Papers, most of whom are Taiwanese firms with offshore banking accounts. It said it was checking the identities of these customers.

The leak earlier this year of more than 11.5 million documents, the so-called Panama Papers, put a spotlight on the shadowy world of offshore companies used for tax evasion, prompting authorities across the world to investigate possible financial wrongdoing by the rich and powerful.

*15.2: NYDFS logo*

# CHAPTER 16
## COLLUSION AND ATTEMPT TO DESTROY NOBU SUE

THIS IS A very serious issue. It began in the fourth quarter of 2013 when the China Investment Fund (KMT) director tried to sell my house near the cemetery where my grandfather is buried, in a suburb of Taipei City. It is unbelievable that US hedge funds such as Monarch and Oaktree, along with Bank of America, Deutsche Bank, Cathay Bank, Shanghai International Commercial Bank, Wilmington Trust, and others, tried to take over my personal assets, before the Chapter 11 case was even over.

The reason? If they could destroy me completely, I would not have the financial capacity to hire US lawyers and fight back. I believe in karma—it's coming!

The plan between Mega Bank, Petros Pappas, HHI, Seward & Kissel LLP, and others was all aligned when the experts got together in New York. It must have gone something like this:

1) Sell to the closed circle just below what's outstanding, so Nobu's personal guarantee will kick in.

2) Make sure Nobu is exhausted, both physically and financially.

3) As there's no equity, no information about the buyers will be disclosed.

Let me recap on a few things here—especially the physical sale of TMT ships by the conspirators. In the first place, OCM Formosa Strait Holdings didn't really exist, not in a physical sense at least. It was a front—a façade. It was used for a few months to temporarily move funds and hide what was really going on, then disappeared after the sales in 2014. JPMorgan Chase (Taiwan) and Oaktree Capital Management (LA) were involved in its creation. According to Ken Leung, OCM Formosa Strait Holdings started to buy loans at the end of 2013. I've already touched on how Ken Leung was involved, along with the ex-head of JPMC (Taiwan)—both were suddenly fired at the end of June 2017, probably with orders to keep their mouths shut, or else!

The concept originated in 2010 in the Oaktree Huntington (Cayman) 6CTB fund, as a lawyer acting for Paul Weiss LLP disclosed to the Chapter 11 court in Houston in 2014. However, it had actually disappeared by that time. Oaktree Capital Management had to buy up all six Whale ship loans in the Chapter 11 process to delete the evidence of what was happening. They had to create OCM Formosa Strait Holdings and Pacific Orca LLC to make the bids. It was a violation of Chapter 11, as the company was changed and, most likely, the final directors and shareholders as well. In 2016, only nine ships of Marshall Islands and Panama registries could confirm that the US$20 million second mortgages were backdated in June 2013. We couldn't find out when these were deleted, as ship sales—Memoranda of Association (MOAs) and Protocol of Delivery—were not disclosed in Chapter 11. The US$20 million second mortgages on those ships didn't show in the Liberian registry (LISCR). However, we had bank invoices showing that ICBCUS33 (Mega's SWIFT Code) had paid US$21,000 for the LISCR fees for seven Whale ships and, two weeks later, Evan Flaschen paid US$21,000 from the DIP loan to the LISCR. Jurisdictions were never disclosed and no good standing was confirmed.

Oaktree had invested US$7 billion in shipping in 2012–2013. In the Oaktree Capital Management business model, it was 10% owned by equity and 90% owned by investors. There's a high possibility that the 90% was Taiwanese funds.

Taishin Bank's US$100 million loan over five years is the key issue—US$100 million cash with low interest for working with Taishin Bank, part of the Shin Kwan Group, with close political ties to the KMT. Actually, Taishin Bank is the bank that knew all the investors in OCM Formosa Strait Holdings. It's highly possible that several ex-bankers sucked the lifeblood from the TMT fleet, but also invested in the ships, earning returns from Oaktree. To clean it up, all the ships and charters were sold in a deal with Onassis Holdings, which today owns most of TMT's Whale and Elephant vessels. The ships currently operated by the Onassis Group are: B Whale, C Whale, D Whale, E Whale, G Whale, H Whale, Fortuna Elephant, And B Max.

I closely monitored a court auction in South Africa. It didn't happen on time and OCM Formosa Strait Holdings and Product Tankers (controlled by Petros Pappas' private company) were the buyers. The address of OCM Formosa Strait Holdings was the same as the Greek office of Petros Pappas. Product Tankers kept the same ship managements as TMT—such as Thome, Fleet Management, and V Ships, so it wouldn't be difficult for lawyers in discovery to find out who the real owners are.

In October 2013, Augustea Bunge Maritime Limited formed a joint venture with York Capital Management. The goal of the new Malta-based company, called ABY Holding Limited, was to operate an independent fleet of dry-bulk vessels. It intended to grow through the acquisition of modern ships and the expansion of the resources available to build a fleet of scale. ABY focused on acquiring first-class quality, dry-bulk tonnage and develop into the global supply chain, which was an integral part of their core business, and they bought E Elephant. I've already outlined how Evan Flaschen helped delay closing a sale and stopped it going to a second Greek buyer, who was willing to pay a higher price. There is evidence of this. Clarkson (Hong Kong) also got a special deal from Flaschen—he gave them the deal with some incentives. The highest bid never got approved by Flaschen, who, in my opinion, didn't tell the truth to Judge Isgur.

You're asking, wasn't Evan Flaschen supposed to be working for me? Of course. But a broker told me Clarksons colluded with him to favor SC Lowy. This is supposed to have happened in April/May 2014 and it proved, to me at least, that Flaschen had already been bought out in late 2013. We found significant evidence in Whitney Bank statements which had ICBCUS33 and ICBC LA (I've already explained what ICBC stands for—incidentally ICBCTWTP011 was the SWIFT code for Taipei) to pay Bracewell & Giuliani's IOLTA account and Evan Flaschen's Hartford, Connecticut, account. My previous experience suggested to me that the organization gave a satellite office the opportunity and freedom to easily create unregulated documents and trading transferrals.

SC Lowy and Lee & Li Law Firm (Taiwan) are under the same name of SC Lowy Investment (Cayman Islands). In the Panama registry the real name traded and the buyers involved were not a Hong Kong company, as SC Lowy is, but a Cayman paper company. Why? The A Duckling deal, 100% owned by Mega Bank, was a gift to SC Lowy. Furthermore, the money wasn't paid by SC Lowy until A Duckling was sold to K Line in Korea. SC Lowy's Mr Kim was restructuring K Line at the same time and had close connections to Allen Tsai, Madam Chow's son-in-law. So you can see how the people involved were all connected in one way or another and how the extent of the collusion was to make as much money as they could for themselves, along with helping Mega Bank to get KMT funds out of Taiwan.

I'm currently following class action lawsuits by Mega Bank and other Taiwan banks against McKinney Tsai. I'm studying the possibilities of losses filed by shareholders of the Taiwan banks. It's very common in the USA. However, we can't find any impaired loss in Mega Bank financial statements for 2012, 2013, or 2014. It's amazing that the MOF ordered the loss to be cut in half in 2013, just two weeks after TMT filed for Chapter 11 bankruptcy. The real story is that the same fund had supportive investment to cover up.

Was it a perfect crime? TMT's unsecured loan payment was late—not the full amount of US$40 million, but the monthly installment. Should the entire loan have been defaulted? Of course not! Why didn't TMT get back the equity from Ladybug? Seward & Kissel was representing everybody at the same time and they deliberately wiped out any equity.

The "sudden-death" note from Mega Bank, served to TMT on April 15, 2013, was the key. Was it because, exactly eight months later to the day (December 15, 2013) it became part of the sale of all the loans, initiated by Shanghai Commercial Savings Bank? I'd say that's very likely. Each time a loan was sold, a US$20 million second mortgage was sent to the buyers with the loan documents. This had no impact on any of the Taiwan banks' financial statements. Shanghai Commercial Savings Bank loan sales documents were all typed on error message paper and signed by Deutsche Bank. They had no legal documents nor POA letters. Were they lumped together with KMT funds?

I know it all sounds so complicated and you'd need to be a commercial lawyer to get your head round most of it. To understand it better we might want to read the announcement published by the Taiwanese Minister of Finance on July 7, 2014. If you remember, and I've mentioned this several times, in the announcement he ordered all Taiwan banks involved with TMT to cut their outstanding loans by half. I've already asked how could this have happened without independent valuations and without the government knowing the internal details of private businesses. To find the answer we asked a well-known certified public accountant to analyze the 2013 audit statements of most Taiwan banks involved in the TMT case. None of them listed the TMT loans. Where did they go?

Here's the answer.

As you know, a US$20 million DIP loan was arranged by Macquarie Bank, with one condition: all 16 ships had to have US$20 million second mortgages as securities for the US$20 million loan. Who got the 1% commission? Macquarie Bank or the arranger? After the cut in half of TMT loans in the third quarter, by order of the Taiwan Minister of Finance, the Chapter 11 banks accepted second mortgages for Panama-flagged, Marshall Island-flagged and Liberia-flagged ships, then sold the fragmented loans on an almost daily basis, starting on December 15, 2013. The issue with Panama was how to backdate a US$20 million second mortgage loan from 2014 to 2012. Any pre-Chapter 11 wrongdoings needed to be camouflaged. On January 8, 2014, at the sales hearing of Ladybugs, Judge Isgur, without prior notice, agreed all the terms of the DIP loans, including backdating the US$20 million loans and allowing each ship to have a US$20 million second mortgage.

We'd conducted inquiries in the Marshall Islands, Panamanian, and Liberian registries. In 2016 only nine ships of Marshall Islands and Panama registry could confirm that the US$20 million second mortgages were backdated. We couldn't find out when these were deleted, as ship sales, MOAs, and Protocols of Delivery were not disclosed in Chapter 11. However, as I've already said, we had bank invoices showing that ICBC NYC (Mega Bank's SWIFT Code) had paid US$21,000 for the LISCR registry fees for seven Whale ships and, two weeks later, Evan Flaschen paid US$21,000 from the DIP loan to LISCR. After that, the US$20 million second mortgages for all 16 ships were confirmed.

Mega Bank involved Oaktree as early as June 2013. Ken Leung, who was from Hong Kong and lived on the west coast, worked as Oaktree's general counsel from 1988. He was head of shipping and behind Star Bulk investments and many other accounts. He was heavily involved in this deal, as was the former head of JPMorgan Chase (Taiwan), who was running a successful US$100 billion asset management at that time and was later fired by JPMC NY toward the end of June 2017. According to Ken Leung, Oaktree Huntington (Cayman) 6CTB started to buy loans at the end of 2013. It bought out all the Whales in the TMT Chapter 11 filing, under the name of OCM Formosa Strait Holdings, which had been created to facilitate the temporary moving of funds and which disappeared after the sales of January 2014, to eliminate the evidence of fund movement.

The former Taiwan ambassador returned to Taiwan at the end of February 2014. The Plan X mission having been accomplished.

In short, the US$320 million was moved perfectly. It was invested internally as US$20 million second mortgages, so the loss was zero on Mega Bank financial statements. The loss of US$20 million in other Taiwan banks was covered up with 'other business'—except for Cathay United Bank, which used Fortuna Elephant to make a profit of US$20 million. Since Oaktree bought it at such a cheap price, when its mission was complete it allowed investors to withdraw US$20 million from its account and paid less money to the KMT nominated account.

Let me explain. Money could be transferred by TMT ships to nominated accounts nobody knew about, apart from Oaktree and Monarch. It might be the London, Panama, or Abu Dhabi branches of Mega Bank—lately, Mega Bank has been closing many of its overseas branches. I wonder why?

By 2014 my relationship with TMT's financial advisors had deteriorated. There's an email from Evan Flaschen of AlixPartners to some lawyers stating that they are 'going to destroy TMT and close the deal.' I need to investigate this further and I am trying to locate all communications between Flaschen, Kelley, Schreiber, and others.

So, for now I will write—to be continued …

## COLLUSION AND ATTEMPT TO DESTROY NOBU SUE

*16.1: Cargo ready to be loaded for Ro-Ro Line*

# CHAPTER 17
## DELETE AND DESTROY THE EVIDENCE

THE FIRST THING I need to say here is that SC Lowy fronted too many ships' loan transactions:

- A Whale: January 8, 2014—SC Lowy and Monarch
- A Duckling: December 2013—100% Mega Bank
- C Handy: Shanghai-Chunghwa-SC Lowy-Solus (SOLA, Ultra Master Fund)
- B Max: Shanghai-Changhwa-SC Lowy-Solus (SOLA, Ultra Master Fund)

Shanghai Bank sold to Macquarie, then to SC Lowy—strange commission deals.

Then there's the Dynasty syndrome of keeping it in the family.

I've already written about Allen Tsai in Chapter 5. You'll remember that he married the daughter of President and Christine Ma. He was a banker in Deutsche Bank in early 2000. Then he was a colleague of people in SC Lowy and Solus Asset Management. Solus Asset Management was set up by the former head of Deutsche Bank's Distressed Products Group. This is where it gets complicated again. George Soros had dealings with York Capital and with Angelo, Gordon & Co (investment advisors)—Solus/Soros, similar but separate names and it's easy to get confused. George Soros' lead fund organized the Angelo, Gordon & Co deal in 2008, which was connected to Pappas' Star Bulk and Oceanbulk mergers and to George Solos' York Capital, who are the largest shareholders in Vantage Drilling International. So, as I've said several times, you can see how incestuously interlinked this group of people and partnerships are.

SC Lowy 'is a market leader in secondary loan and high-yield bond trading across Asia-Pacific, the Middle East and Australia'—according to their website. I've outlined how the company was set up under SC Lowy Financial (HK) in 2009. I suspect the money was supported by Deutsche Bank and possibly China Investment Fund (need to investigate further). This would have involved Deutsche Bank's London, Hong Kong, and New York branches in a close relationship, buying and selling distressed loans.

I've already mentioned Carl Chien, the son of ex-Taiwan foreign minister Chien Foo, who was a leading member of the KMT under Chiang Kai-shek and his son, Chiang Ching-kuo. This smart kid played an important role in both Goldman Sachs and JPMorgan Chase N.A. As the head of JPMorgan Chase (Asia) he controlled the region, including China, Taiwan, and southeast Asia. We can see how the son-and-daughter fine of US$264 million in October 2016 was such an important event. It showed that, even after Mega Bank being fined US$180 million because of AML, JPMC's Asian establishment was fined a further US$264 million for ongoing financial misconduct. There are many other such instances of impropriety, such as the China Railway funding scandal. My point is that all these instances are connected—through the Dynasty that had controlled the financial and associated institutions since the KMT first arrived in Taiwan.

But let's get back to deleting and destroying evidence—Robert Seiden is a former prosecutor, lawyer, global forensic investigator, court-appointed receiver, and founder of Confidential Global Investigations. He was a senior prosecutor in the Manhattan District Attorney's office, New York City, from 1988 to 1999, where he investigated and prosecuted cases of money laundering, fraud, embezzlement, and other financial crimes. One of his investigations uncovered US$250 million in loans given to Macquarie Bank by Mega Bank—in other words, the China Investment Fund. This may very well be related to the initial US$25 million loan given to TMT, which was ultimately increased to US$40 million secured by pledging A Ladybug. The original unsecured loan was not reported in the Chapter 11 court, neither was the fact that it was sold to Macquarie Bank for less than it was worth, causing financial loss to TMT. It might not seem like it, but this case is very important in the context of the jurisdictions of Taiwan, Panama, and the USA—more will be written about that later.

Furthermore, a liquidation analysis presented by me to Judge Jones in a mediation attempt in 2016, showed that Taishin Bank owned 15% of Fortuna Elephant, which was never in the Chapter 11 transfer notice. Remember I spoke earlier about the 85% and the missing 15%—well, here was one 15%, neatly tucked away in Taishin Bank. But that's just one of many percentage splits of the loans, done to cover the tracks and confuse any subsequent investigation or audit.

The oddest thing was that loan sales to Western banks had no lawyer statement fingerprints. Only one proper legal document was certified by the bank's own stamp, according to compliances that showed proper lawyer name involvement in September 2012, and that was for the A Ladybug loan agreement. However, separate documents for the transferred loans were not disclosed. Macquarie Bank's POA on November 22, 2012, issued in Sydney and another POA on November 23, 2012, issued in New York, were based on compliances of Macquarie Investment Bank. Both had numbers to show internal control. All other documents involving large financial institutions lacked those certified stamps throughout the whole of Chapter 11. I cannot believe that the hundreds of lawyers involved in Chapter 11, including paralegals and other associates, didn't pay sufficient attention to those documents. The irregularity in the documents is very clear—details will be pointed out in my next book. I realize this may be difficult to follow for the average person, but the inference is that Madam Chow (Christine Ma), using bank resources and taxpayer's money, involved a special team of Wall Street professionals as consultants to disguise the scam.

You remember I told you about the meeting I had in October 2013 at the Bracewell offices, with three young ladies from Macquarie Bank, in the presence of Lisa Donahue, Evan Flaschen, and Bob Burns, who came to Taiwan before I filed for Chapter 11 and met my family. Lisa Donahue (AlixPartners) said she and Bob Burns were both Irish, but they'd never met each other—that wasn't true. Later, I found out that Bob Burns, working in Bracewell & Giuliani LLP, was a former general counsel of Monarch Capital. Monarch and major shareholders in Star Bulk Carriers had bought A Whale just two years previously. The lawyers most likely pretended they didn't know each other to avoid a "conflict of interest" and to make as much money as they could from the Chapter 11. It wasn't only that. The Seward & Kissel lawyer, Ahmed, always stayed with Evan Flaschen and it's obvious, to me at least, that the UCC lawyers and the debtor lawyers got together in the Bracewell & Giuliani offices and worked on the scenario they were going to present to Judge Isgur in court the following day. I'm convinced the New York lawyers, led by Charles Kelley, got together in the Mayer Brown offices and shared information with Vidal Martinez and the Vantage lawyers in Houston. If that's not a conflict of interest, I don't know what is.

Anyway, that meeting at the Bracewell offices only lasted 30 minutes and the Macquarie ladies had no interest in shipping, or how the ship properties were related to the case—they were only interested in working with the debtors to transfer the debt. Investigations done by my team have shown that special bankers from Taiwan and

Hong Kong visited Mega Bank in New York during 2013 and early 2014, to give instructions on how to transfer the debt. In other words, to launder KMT money and get it out of Taiwan.

They all thought the cover-up was airtight.

But it wasn't.

*17.1: Destroying the evidence (© orangeline/123RF)*

# CHAPTER 18
## THE SAMSON WU STORY: FAKE NEWS?

IN 2002/2003 THERE was a mysterious legal battle between Mega Bank Panama and the USA called the Samson Wu story. This was reported in the Taiwan news media about the same time as the NYDFS $180 million AML case should have been the big news media item in Taiwan. Let's talk about the Samson Wu case—was it fake news, to camouflage the real story of what was happening?

For those who don't know, Samson Wu was accused of stealing the intellectual property of Super Vision International (NASDAQ: SUPVA), a leading manufacturer of fiber-optic and LED lighting products. The legal battle involved stolen trade secrets, private investigators, shredded evidence, and threats. It all supposedly started when Super Vision began exploring opportunities in the China market. Chinese competitors, led by Samson Wu, were said to have offered a Super Vision employee more than US$1 million to steal technology and advanced manufacturing equipment. Wu was also supposed to have hired people to intimidate Super Vision employees and their families. After seeing the market flooded with half-price "counterfeit" products, Super Vision took legal action. They hired private investigators to masquerade as wealthy Arab Sheiks and purchase the "counterfeit" products via hidden surveillance cameras.

It all sounds a bit like a thriller novel, doesn't it?

The "evidence" was used to convict Samson Wu and others in a jury trial (Case # CI-99-9392) where the defendants refused to answer any questions, citing their

Fifth Amendment privilege. A final judgment in the amount of US$41.2 million was awarded to Super Vision after the defendants were found liable on all counts of fraud, civil theft, conspiracy, misappropriation, and the destruction of evidence. But, by the time the final judgment was entered, Samson Wu had liquidated all his US holdings and wired the funds out of America via 'methods consistent with money laundering.' Brett Kingstone, the Founder, President and CEO of Super Vision, wrote a book about the case (The Real War Against America from Specialty Publishing, ISBN 0-9755199-2-1).

Now, why would I say that this may have been an example of fake news? Well, it was done to control the media and distract attention from what was really going on. Consider the following article by John Hsieh (the name is fake, btw; and the article was online in March 2005 but has since disappeared):

> Mega International Commercial Bank (MICB) is a state-run bank with rich experience in international banking clearance, but how was it involved in a lawsuit and penalized by NYDFS? As Taiwan President Tsai Ing-wen said, 'It had damaged Taiwan's reputation and created public mistrust about supervision of the financial sector.' Well, let's review it from the press release by NYDFS on 19 August 2016, and the decision and order of the Supreme Court, Appellate Division, First Department entered 11 August 2015.
>
> On 16 June 2003 a Florida court entered a judgment in excess of $41 million in favor of Super Vision International Inc. against Caruso (debtors) in counterfeiting, civil theft and the misappropriation of its propriety information. Debtor Samson Wu must disclose all accounts that he was authorized to draw. On 24 March 2009, Super Vision assigned its rights against debtors to B&M and the judgment was entered and recorded in Nassau County in New York State in favor of B&M. On 7 August 2014, B&M served Mega Bank with subpoena duces tecum and an information subpoena with a restraining notice and questionnaire that asked, among other things,

whether Mega had a record of any account in which each judgment debtor may have had an interest and whether the judgment debtor was indebted to Mega in any manner. On 14 August 2014, Mega responded in a letter stating that its New York branch was not holding any account or other property for the judgment debtors and they were not indebted to it. On 27 August 2014 Mega responded to the subpoena duces tecum stating that its New York branch was not in possession of assets belonging to any judgment debtor, and objected to the subpoena to the extent that it sought records located in Mega branches outside New York. On 10 September 2014, B&M filed a petition signed by Super Vision founder Brett Kingston pointing out that Mega was intimately involved with the judgment debtors, especially Wu, who concealed debtor assets—including, through transactions in Panama—where Mega Free Zone branch manager Angel Caballero was an officer of companies owned by Wu.

Mega argued that the 'separate entity' rule precluded enforcement of subpoenas and restraining notices to Mega branches outside New York. It also argued that principles of international comity precluded compelling international compliance with the subpoenas. However, Mega consented to the necessary regulatory oversight in return for permission to operate in New York, and therefore is subject to jurisdiction requiring it to comply with the appropriate information subpoenas.

In order to benefit from the advantages of transacting business in this forum, a foreign bank must register with and obtain a license from the Superintendent of NYDFS, and file a written instrument 'appointing the superintendent and his or her successors its true and lawful attorney, upon whom all process in any action or proceeding against it on a cause of action arising out of a transaction with its New York agency or agencies or branch or branches.' On 11 August 2015, Supreme Court, Appellate Division First Judicial Department, Justice Rolando T. Acosta, J.P. made an order of the

Supreme Court, New York County (Geoffrey D. Wright, J.), entered 19 September 2014, which, to the extent appealed from, granted the petitioner's motion to direct respondent to fully respond to an information subpoena, should be affirmed, with costs.

In October 2015, the US Federal Reserve visited Taiwan's Financial Supervisory Commission to discuss financial technology, but nothing related to Mega Bank, according to Banking Bureau Director General Austin Chan. Former Mega Bank chairman McKinney Tsai, however, confirmed that the US Federal Reserve visited Mega Bank's Taipei headquarter on 5 October 2015, but he wasn't there due to a Legislative Yuan Committee meeting. Hence Tsai had been well aware since October 2015.

In February 2016, NYDFS issued a Report of Examination which found that the position of BSA/AML officer in Mega's New York branch was held by a person from Mega International's head office who possessed little familiarity with US regulatory requirements. Similarly, its Chief Compliance Officer lacked adequate knowledge of BSA/AML and OFAC requirements. On 24 March 2016 Mega Bank submitted a response that refuted a number of NYDFS's examination findings. It declared that certain types of activity were not suspicious, and insisted no AML regulatory guidance related to filing 'Suspicious Activity Reports' on such types of transactions. Therefore, such transactions did not constitute suspicious activity. This extremely troubling response to the examination was totally unacceptable. Financial Services Superintendent Maria T. Vullo said 'NYDFS will not tolerate the flagrant disregard of AML laws and will take decisive and tough action against any institution that fails to have compliance programs in place to prevent illicit transactions.'

On 19 August 2016, Vullo announced, 'MICB will pay a US$180 million penalty and install an independent monitor for violating New York's anti-money laundering laws,' and released a Consent Order signed by Hann-Ching Wu, then-president of Mega International Commercial Bank Co., Ltd., Vincent S.M. Huang, senior vice president and general manager of MICB-NY Branch, and Maria T. Vullo, Superintendent of Financial Services.

The Mega scandal is a typical example of criminal acts carried out by the KMT in Taiwan. They connected the national treasury to their party account in the old days, and then hid the stolen money all over the world. It occurred in Ma Ying-jeou's administration, but successor Tsai Ing-wen's government got the blame. What kind of logic is that? It simply does not make sense at all. Party politics asks that the ruling party be responsible for whatever happens in the nation. The water that bears the boat is the same that swallows it. If the DPP administration does not know how to fix the headaches left by the KMT government, then the Taiwan people will show the DPP government how to fix it.

Now that former Mega Chairman McKinney Tsai has been indicted and is under investigation, a new chairman and new general manager has been appointed. President Tsai Ing-wen said, 'We must review our financial supervision, promote reform, and not allow this ridiculous and unbelievable matter to happen again.'

I hope Taiwan will learn a good lesson from this Mega scandal.

This was what was reported in the news media. However, they didn't have the proper evidence as to what the real issues were. The Samson Wu story was obviously created to cover things up when McKinney Tsai quit as Chairman of Mega Bank and moved to Cathay United Bank as a director. Circumstantial evidence to support the scandal is plentiful. Taiwanese people had been crazily buying real estate in California ever since Taiwan left the United Nations (UN). More than 8,000 people had left the Taiwan banking industry due to early retirement and the banking industry was (and still is) in serious chaos. SinoPac, Chinatrust, Cathay United Bank, First Bank, Shanghai

Commercial Saving Banks, and many other banks had moved offices, or left Taiwan. These banks' overseas scandals were quietly being extinguished in the media. The FSC and SEC in Taiwan were also unwilling to investigate, stating it was against the public interest.

What has now been exposed is how this is all connected to KMT Dynasty insiders and ex-President Ma Ying-jeou.

*18.1: Brett Kingstone's* The Real War Against America

# CHAPTER 19
## AML: US$180 MILLION NEWS

I'VE MENTIONED MEGA Bank's AML case already, but let's take a closer look at the US$180 million fine and other related issues. As I've said, the NYDFS ordered MICB to pay a US$180 million penalty and install an independent monitor for violating New York's AML laws. The fine was part of a consent order entered into with the NYDFS in which Mega Bank agreed to take immediate steps to correct violations, including engaging the independent monitor to address serious deficiencies within the bank's compliance program and to implement effective AML controls. Maria Vullo (NYDFS Superintendent) said in a NYDFS Consent Order on August 19, 2016:

> The compliance failures that DFS found at the New York branch of Mega Bank are serious, persistent and affected the entire Mega banking enterprise and they indicate a fundamental lack of understanding of the need for a vigorous compliance infrastructure. DFS's recent examination uncovered that Mega Bank's compliance program was a hollow shell, and this consent order is necessary to ensure future compliance.

What were the details of the NYDFS' findings?

Well, they found that the bank's head office was indifferent toward risks associated with transactions involving Panama, recognized as a high-risk jurisdiction for money laundering. Mega Bank had a branch in Panama City and another in Panama's Colon Free Trade Zone. NYDFS' investigation identified a number of suspicious transactions running between Mega Bank's New York and Panama branches. It's well known that Panama was a diplomatic ally of the KMT, who spent a lot of money to maintain close diplomatic relationships. According to NYDFS, the investigation also determined that a substantial number of customer entities, with accounts at other Mega Bank branches, were formed with the assistance of the Mossack Fonseca law firm in Panama. Mossack Fonseca is one of the law firms at the center of the formation of shell company activity, designed to skirt banking and tax laws worldwide, including US laws designed to fight money laundering—and is now at the center of the Panama Papers scandal.

Among the findings of the NYDFS investigation were:

• The BSA/AML officer for the New York branch, who was based at the bank's Taiwan headquarters, and the branch's chief compliance officer both lacked familiarity with US regulatory requirements. In addition, the chief compliance offer had conflicted interests because she had key business and operational responsibilities, along with her compliance role.

• Compliance staff at both head office and branch failed to periodically review surveillance monitoring filter criteria designed to detect suspicious transactions. Also, numerous documents relied upon in transaction monitoring were not translated to English from Chinese, precluding effective examination by regulators.

• The New York branch procedures provided virtually no guidance concerning the reporting of continuing suspicious activities; had inconsistent compliance policies; and failed to determine whether foreign affiliates had adequate AML controls in place.

• The last clause of the press release has an option to click on all the described details. I found it very interesting that one technical company with similar bank accounts was involved in the Colon Free State Zone. Who that was is still a mystery.

Under the consent order, Mega Bank was to install an independent consultant within ten days of the selection by NYDFS to implement changes to its policies and procedures and immediately address compliance deficiencies at the New York branch. The order also called for the bank to engage an independent monitor for two years within 30 days of its selection by NYDFS to conduct a comprehensive review of the effectiveness of the branch's compliance program.

The independent monitor should also commence a transaction and OFAC Sanctions Review to determine whether transactions inconsistent with or in violation of the OFAC Regulations, or suspicious activity involving high-risk customers or transactions were properly identified and reported from 2012 to 2014. The monitor would be selected by and report directly to NYDFS. The NYDFS action against Mega Bank was notable because it represented a substantial penalty for a first violation—when I say first, I mean a first investigated violation. Mega Bank were violating AML laws before then and getting away with it. In addition to the bank's failure to properly monitor suspicious transactions, NYDFS found that Mega Bank's chief compliance officer was not US-based and had little familiarity with US AML requirements. The case against Mega Bank was one of the first, if not the very first, cases linked explicitly to the Panama Papers.

So, let's look at the Panama Papers and the connection with Mega Bank.

The Panama Papers are 11.5 million documents that detail financial and attorney–client information for more than 214,488 offshore entities. They were leaked in 2015 by an anonymous source and reveal a murky financial underworld of fraud, tax evasion, and money laundering by politicians, celebrities, and sports stars using shell companies for illegal purposes. A shell company exists only on paper and has no offices and no employees—it may have a bank account, or hold investments, or be the registered owner of assets. Some of the documents date back as far as the 1970s and they were taken from Mossack Fonseca, the Panamanian law firm and corporate service provider mentioned already. The personal financial information about wealthy individuals and organizations in the documents had previously been kept private.

The whistle-blower who leaked the documents to German journalist Bastian Obermayer from the newspaper Süddeutsche Zeitung, remained anonymous, even to journalists who worked on the investigation.

'My life is in danger.'

That's what he told them. He said he leaked the documents to expose the scale of the injustices they described. Journalists from 107 media organizations in 80 countries analyzed the documents for a year before the first stories were published in April 2016. The documents were called the Panama Papers because that's the country they were leaked out of.

How was Mega Bank involved? It has already been established that Mega Bank, through the KMT, had very close relationships (both financial and political) with Panama. The bank had "suspicious" accounts that were set up by Mossack Fonseca and, on October 5, 2016, my old "friend" McKinney Tsai was arrested in Taiwan and taken into custody on suspicion of insider trading. '*The former head of a Taiwanese bank linked to the Panama Papers and his top aide [Wang Chi-pang] have been detained on suspicion of violating banking and securities laws*,' officials at the Taipei district prosecutor's office said. According to Apple Daily, Tsai offloaded stocks ahead of Mega Bank being fined US$180 million in the NYDFS AML case.

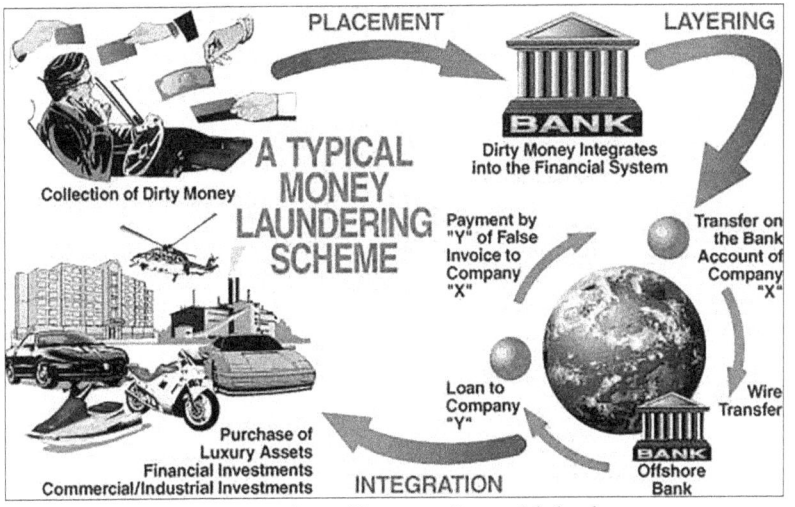

*19.1: Laundering "dirty money" on a global scale*

# CHAPTER 20
## MEDIATION AND TRUTH COMING OUT

THE MEDIATION PROCESS took about ten months. There was an unexpected call from the UCC to start mediation after the NYDFS news came out in September 2016. Evan Flaschen suddenly requested mediation, together with silent participants Kelley Drye LLP, the lawyer firm that took over after Seward & Kissel were fired. Very odd! It took three months for Deirdre Brown and HooverSlovacek to persuade me to go to mediation, finally convincing me by saying that if I didn't like it, I could back off. It was, basically, lawyers and advisors vs Nobu Sue. However, the strange thing was that all the mediation information was leaked to the lenders, who tried to run away after the Chapter 11. It became so obvious. I raised the question—if the lenders aren't willing to come for the global settlement, then what's the point? The patent litigation was put aside, but all the lenders weren't involved directly in the mediation. Odd.

As I said, the first three months were spend deciding whether to go to mediation or not. It was a very ambiguous solution to the settlement process. The new UCC lawyer who succeeded Seward & Kissel, Kelley Drye LLP (also JPMC's lawyers for over 100 years), said 'let's agree matters and forget all the details.' It surprised me that the process didn't include all parties, but only the debtors and myself, along with unsecured creditors. It wasn't easy to understand why the global settlement wasn't done in Chapter 11. It was like, in Chapter 11, some money had to go to unsecured creditors so it looked like all parties agreed. The secured lenders had already sold ships cheaply and swallowed up all the valuable assets. The silent lawyers made a show of getting more money, which was unbelievable. It was like giving a donation to the poor at Christmas so they all felt good about themselves. It was pathetic.

The voting was important, but it all depended on the judge's decision. It was so subjective and riddled with political maneuvring, and posturing, and status-strutting within the American legal establishment. I learned a lot going through the Chapter 11 bankruptcy procedure in the USA. It cost me US$120 million and all the lawyers were charging up to $1,000 an hour—in the end, everybody made money except me. All they wanted to do was make as much cash as possible. There were US$9 million left and it was quickly depleting to US$8 million. Yet no one was talking about how to get money from creditors, or from the equity from ships that were sold and the US$400 million made from those sales. It amazes me how none of those people could see the overall view—from an aerial perspective. They all just followed the textbook interpretation of Chapter 11 doctrine and special terms. It was like someone who'd just passed their driving test and adhered to all the rules they'd recently learned. Novices. Whereas experienced drivers around them would use their initiative and intuition—none of those high-priced lawyers used any initiative, imagination, or intuition. They just went through the motions of running up huge legal bills.

It's shocking to me that all the documents for final approval were written up by the lawyers at the last minute and the judge signed them without, as far as I can tell, even understanding them. It was like they all got together and came up with something that was agreed between them. But it wasn't the truth.

The truth wasn't told in the Chapter 11 court!

I would never have agreed to the sale of the loan to Macquarie Bank and I had a valid cause for dispute with Mega Bank over that. Also, the debtors' counsel usurped control of the case, which made things messy for the Chapter 11 judge—Esben Christensen of AlixPartners controlled all the debtors and I believe he breached his duties in doing so. Christensen made a deposition in New York in October 2017, which stated that 'synthetic revolvers' was the term AlixPartners used to move money in and out of over 30 accounts, so nobody could consolidate. In actual fact, the judge relied on all the big-firm lawyers to be honest, but—as far as I'm concerned—they weren't. The UCC was asserting itself a lot more than it did in the past—the debtors (ship corporations) wanted me to back out so I looked like the bad guy and they looked like the good guys. The debtors also worried that what they did would be discovered—all the sales took place in jurisdictions outside the USA, where the Chapter 11 court had no control. Credit bids were improper and didn't follow statutes. Judge Isgur knew there were problems—I mean, Evan Flaschen asked for all documents to be destroyed (why would he want that, unless there was something to hide?), but the judge wouldn't allow it.

Now the debtors were working hand-in-hand with the lenders. They wanted to stop me from litigating—they wanted to stop me from doing discovery. The DIP lender had authority, under the DIP loan, to take second mortgages of US$20 million on every vessel. And they did. Evan Flaschen was the designee who signed off on those second mortgages. I've said this already, but I'll say it again, something definitely didn't add up with Macquarie Bank (DIP lender). There was impropriety. This was documented by Macquarie lawyers in March 2014 but backdated to the date of the bankruptcy petition filing. Either Flaschen was complicit or he was incompetent. I think he was complicit. How can you oversee a foreclosure sale without seeing all the loan documents?

There's still a lot of ongoing litigation that I can't discuss, but the power was with the litigation trustee. Evan Flaschen had no power in mediation, the litigation administrator could pursue claims, but nobody could "buy" a claim. Let me explain, creditors' committees are increasingly turning to litigation trustees to handle complex litigation in Chapter 11 proceedings. The litigation trustee is a tool for creditor committees when the debtors' assets include potential claims against third parties. Before that, Mayer Brown LLP had sold a claim to Wilmington Trust in Minnesota for US$1.

MAYER·BROWN

Mayer Brown LLP
1675 Broadway
New York, New York 10019-5820

Main Tel +1 212 506 2500
Main Fax +1 212 262 1910
www.mayerbrown.com

November 26, 2014

BY COURIER, FACSIMILE,
AND ELECTRONIC MAIL

Michael F. Lotito
Direct Tel +1 212 506 2521
Direct Fax +1 212 849 5527
mlotito@mayerbrown.com

Mr. Hsin-Chi Su
10th Floor, No. 245, Sec. 1
Dunhua S. Rd.
Taipei City 106
Taiwan
Facsimile: 886-2-8771-1559
Email: ghung@colonmail.com
Attention: Hsin-Chi Su
Greene Hung

Re: Notices of Assignment and Transfer

Dear Sirs:

Enclosed herewith are copies of the following notices:

- *Notice of Assignment and Transfer to Borrower, Other Obligors and Account Bank* with respect to that certain Facility Agreement dated 21 June 2010 (as amended, restated, supplemented, or otherwise modified) made between C Whale Corporation, as borrower, Great Elephant Corporation, as English guarantor, the financial institutions from time to time party thereto, as lenders, Mega International Commercial Bank Co., Ltd. ("**Mega Bank**"), and CTBC Bank Co., Ltd. (formerly known as Chinatrust Commercial Bank Co., Ltd.) ("**CTBC**"), as arrangers, and Mega Bank, as agent and security trustee;

- *Notice of Assignment and Transfer to Borrower, Other Obligors, Other Lenders and Account Bank* with respect to that certain Facility Agreement dated 28 September 2010 (as amended, restated, supplemented, or otherwise modified) made between D Whale Corporation, as borrower, Ugly Duckling Holding Corp. ("**Ugly Duckling**"), as English guarantor, the financial institutions from time to time party thereto, as lenders, Mega Bank and CTBC, as arrangers, and Mega Bank as agent and security trustee;

- *Notice of Assignment and Transfer to Borrower, Other Obligors and Account Bank* with respect to that certain Facility Agreement dated 9 March 2011 (as amended, restated, supplemented, or otherwise modified) made between G Whale Corporation, as borrower, Ugly Duckling, as English guarantor, the financial institutions from time to time party thereto, as lenders, Mega Bank, CTBC, and First Commercial Bank Co., Ltd. ("**First Bank**"), as arrangers, Mega Bank, as agent, and CTBC, as security trustee; and

Mayer Brown LLP operates in combination with other Mayer Brown entities with offices in Europe and Asia
and is associated with Tauil & Chequer Advogados, a Brazilian law partnership.

*20.1a–e: Transfer notice from Mayer Brown to Wilmington*

Mayer Brown LLP

Mr. Hsin-Chi Su
November 26, 2014
Page 2

- *Notice of Assignment and Transfer to Borrower, Other Obligors and Account Bank* with respect to that certain Facility Agreement dated 7 June 2011 (as amended, restated, supplemented, or otherwise modified) made between H Whale Corporation, as borrower, Ugly Duckling, as English guarantor, the financial institutions from time to time party thereto, as lenders, Mega Bank, CTBC, and First Bank, as arrangers, Mega Bank, as agent, and First Bank, as security trustee.

Please review and take notice of the contents therein.

Sincerely,

Michael F. Lotito

ML/ml

Enclosures
cc: Joshua G. James, Vice President, Wilmington Trust, N.A. (by electronic mail)

---

## NOTICE OF ASSIGNMENT AND TRANSFER
## TO BORROWER, OTHER OBLIGORS AND ACCOUNT BANK

To: C Whale Corporation (as borrower, owner and pledgor under the relevant Finance Documents (as defined below), the "**Borrower**")
Great Elephant Corporation (as English guarantor under the Facility Agreement (as defined below, the "**English Guarantor**")
TMT Co., Ltd. Panama S.A. (as subordinated lender under the relevant Finance Document, the "**Subordinated Lender**")
16th Floor, No.200, Sec 1, Keelung Rd., Xinyi District, Taipei City 11701, Taiwan
Attention: Mr. Hsin Chi Su

Taiwan Maritime Transportation Co., Ltd. (as guarantor under the relevant Finance Document)
16th Floor, No.200, Sec 1, Keelung Rd., Xinyi District, Taipei City 11701, Taiwan
Attention: Mr. Hsin Chi Su

Mr. Hsin Chi Su (as guarantor under the relevant Finance Document)
16th Floor, No.200, Sec 1, Keelung Rd., Xinyi District, Taipei City 11701, Taiwan
Attention: Mr. Hsin Chi Su

Mega International Commercial Bank Co., Ltd. (as depository bank of the pledged and charged accounts pledged and charged pursuant to the relevant Finance Documents)
100 Chi-Lin Road, Taipei 10424, Taiwan, Republic of China

Date: 14 August 2014

Dear Sirs

We refer to the following documents:

1. a facility agreement dated 21 June 2010 (together with all amendments, supplements and addenda thereto from time to time, called the "**Facility Agreement**") made between (1) the Borrower, as borrower, (2) the English Guarantor, as English guarantor, (3) the financial institutions named therein, as lenders (collectively, the "**Lenders**"), (4) Mega International Commercial Bank Co., Ltd. ("**Mega**") and CTBC Bank Co., Ltd. (formerly known as Chinatrust Commercial Bank Co., Ltd.), as arrangers (collectively, the "**Arrangers**") and (5) Mega, as agent and security trustee (in such capacity, the "**Existing Agent**", and together with the Lenders and the Arrangers, the "**Finance Parties**"), pursuant to which the Lenders have made available to the Borrower certain secured term loan facilities of Dollars Eighty Four million ($84,000,000) (the "**Loan**") upon the terms and conditions contained therein;

2. the other Finance Documents executed pursuant to the Facility Agreement;

3. a notice of resignation dated 20 June 2014 issued by the Existing Agent to the Finance Parties and the Borrower;

4. a successor agent agreement dated 11 August 2014 (the "**Successor Agent Agreement**") executed by the Lenders and Wilmington Trust, National Association

(the "**Successor Agent**"), pursuant to which the Lenders have accepted the Existing Agent's resignation as agent and security trustee under the Finance Documents and appointed the Successor Agent as successor agent and security trustee pursuant to clause 26.12 of the Facility Agreement upon the terms and conditions contained therein;

5. a transfer certificate dated as of 11 August 2014 (the "**Transfer Certificate**") executed by the Existing Agent in favour of the Successor Agent pursuant to which the Existing Agent has assigned and transferred to the Successor Agent the Existing Agent's claim under the Finance Documents in the principal amount of Dollar One ($1); and

6. a deed of assignment dated as of 11 August 2014 (the "**Deed of Assignment**") executed by the Existing Agent and the Successor Agent pursuant to which the Existing Agent the role and status of the agent and security trustee and all present and future rights, benefits, obligations and liabilities of the Existing Agent arising from or in connection with (a) the Finance Documents, (b) the relevant enforcement titles/orders and ongoing legal proceedings and (c) applicable laws.

NOW WE HEREBY GIVE YOU NOTICE THAT :

1. With effect from the date of the Successor Agent Agreement, the Lenders accept the resignation of the Existing Agent as agent and security trustee under the Finance Documents and appoints the Successor Agent to act as successor agent and security trustee under the Finance Documents.

2. With effect from the date of the Transfer Certificate, the Existing Agent has transferred its claim under the Finance Documents in the principal amount of Dollar One ($1) to the Successor Agent.

3. With effect from the date of the Deed of Assignment:

   (a) The Existing Agent has assigned and transferred the role and status of the agent and security trustee and all of its present and future rights, benefits and obligations arising from or in connection with (A) the Facility Agreement and the other Finance Documents (as defined in the Facility Agreement), (B) the relevant enforcement titles/orders and ongoing legal proceedings and (C) applicable laws to the Successor Agent.

   (b) The Successor Agent has accepted and assumed the obligations of the Existing Agent under the Finance Documents and shall perform and comply with such obligations under the Finance Documents as if originally named as an original party thereto.

   (c) The Existing Agent is discharged from all its obligations and liabilities in respect of the Finance Documents whether present or future, actual or contingent. The rights of the Borrower and the other Obligors against the Existing Agent shall be cancelled.

> (d) All notices and communications to the Successor Agent under clause 31 of the Facility Agreement and any analogous provision in any of the other Finance Documents shall be delivered to the following:
>
> Wilmington Trust, National Association
> 50 South Sixth Street
> Suite 1290
> Minneapolis, MN 55402
> Attention: Joshua James
> Facsimile: 612-217-5651
>
> (e) All notices and communications to the "Agent" and "Security Trustee" under the Finance Documents should be addressed to the Successor Agent only.
>
> 4. All other terms of the Finance Documents remain unchanged.
>
> This Notice and your acknowledgment hereto shall be governed by and construed in accordance with the English law.
>
> Yours faithfully
>
> For and on behalf of
> MEGA INTERNATIONAL
> COMMERCIAL BANK CO., LTD.
> (as Existing Agent)
>
> Name: Priscilla Hsing
> Title: Vice President and Deputy General Manager
>
> For and on behalf of
> WILMINGTON TRUST, NATIONAL ASSOCIATION
> (as Successor Agent)
>
> Name:
> Title:

Charles Kelley, the creditor lawyer for Mayer Brown, attacked me on the order of Wilmington Trust over my personal guarantee. I fought back and, eventually, that case had nowhere to go. They dug their own graves and I got discovery from them. Kelley made the mistake of filing the wrong date, which was cited by my lawyer, Deirdre Brown—so he quit. Or maybe he finally realized that he was being used by MICB and the KMT? This is why Mayer Brown's

## MEDIATION AND TRUTH COMING OUT

offices in New York, Hong Kong, and London need to be investigated, as they were key players in the entire Mega Bank/KMT scandal.

The thing about this case is, they say I'm eccentric and egocentric and they say I allege outrageous things. If that was the case, they would have come after me hard by now and tried to completely destroy me. Why haven't they? Because they're afraid of the evidence I have. If I had nothing, I'd be dogmeat by now. They're worried about the evidence that's out there.

They're very worried!

Of course, they could also try to have me killed. There have already been death threats, which I'll tell you about in the next chapter.

*20.2: Nobu Sue at Bankruptcy Court*

# CHAPTER 21
## TELEVISION EXPOSURE AND DEATH THREATS

THE SPECTER OF the "revolving door" appears briefly, then disappears back into the financial fog. In 2010 TMT was given the first loan of US$25 million for A Duckling Corporation, after being approached by Mega Bank, who requested the financial relationship. Ding & Ding drafted the loan documents, which were "unusual" to say the least. The documents took no account of the first lien ship pledge and TMT was unfamiliar with ships' loans. The emphasis was all about the event of default, with more than 50 pages about how the pledge worked in the event of such a default. The bank could take over A Duckling Corporation and its guarantor (Ugly Duckling Corporation) and do whatever they wanted, at any time they wanted. They seemed more like corporate finance documents than simple shipping loan documents. The Panamanian company, A Duckling Corporation, gave full authority to the lender, Mega Bank, to create and sell to new companies, without my consent. It's all too clear now that it was a set-up. TMT was being targeted from its first loan in 2010.

It was very clear to me that Madam Chow must have made her plans before sanctioning the loans—probably with financial lawyers in New York and Wall Street advising on the documentation. Mayer Brown's key lawyers in Hong Kong, Houston, and New York were heavily involved in the Mega Bank vs TMT case in 2013 and 2014, but the name of Mayer Brown New York never officially showed up in TMT's Chapter 11 case—cited by TMT lawyer, Deirdre Brown. Chang Ting Hua, the former Deputy Manager of Mega

Bank, was involved. I asked lawyers from Ding & Ding to come to TMT's offices after Mega Bank's money laundering was exposed. They showed up once, but never came back. It happened one month after the US$180 million AML, about September/October, in Taipei.

If Plan X was prepared by Madam Chow, then it follows that she must have decided, through her family and top legal advisors, who would be nominated as bank CEOs, which included Mega Bank, First Bank, Kaohsiung Bank, Chang Hwa Bank, Taiwan Cooperative Bank, Land Bank, Hua Nan Bank, private sector Chinatrust, Cathay United Bank, Bank SinoPac, SCSB, and Taichung Bank. She probably gave them separate instructions on how and when to conduct transactions. This would ensure that nobody saw the full picture. The full picture was Plan X.

People within the KMT began to whisper about it in 2014, after the brilliant success of Plan X. As well as that, it's almost certain that greedy people became further involved. These included top KMT politicians, including chairmen of banks who tried to profit from the sale of TMT assets. Further investigation is required here and answers to questions will be forthcoming.

Conspiracies always have unforeseen consequences. The most difficult thing to do is completely destroy the evidence. Cracks appear and details leak out—here are some, which I'll outline, one by one.

1) The TMT Chapter 11 case was the result of concerted actions carried out by the lawyers of the lenders, DIP lenders, debtors, and unsecured creditors.

2) The TMT Chapter 11 case was used to move money abroad from Taiwan, by prearranged SWAP contracts among parties, using a few routes. The main ones were Macquarie Bank, JPMorgan Chase Bank, Deutsche Bank, and SC Lowy Financial (HK).

3) The geography and timing of the loans were divided into many components, so it was difficult to comprehend the full picture without performing a big data analysis.

4) The parties involved applied an approach whereby jurisdiction fell outside Taiwan—that way, they could avoid a criminal case in Taiwan.

5) The establishment Dynasty held the power to nominate the chairmen and CEOs of banks, along with total power over the legal system.

6) The scale of money involved was between US$10 billion and US$100 billion over 60 years, once you understand how it moved through the history of the Chinese dynasties to the last Emperor of the Chin Dynasty. It's estimated that, in the 1950s, Chiang Kai-shek and his wife had four times the value of the Chinese GDP, in cash, in the USA—they were taking money from opium and military aid and other sources.

7) Over-the-counter SWAP was used so there would be no SWIFT payment records. The lawyers involved were from internationally recognized firms—Mayer Brown LLP, Johnson Stokes & Master, Paul Weiss Rifkind Wharton & Garrison LLP, Kelley Drye LLP, Winston & Strawn LLP, Norton Rose Fulbright, and many other famous Texan bankruptcy lawyers.

8) The story created in the Taiwan media about Samson Wu and Super Vision was "fake news" to draw attention away from Mega Bank's money laundering.

9) This scandal was gigantic, involving at least ten branches of Mega Bank, including those in Singapore, Hong Kong, Taipei, Tung Nan, Colon, Panama City, Los Angeles, Chicago, and New York. More than 30 other major Taiwanese bank branches were also suspiciously involved.

The DIP loan on January 8, 2014, with Judge Marvin Isgur was strangely inconceivable. The judge was told by Charles Schreiber (Winston & Strawn), Evan Flaschen (Bracewell & Giuliani), and Charles Kelley (Mayer Brown), all most likely under instruction from Kim Pu-tsung, to allow the securities for the second mortgage to cover the US$20 million DIP loan—the DIP loan was used as working capital to move ships and pay legal fees for lawyers and professionals. This is an assumption, as Pu-tsung graduated from Texas University and he visited Texas many times, including when we filed for Chapter 11 in June 2013. Oddly, on the first document, the DIP lawyer didn't reveal the conflict of interest, of Macquarie also being a lender, to Judge Isgur. The US$20 million loan was typed as plural on these documents, not as a single loan. This meant the 16 ships could be pledged for a total of US$320 million second mortgages with only US$20 million DIP second mortgages. This was weird, only US$20 million was borrowed and secured by Vantage shares—why more? Importantly, I brought this up and argued with my lawyer about the case in terms of mathematical fraud, but my lawyer insisted this was common practice in bankruptcy law. I was sure the judge didn't read it as second mortgages (plural)—he must have read it as a second mortgage (singular) and relied on the honesty of the US lawyers. My theory is that, by the MOF in Taiwan reducing the loans by half, China Investment Fund could add more money on top of the US$20 million finance and make it seem like the sales were profitable. The intended buyers were set up. Oaktree paid money to the designated accounts anywhere in the world, then the US$20 million was separated from the source of funds so that Oaktree owned 100% after sales in February and March 2014.

Let's be clear, Kim Pu-tsung had extraordinary power under President Ma and Christine Chow. He was sent to Washington DC as Taiwan's ambassador at the end of 2012, the same time as the A Ladybug guaranteed loan was sold to Macquarie Bank. Macquarie's Taiwan office is only 30 meters away from the KMT headquarters in Taiwan and there were obviously strong connections between the KMT and Macquarie in Sydney and New York, as well as in Taiwan. Furthermore, the Macquarie DIP loan was organized by Winston & Strawn, signed by Evan Flaschen, the designee at the time, then given super priority in March 2013. Winston & Strawn had a lawyer in Washington DC who was involved in the US$20 million second mortgage signatures—was that lawyer under instructions from Kim Pu-tsung? These questions have to be asked.

The Formosa Television (FTV) program PTT (a blog used by seven million Taiwanese to discuss political and economic policies on a daily basis) started to cover the TMT case from June 28, 2017. Within a week, four million Taiwanese citizens were following the case on social media and this resulted in death threats against FTV and myself. The FTV program was aired from June 28 to 30, 2017. Interesting things began to happen: JPMC fired its Taiwan CEO and ten other bankers at the end of June 2017; FTV received the first death threat from a source close to the KMT, telling them to stop broadcasting the TMT story on June 28, 2017; a second death threat was made against newscasters, their families, and other people involved, including myself. In the threat a male voice stated that "they" controlled the financial and legal establishments in Taiwan, so we couldn't defeat them. The newscasters had to stop reporting and leave Taiwan for their own safety and I had to fly to the USA to protect myself.

Where did the money come from that was deposited in US and other international banks? This very simple question is being asked again today. The Dodd-Frank regulations that were introduced in 2010, after the financial crisis of 2008–2009 (and are now being diluted by Republican politicians) made it necessary to carry out KYC procedures, so the ultimate identity of companies and the origin of the money could be known. The funds arrived in the USA—presumably via Los

Angeles, Chicago, and New York—and were kept in Mega and other Taiwanese banks involved in this scandal.

Evidence of where that money came from must be disclosed.

*21.1: Formosa Television*

As I said, TMT's story was broadcast on Taiwan's FTV in June 2017 and it continued for three days. During the final couple of days, there were two phone calls to the newsreader from her former boyfriend, who told her not to continue with the broadcasts.

'Why not?'

'Because it's dangerous.'

She ignored the warning and continued the following day, when myself and Mr Tobisaka san (a Japanese financial expert) appeared in an FTV interview with the Taiwan FSC. Further anonymous death threats followed, and we were told that everyone concerned with the program was in danger. We left Taiwan over the next few days and all broadcasting stopped.

This confirmed that TMT's case was real—it was true—I had something to say and certain people were afraid of what that was. I felt vindicated. Since then, however, I have not felt safe. I cover my tracks when I move around the world because, as you know, 'accidents can happen'—people commit suicide, even though there's no reason why they should. And, in most cases, it's very hard to prove they weren't accidents or suicides at all.

However, it hasn't stopped me investigating the global financial situation and my third book, which I am now in the process of writing, will be a comprehensive exposé of international financial corruption that will lift the lid off a lot of secrets and open a Pandora's box of corruption, fraud, and money laundering that goes right to the top of governments and the banking elite.

Watch this space!

Late news—FTV news media were shut down by the Taiwan government in 2018. Nobody knows what's happening at the time of writing this book.

*21.2: Assassination*

# CHAPTER 22

## CORRUPTION AND THE FALL OF THE MA-KIM DYNASTY

THE STORY OF the KMT is fascinating. It wasn't allowed to be spoken about for many years in Taiwan. You could go to prison for even mentioning anything bad about the KMT or insinuating they were corrupt—which they were. They were also untouchable. The NYDFS AML investigation and the US$180 million fine opened people's eyes, if they weren't already open. But why did 23 million Taiwanese have to wait until a foreign authority exposed the truth? Because the information they were fed by the media was controlled.

Mr Kim Pu-tsung was the grandson of Puyi, the last Emperor and member of the Manchu Aisin Gioro clan—the twelfth and final ruler of the Qing Dynasty. In his capacity of ambassador, Kim Pu acted as personal secretary to Ma Ying-jeou. Ex-President Ma and Kim Pu are regarded as an inseparable pair in Taiwan politics. They both worked for Chiang Kai-shek's son, Chiang Ching-kuo. They held huge power as close advisors to the uncrowned king for many years and were able to dispose of all their rivals—until 2016. Even their underlings had great power—one individual, Mr Chien, was reputed to be able to make billion-dollar mergers with just a phone call and to intervene in the lending practices of banks with the authority of "god's voice."

Kim Pu-tsung reigned as US Ambassador between 2012 and 2014, which totally matches with A Ladybug and all TMT ships being sold in Chapter 11. He was also involved with

Winston & Strawn LLP in Washington, who handled the DIP loan case in TMT's Chapter 11. Was this a coincidence? I don't think so. My research continues and more will be revealed in future publications.

The relationships between Taiwanese banks and JPMC, ANZ Bank, Barclays, Standard Chartered Bank, and HSBC are long and intimate. So, it was easy to assimilate KMT money into the international banking scene—they had enormous connections in private and corporate banking.

When we look closely at KMT personnel and their financial relationships, it becomes obvious that they would be able to target TMT with the help of their banks in Taiwan and their banking friends overseas. There are a couple of major matters to consider here:

1) The junk CDOs/CDSs that caused the 2008 Western financial crisis were heavily traded in Taiwan in subsequent years (2009–2011). Taiwan became the derivatives center after many Western banks and holding companies set up there.

2) Why Taiwan? Because the MOF allowed it, maintaining that it wasn't against the interests of Taiwan. But why did Taiwan banking laws allow this clean-up of insolvent CDOs/CDSs from the Western crisis-hit financial system? Because of collusion between the KMT and JPMC.

Don't forget, Ma Ying-jeou and Christine Ma's son-in-law, Allen Pei-Jan Tsai was installed within JPMC and in the perfect position to facilitate the collusion. Consequently, the big Western banks owed the KMT a favor and JPMC was able to invest in TMT's 16-vessel loan sales—leading to the spiriting away of KMT money from Taiwan in a SWAP/AML process.

Eventually, this incestuous relationship resulted in the FPCA of Hong Kong's US$264 million son-and-daughter penalty, just two months after the NYDFS AML US$180 million fine in August 2016. Another question to be

# CORRUPTION AND THE FALL OF THE MA-KIM DYNASTY

answered is this—what was the real story behind the sudden announcement on June 28, 2017, of the firing of JPMorgan Chase's (Taiwan) head lady and ten bankers? JPMC didn't disclose the real reason but announced a 'violation of internal compliance.' The head of JPMC Hong Kong had to quickly jump into the vacancy.

*22.1: JPMorgan Chase sign (© Felix Lipov/123RF)*

*South China Morning Post*—November 16, 2016

What's wrong with hiring rich kids?

JPMorgan Chase & Co will pay US$264 million to the US government to settle allegations that it had hired the children and relatives of influential Chinese policymakers or officials in the hope of winning their business, the US Securities & Exchange Commission said in a statement Thursday.

The settlement ends a three-year investigation into whether the hiring practice at the New York-based bank had breached US anti-bribery laws. At issue was whether JPMorgan was systematically targeting to hire the relatives of China's most influential officials, policymakers and business leaders to curry favor with the country's decision makers.

JPMorgan will pay the SEC US$130 million. It is also expected to pay US$72 million to the Justice Department and US$61.9 million to the Federal Reserve Board of Governors, according to the SEC statement.

'JPMorgan engaged in a systematic bribery scheme by hiring children of government officials and other favored referrals who were typically unqualified for the positions on their own merit,' Andrew Ceresney, director of the SEC Enforcement Division said in the statement. 'JPMorgan employees knew the firm was potentially violating the Foreign Corrupt Practices Act (FCPA), yet persisted with the improper hiring program because the business rewards and new deals were deemed too lucrative.'

The regulator said JPMorgan's Asia unit created a hiring program that allowed clients and influential government officials to recommend potential job candidates. Those referred under the program bypassed the firm's normal hiring practices and received 'well-paying, career-building JPMorgan employment,' the SEC said.

About 100 interns and full-time employees were hired over a seven-year period. JPMorgan won or retained business resulting in more than US$100 million in revenues because of the program, the SEC said.

'We're pleased that our cooperation was acknowledged in resolving these investigations,' JPMorgan's spokesman Brian Marchiony said in an emailed statement. 'The conduct was unacceptable. We stopped the hiring program in 2013 and took action against the individuals involved. We have also made improvements to our hiring procedures, and reinforced the high standards of conduct expected of our people.'

JPMorgan hired the friends and family members of executives at three-quarters of the major Chinese companies that it took public in Hong Kong, The Wall

Street Journal reported in December 2015, citing the bank's document compiled as part of the US government investigation.

The program lasted from 2004 to 2013 and was known internally as Sons & Daughters, according to the Journal report.

US investigations into JPMorgan have claimed the jobs of at least two senior bankers. Todd Marin, vice chairman of Asia-Pacific investment banking, and Catherine Leung, vice chairwoman of Asia investment banking, left the bank in February 2015, Dow Jones Newswires reported.

No individual JP Morgan employees were named in the SEC statement, nor did the US authorities announce any criminal charges against either the bank or its employees.

The Chinese officials whose children or relatives are tied to JPMorgan's hiring program read like a Who's Who of China's policymaking and businesses.

Gao Jue, son of commerce minister Gao Hucheng, got a job at the bank. Tang Xiaoning, son of the China Everbright Group's president Tang Shuangning, also worked at the bank, in addition to also having worked at Goldman Sachs and Citigroup.

Some officials also referred relatives or their friends' children to intern at the bank.

Peter Pang, deputy chief executive of the Hong Kong Monetary Authority, referred his son to JPMorgan for an internship in 2006.

Charles Li, current chief executive of the Hong Kong Stock Exchange, referred the daughter of former China Securities Regulatory Commission's official Huang Hongyuan to an internship while he was chairman of the bank's China business from 2003 to 2009.

JPMorgan wasn't the sole bank to be investigated. HSBC, Goldman Sachs & Co., Credit Suisse, Deutsche

Bank and UBS have all been queried about their hiring practices.

'In financial services, if you have relationships and you can use those to get business, that's part and parcel of investment banking, particularly in the current difficult business environment,' said John Mullally, director of Hong Kong & Shenzhen financial services at Robert Walters. 'China is not particularly different from what happens elsewhere in the world.'

Earlier this year, Libya's sovereign wealth fund alleged that Goldman Sachs tried to influence the fund's then-deputy chief into purchasing some derivatives from the bank by granting an internship to his younger brother. However, a London judge ruled in October that the offer did not have a material impact on the Libyan Investment Authority's decision to enter into the trades.

China's Communist Party, which has been cracking down on corruption since President Xi Jinping took the reins of power, doesn't bar cadres' children from seeking jobs in foreign banks.

'These children are not public servants themselves, and can have full freedom when it comes to employment,' said Zhuang Deshui, an anti-corruption expert at Peking University. 'But the officials are required to fill in where their spouses and children work in the reports about their personal information that they hand to the party.'

The "British connection" in Taiwan is through RBS, Macquarie Bank, ANZ Bank, Standard Chartered Bank, HSBC, and Barclays. All are connected to the clean-up of the Western financial crisis of 2007–2009, assisted by the KMT and the Taiwan MOF.

It's a small (financial) world, isn't it?

In the context of such a small world, I would like to reiterate Mega Bank's relationship with Petros Pappas and his Star Bulk Carriers Corporation. As you know, in April 2010 A Duckling had two ships registered in only one company and this is when Pappas and Mega got very friendly with each other. Ultimately, Pappas also stood to benefit from the demise of TMT and he would have been only too happy to assist Mega with their plans to that end.

Then there's the sons and daughters hiring program that I've mentioned previously. Let me elaborate on that here. In November 2016 JPMC had to pay US$264 million in fines to settle civic and criminal charges involving a systematic bribery scheme spanning 2006–2013, in which the bank secured business deals in Hong Kong by agreeing to hire hundreds of friends and relatives of Chinese government officials, resulting in millions of dollars in revenue for the bank. And this practice wasn't confined to Hong Kong—I mean, McKinney Tsai's son worked for Standard Chartered Bank and we've already discussed how Big Mama's son-in-law got to be a big cheese with JPMC. They were called the Kuanxi Kids (Kuanxi or Guanxi in Chinese describes the basic dynamic in personalized networks of influence), it's a central cultural idea in Chinese society. They had better salaries and working conditions because of who they were related to.

It's one thing to tip people in a restaurant in appreciation of their hard work and good service. It's quite another thing to offer bribes, which these jobs were, in return for favors. But history is littered with such instances—Lockheed, Siemens, Kellogg Brown, BAE Systems, Raphael Hui, and Thomas Kwok—Japan, Argentina, Nigeria, Bangladesh, and so on, and on.

It was this prevailing climate of corruption in high places that facilitated the KMT plan, to utilize the top-guns in banking, accounting, law, politics, and the media with impunity and a complete disregard for the law. In the case of the KMT, the law didn't apply to them. They also used a small network of world leaders, as a plan on that scale could not succeed without the secret cooperation of selected leaders.

But now the lid is off the box and the dirty secrets are escaping. This has already led to the political downfall of the

Ma-Kim Dynasty. How long before the legal downfall? How long before this Dynasty is sent to prison for its crimes?

Because that's where it belongs.

22.2: *Bribery and corruption (© Andriy Popov/123RF)*

22.3: *Bank robbery*

# CHAPTER 23

## SHIPBUILDING FRAUD

A SUMMARY OF the news was 'A consortium of Taiwan's largest private shipbuilder Ching Fu Shipbuilding Co Ltd., US defense firm Lockheed Martin Corp and Italian firm Intermarine SpA have won a contract to supply six mine countermeasure vessels for Taiwan's navy.' It was in 2014, at the height of the KMT money-laundering enterprise. To me, there were too many deliberate leaks coming out in a single month, apart from the key data—that never came out. Key data would have been:

- A comment from the Chairman of Ching Fu Shipbuilding.
- Details of the payment and delivery dates for the new ships.
- Refund guarantee of banks and contractors.
- Government guarantee for payment to the shipyard.

My first thought was: 'Why not ask CSBC (China Shipbuilding Corporation)?' After all, they are the largest shipbuilding and industrial machinery group in Taiwan. They have much more capability than Ching Fu. Was there an element of dual private/government control? Normally, the qualification and financing status affect the performance guarantee issued by the Defense Minister—the policy for government guarantee is that the country's naval ships will be built by the country itself.

One answer was leaked by the Chairman of Ching Fu, in a letter written by Mr Chen Ching-nan that urged ex-President Ma to support the 'own ship/own country' policy, which was approved three months before he retired after eight years as president.

There are other anomalies—how can the ships be built in two years, as 80% of the equipment needed to produce them is being prepared in Europe or the USA? It's not yet delivered and may not be even fully secured in the procurement process. Normally, the Navy and Ministry of Defense will have been involved in the details and will have agendas for timing and delivery. This equipment would require first-class guarantees from Taiwan banks and then a government guarantee for the finance. All this supply chain management information needed to be disclosed by Ching Fu Shipbuilding's Chairmen, Mr Chen, but we don't have it.

As well as that, the down payment from the navy, who ordered the ships, is really not enough. And what was actually paid to Ching Fu Shipbuilding by September 17, after three years of the contract? Ching Fu value added is a maximum 20% of the construction. There was an alleged 10% commission in the contract and, yes, this would be to try to make money to support shipbuilding but wouldn't be paid on the signing of the contract. Normally, it would be paid in installments.

Normally, the installments would be 20% x 5:

1) Sign up

2) Order equipment

3) Steel cut/keel laying

4) Commissioning

5) Delivery of ships.

I wondered why only a maximum of 40% was paid to Ching Fu Shipbuilding. What could be the real news behind this fake news? It showed a total of US$600 million loss and each syndication loan lost 40%. Yes, 40% of money paid for 100%

finance. However, most of the money was paid for equipment, so that Ching Fu Shipbuilding hadn't technically lost money, as long as it didn't actually begin full construction. The ships' parts were still only "parts" and not assembled.

Then I was proved right. In August 2017 the fraud was exposed and Ching Fu Shipbuilding, Taiwan's largest private shipyard, was taken over by creditor banks. Chen Ching-nan was found to have used a fake navy ship contract to secure loans of US$498 million from a consortium of Taiwanese banks between 2014 and 2016. According to prosecutors, the shipyard also set up a number of overseas shell companies for money laundering. Several senior officials of the shipyard were arrested and the creditor banks took over the financial management of Ching Fu Shipbuilding in an effort to maintain business operations and avoid bankruptcy at the shipyard.

What has all this to do with TMT and Nobu Sue?

Well, as I said, the fraud took place in 2014 and it's my belief that the fake news was created to camouflage the TMT case and the outflow of money from Taiwan by the KMT to overseas accounts from 2012 to 2015.

The real truth of the matter will come out once questions are answered about: construction contracts; refund guarantees to Italy, France, and other Western military equipment suppliers; procurement contracts; deadlines, delivery dates and payment schedules. There has been no defense spokesman to explain the military orders, just a discussion about government bank losses.

*23.1: Ching Fu Shipbuilding*

# CHAPTER 24
## PANAMA

IN THE FOURTH quarter of 2016, Taiwan lost diplomatic relations with São Tomé and Principe—a small island nation close to the equator, off the coast of West Africa. This became big news in all media and the diplomatic reputation of the Tsai Ing-wen administration was in deep trouble. The ROC had guaranteed to invest more than US$250 million to develop the country—including port and infrastructure development. Equal to almost a year of São Tomé and Principe's GDP.

But Taiwan had spent very little money since São Tomé and Principe's independence in eradicating malaria and providing support for agriculture and fisheries.

Then, suddenly, Taiwan's much bigger diplomatic relations with Panama were cancelled. The Tsai administration admitted that they were only given a few hours notice from Panama. Is it possible that Taiwan spent a lot of money financing the Panama canal so that it was allowed to open 175 accounts for money-laundering purposes? Was it planning something similar for São Tomé and Principe, instead of developing that country's infrastructure?

Chinese and Taiwanese diplomacy is so connected, as are the KMT's relations with China, that it seems highly possible that the Taiwan MOF was heavily influenced by KMT insiders to hide evidence of the Panama scandals—and to avoid direct prosecution if the 175 accounts were found.

The Taiwan Congress agreed to keep those 175 accounts open for ten years, without being disclosed. The National Securities and Confidential Law was passed with agreement between the DPP and the KMT (ruling party and opposition party together). It raises suspicions that the inside story is not being told. The Taiwan government had nothing to say for a few months—it just cleaned up the news and nobody complained. Have you ever had that powerless feeling?

Why am I writing this chapter? Because the Mega Bank scandal began in Panama and ended in Panama. The plan targeted TMT's Panama-registered vessels because the KMT had strong connections with that country. They knew that TMT had had many Panamanian companies in the past—it had registered over 100 ships and had used many Panamanian lawyers. Madam Chow could easily discover all she wanted to know about TMT from those lawyers and from the registry—A Duckling, A Ladybug, and so on.

It all began in 2010. The A Duckling contract was not a shipping contract at all. It was corporate finance and clearly stated—in a special clause called 'source of the funds'—that it could be assigned and the contract novated. A normal ship finance contract would never have a clause to notify the borrower of where the money comes from. Mega Bank planned the use of Ding & Ding as the law firm to front the scam. It was a set up. There was most likely a Mega Colon Free Trade Zone branch to open and close accounts as it wanted.

The power of the KMT is huge. With billions of dollars in funds, it can buy off opposition parties to stop them looking too closely at what happened in the past. After 2016, the DPP and the KMT were in the same boat, which is why information on AML news and fines from the NYDFS and the Federal Reserve in Washington DC were, and still are, suppressed. They hardly registered as news in Taiwan. The entire country tried to keep it quiet. I'm not sure of the real reason, but I suspect it may be because they are afraid Regulation K will be suspended. Only time will tell.

Why?

State control and so many individuals and institutions are involved in corruption.

I need to be a bit subtle here, as there's more than a year's observation period left, of the Taiwan banking system by the USA. What will happen is still unknown and we need to wait and see what the outcome will be. So, let's not speculate too much in this book, we'll have to wait for future revelations—which will come.

For now, let me reiterate some of what I've already written in this book. Plan X was set up at the beginning of 2010, that's when TMT came to the attention of the KMT. Checking the ships from the fleet lists was easy. The plan to move the funds from Taiwan to various destinations throughout the world was most likely conceived with the help of Mayer Brown LLP in Hong Kong and New York.

The granting of Regulation K to American branches of Taiwan banks helped a great deal and this concession was probably influenced by Madam Chow, McKinney Tsai, and others who regularly visited America and had many financial friends there. From the Central Bank to the MOF, the entire escape plan was carefully constructed.

After us, Panama was the key—the KMT and MICB had a lot of power there. The team from Mega Bank utilized two of its branches in Panama (Colon Free Trade Zone and Panama City) and ten Panamanian law firms. The Free Zone in particular gave them lots of freedom to conspire and plot.

The plan started with the first A Duckling loan in April 2010—TMT was targeted from there. It was easy for the small circle of law firms (at that time) to work with a cluster of Wall Street experts who had manipulated the 2008 financial crisis and who knew how to operate the SWAP scam. The key was to make sure that evidence of the whole plan was fragmented and could never be revealed in its entirety by any one entity. That's when the second loan of US$84 million to C Whale from the original two banks (Chinatrust and Mega) was transferred to eight other banks.

The mistake was made in the Panama registry—by registering TMT Panama S.A. as a lender. The C Whale deed of registry in Panama stated that the secondary put TMT Panama S.A. as lender—they never played the role of lender. Why would the borrower put their Panama companies as lender in June 2010?

June 21, 2010—TMT Panama S.A. as Subsequent Creditor.

August 25, 2014—TMT Panama S.A. as Subsequent Lender.

It was clearly designed to camouflage the money laundering under the TMT name. Big mistake. Even so, it took TMT six years to find that document.

The filing for Chapter 11 bankruptcy was a surprise that threatened to foil the plan, but the plotters got their act together and were able to manipulate the court by means of collusion, bribery, and conflict of interest, much of this already outlined by me.

Once it was all done, the culprits disappeared—lawyers, politicians, and bankers—all hiding the parts they played in Plan X and hoping their crimes will never come to light.

But I'm here with my torch, shining it into the dark and dirty corners.

*24.1: Panama*

# CHAPTER 25
## STAR BULK/KMT/MACQUARIE BANK ORCHESTRATION

WE HAVE THE Petros Pappas/Seward & Kissel LLP New York/Ellenoff Grosman & Schole LLP relationship—lawyers who were fired in 2014 by Judge Isgur. Emails from Pappas to Seward & Kissel show how to make an initial public offering and how small shareholders won't make a fuss if their company does unlawful things. It seems clear that Enron's "children" in New York became the center of financial crimes against TMT. These people also advised HHI in a US$3.3 billion TMT order—they used TMT new shipbuilding to advise HHI and HSHI in scams over US$1 billion.

Mega Bank knew of the existence of TMT Panama S.A., so they used Mayer Brown LLP to create TMT Panama S.A. as subordinate creditor, with Ugly Duckling Panama as an English guarantor (we gave shares to Mega).

So, we were naked and vulnerable for Mega to create many corporate accounts in Panama and London. If this is true (and I believe it is) then it explains the whole scam.

Here's the line-up in Panama:

1) Mega Bank Panama (largest in Central America)

2) Mega Bank New York

3) Bank of China in Taipei (representative office in same building as Mega New York)

4) Potential opening and closing of 175 accounts by Mega Bank

vs

1) TMT Panama S.A.

2) Ugly Duckling Corporation Panama

3) A Ladybug Panama

4) A Duckling Panama

5) C Whale Corporation Liberia

6) D Whale Corporation Liberia

There were many connections and orchestrations. It looks like TMT Panama S.A., Ugly Duckling Holding Panama, and Great Elephant Corporation Liberia all played a role, and there were communications with Mega Bank's legal departments/international divisions.

From the very beginning, the A Duckling loan document was suspicious:

1) Allowing of funds clause was very unusual

2) Many clauses about the event of default

3) Many condition precedents

4) Not a normal ship loan, but like a corporate loan

5) Panama registration and ship's particulars not specified in contract

6) Two corporate loans, one TMT and one Ugly Duckling Corporation Panama

7) Mayer Brown subordinate creditor, plus English guarantor—why were both needed?

8) Taiwanese and English law used in one contract

C Whale was the second loan. It was planned and exchanged with TMT in June 2010 when they knew I was away, involved in the Gulf of Mexico oil spill—a very opportune time for them. All legal documents needed to be signed in Taiwan, for jurisdiction purposes. So I couriered my signature, but Mega Bank switched documents with new amendments of the contract on July 8 and 12, 2010, knowing I was on board A Whale and couldn't check them.

It seems Mega Bank had created an English company and a Panamanian company—the Panamanian company lent the money with the English company as guarantor.

It emerged that the loan sold by Mega Bank to JPMC was signed by two bankers in the London office. JPMorgan Chase N.A. was never involved, which indicates that the money never went through New York. The money amounted to billions of dollars and transferring it in this way can be considered money laundering.

Here's the trick of the C Whale second loan:

1) Deed of trust with Mayer Brown was eccentric

2) There were two sets of legal documents

3) Amendments were faked

4) Eight banks were involved

5) TMT Panama S.A. account was paid from retention account

6) Assignment of retention account —why?

On March 13, 2013, a secret meeting between three parties emerged from E Whale transactions. You have to ask, why did Pappas and Mega Bank send a record of that meeting to the auction process in South Africa? Whatever the reason, it means that Pappas and Mega Bank had been orchestrating things for a long time.

I found that the most likely reason for the disappearance of Charles Kelley after August 2016 was the dual deed in the Panamaian and Liberian registries—the Mayer Brown team in Hong Kong was probably involved, and possibly the New York team as well. This inclines me to believe that out of Mayer Brown, Seward & Kissel, Bracewell & Giuliani, Gardena, Winston & Strawn, none had all the information, or all the related documents from the Panama registry. This, of course, was to muddy the waters and prevent discovery of the full plan.

So, we can now see that it all began with the purchase and registration of A Duckling. Investigations into TMT began in Panama, Liberia, and the Marshall Islands, probably carried out by Mega Bank branches in Korea, Panama, and London. There was an exchange of information between Mega's Chan Tin-Hwa and TMT's Green Huang around August 2009. Green was asked to disclose TMT's corporate structure in full, so Plan X could be devised and activated. Then Mega Bank made the offer to finance eight Whale ships on October 15, 2009. It's very likely that, once Mega Bank consulted with Madam Chow, they probably realized they'd have to set up entities in Panama to fit with TMT's structure, which they now knew. Mega had so many overseas branches that it was easy to target the Panama flagship. The interesting part of the plan was to set up an English guarantor, to avoid money flowing through New York, which could be discovered by the NYDFS—but that part of the plan didn't work, the NYDFS still found evidence of money laundering, hence the AML case. The English guarantor involved the London branches of Mega Bank and JPMC—I've already mentioned Chris Craig's role in the plot.

The largest Capesize Panama flag was A Duckling, which was bought for US$42 million from Belgian owners—it had the same name as the other A Duckling sold to Star Bulk in 2007. Mega Bank's law firm was Mayer Brown LLP of Hong Kong and New York and there was a high possibility of collusion with Petros Pappas' lawyer, Seward & Kissel LLP. TMT's Panama Lawyer was Quijano & Associates and there's an interesting record of the Quijano Panama registration. Furthermore, a Marshall Islands Greek law firm was involved in the 85% registration that I've already written about. They must have noticed the strange loan documents, with major lenders as financiers and the few vessels that were syndicated out from day one. This was very abnormal. I need to locate emails between Quijano and other Panamanian lawyers—Aries Law, Morgan & Morgan PA, and Torrijos & Associates—as they were all involved and it will link this book up with my next book.

As far as the Macquarie/KMT relationship is concerned, they were situated only 50 meters away from each other in Taipei. Mega Bank's Sydney branch had long-standing relations with Macquarie Bank—consequently, the relationship between Macquarie Investment Bank and the KMT would naturally be a very deep one. It's quite possible that financial transactions between Macquarie and the KMT had been occurring for a long time. Furthermore, Yan Ming Shipping Line, China Shipbuilding, China Steel Corporation, Taiwan Navigation, and Evergreen Group all had similar banking relationships with Mega Bank. This clearly shows expertise in structural finance which would imply a kind of perverse professionalism when it came to the October 15, 2009, offer from Mega Bank to TMT. The latest findings from the many shipping and corporate lawyers used by Mega Bank indicates that the "experts" in the Taiwan financial marketplace were all eager to join in the scam.

The problem was, as I've said, the aftermath. How to disguise such large amounts of monetary transactions is virtually impossible. They had to go through international banks such as Macquarie Bank, JPMC, Deutsche Bank, Barclays, ANZ Bank, Standard Chartered Bank, and Bank of New York Mellon—all of which have Taiwan branches. It will be interesting to chase the money and see what happens in the future. The latest wind turbine project in offshore Taiwan shows that a new scandal has started. Macquarie Bank has won 50% of the investment in a 20-year contract. However, the deal includes a no-claim, no-default, and free-to-sell exit clause. Basically, people in Taiwan will pay even if no wind blows. The US$600 million loans are from government-related Taiwan banks again, plus an unsecured loan. This is another amazing story—to make the loan possible, the money has to go outside Taiwan, then come back to Taiwan.

The symptoms are back again—will history repeat itself? It usually does when it comes to financial fraud. We'll see how this develops in my third book.

*25.1: Nobu Sue on television*

# CHAPTER 26
## CONCLUSION

THE BASIC NATURE of Plan X seems very simple now. It was robbery. Taiwan government-owned banks and private banks robbed TMT in order to send money overseas without leaving a trace. They targeted TMT—and me. We lost a family business because we weren't 'insiders.' We were outside the 'system.' How could they get away with criminal behavior like that? It had to go through whoever negotiated in New York to obtain Regulation K from the NYDFS. Was it Madam Chow and her former Deutsche Bank and current JPMC banker son-in-law, Allen Tsai? I will let the readers make up their own minds on that question. What is clear is that it was all planned as far back as 2010/2011. Without having an intimate knowledge of the country's incestuous banking practices, the NYDFS inadvertently allowed Taiwan's financial 'values' to be established in the state of New York and the opening up of holding companies that combined commercial banking with investment banking activities.

It was difficult—but it was done.

When banks use a SWAP deal, they use a loan or contract not related to pure commercial lending. It has to involve the sale and purchase of a contract done by the investment sector of the bank. It's like a low interest lending business, not profitable in the low interest yield, but in the buying and selling of troubled assets. The US SEC supervises investment banking activities, while Taiwan's FSC is involved mainly in commercial lending activities. In Taiwan, the first eight months of the Mega Bank money-laundering investigation was put on hold, until the scandal itself was officially announced—because the SWIFT code payments between Taiwan and New York didn't exist. Consequently, the new government, elected in 2016, couldn't find any evidence of money laundering—there was no digital trace. Only a SWAP with more than two parties could repatriate money without a SWIFT code.

TMT alerted Taiwan's FSC to this in September 2016. TMT supplied some of the firsthand evidence it had accumulated to Taipei police in the same Taipei district where Mega Bank's head office was located. However, the FSC didn't respond, and didn't answer calls during the investigation. The Taiwan financial and legal establishment didn't react until FTV began to cover TMT's case and broadcast its findings. The reaction was astonishing and long overdue—they considered that this true story could seriously threaten the international banking community.

The analysis of Chapter 11 court documents proves the process was extremely suspicious and fraudulently structured. It was very obvious that it involved forgery, misrepresentation, and malpractice. The lawyers charged US$500 to US$1,200 per hour, depending on how smart they thought they were, but now they're sitting on a volcano that's threatening to erupt and expose one of the biggest financial scams in history. Some lawyers told the judge they had more than 20 years experience in US bankruptcy law, but had never been involved in this kind of case. Neither had I. But it soon became clear that the complexity of the case was beyond the imagination of even US lawyers specialized in bankruptcy. Over 100 lawyers read the documents in dockets—too many documents, the gist of which most ordinary people would not be able to remotely understand. Too much information is no information at all. Great amounts of taxpayers' money were spent behind the scenes on law firms in Houston, Dallas, New York, and Connecticut by the Taiwan banks, sanctioned by top government officers.

## CONCLUSION

Most covert plans usually involve only a small group of people—they need to keep their cards close to their chests when dealing with both insiders and outsiders. When a large group is involved, the plan has to be broken up so that it's still controlled by only a small group and the rest don't see the full picture, as one hand doesn't know what the other hand is doing. This requires meticulous timing and coordination, from top to bottom. TMT's Chapter 11 case with Mega Bank was just such a complicated and convoluted scheme. A lot of money was involved, and the performance was played out in the Chapter 11 court with all the lawyers playing their individual parts, interacting with each other in a sleazy and grotesque ballet.

It was, and still is, difficult for me to find the truth. I have been fighting for five years and have spent millions of my own money trying to discover the reality of it all. You may say I'm crazy, but I believe it's important to expose how top lawyers can work for their own interests and for money, rather than for the truth and the overall good. It's happening everywhere, not only in the TMT Chapter 11—Wall Street, Lehman Brothers, RBS, and many, many more. The rich have this insatiable lust for money, the more they have, the more they want—at the expense of the people who make the wealth in the first place—the ordinary people who go out to work and create things. All these parasites do is create lucre for themselves.

What if TMT hadn't filed for Chapter 11 bankruptcy? It may have been rescued by other means, but the name of Nobu Sue would have been slandered as criminal throughout the world by the people who wanted to destroy me. But TMT did file for Chapter 11 and this facilitated the collusion between Western and Eastern banks and we are now in a new era of banking scandals, which will go beyond national borders and regulations. There is a solution—I began to realize that I had already filed patents for event-driven software communications with servers. This is decentralized architecture, which originated in Tokyo in 2001–2002. I had to concentrate on the shipping business and didn't give it much more thought for the next 15 years. Now, however, the world is finally seeing the potential of bitcoin and blockchains. Utilizing my inventions, I believe we can create a better and more honest banking and economic system. My investigations have made me an expert on the seamy side of the global banking system—from front-running to AML—and I know we can use the digital revolution to mend what, in my opinion, is terminally broken.

In my next book, I plan to dig deeper, but this case will affect the political and economic landscape of Taiwan and, to a lesser extent, the greater Chinese culture. Five thousand years of Chinese history was based on the system of dynasty and kingdom. This institution was supported by an enormous bureaucratic machine, with legal systems and other institutions built up over the millennia. It's rock-strong and will not change overnight. A new understanding of history and its organic system is what I hope for in this book, *Dynasty Escape*. We are at a turning point—we need to break down the façade of establishment elitism and understand what's good for everybody, not just the privileged few. That's the only way to guarantee a better life for generations to come.

The future is something we must think about now—in the present. As an inventor, I thought about my future back in 2000 and I have more than ten IT-related patents that have come to fruition today. I thought about it back then, and now it has happened as I predicted. The future is in our hands—right now! I hope this book will encourage people to think about that future—it will affect all our children and grandchildren, not just the children and grandchildren of the manipulators, the greedy and the powerful.

In conclusion—there are no definitive conclusions to this book—yet.

It is ongoing.

My next book will make history!

# CONCLUSION

*26.1: Taiwan's flag*

# AFTERWORD

THE STORY OF Mega Bank's scandals may be in US bookstores, but this is the book people in Taiwan and Chinese elsewhere will want to read. However, it only reveals the tip of the iceberg. The true story always comes with great sacrifice. Priscilla Hsing, who was a former deputy president of an international bank, was appointed the new General Counsel of Mega International Bank at the end of 2012. She was involved in TMT's Chapter 11 case and the NYDFS US$180 million AML case directly. Normal compliance needs a balance of checking function. This case is an example of reverse-conflict, where whoever knows the Panama scandal will best become the legal head at Mega Bank—and Madam Chow was the legal head of Mega Bank until 2008.

It was the biggest financial scandal in modern Taiwan history. Many people involved in my case have now placed their lives in danger—the threats are frightening and unprecedented. It's because we pursued justice by exposing violations of international law. We received threats on Twitter and Facebook from government people and over the phone in the form of anonymous calls. The newscaster who covered our case on FTV was offered a bribe not to air her report. When the bribe failed, her family were threatened.

It's important to tell people the true story, not fake news. Readers must ask questions of themselves before choosing their next president. We have one of the most advanced democracies in the world, but that democracy has been shanghaied by a dynasty for so long, its legal and financial

## AFTERWORD

systems are unrecognizable and are not the fair, independent entities they ought to be.

Mayer Brown LLP, Bracewell & Guiliani LLP, Seward & Kissel LLP, Kelley Drye LLP, Paul Weiss, and so on—all these legal firms and individuals represented banks and governments during the Western financial crisis of 2008. They knew how that crisis was utilized to obtain huge amounts of money. Charles Kelley, the chief of Mayer Brown LLP disappeared, knowing all about the scam. Mr Black from Winston & Strawn LLP told a colleague of mine that 'something was funny in the TMT Chapter 11 case.' By writing this book I hope to let people know how the case evolved. My next book, if I'm allowed to live long enough to write it, will cast doubt on all the books written about American history, Chinese history, and European history over the past 100 years. I want to tell the true story, even though my life has been threatened. Any reader can draw his or her conclusion as to what is true and what isn't—but in a court of law there's only one truth, one conclusion—that of the judge. This is irrefutable, whether it's right or wrong—and, in the case of TMT's Chapter 11, it was wrong. The legal system is a strange animal, my direct experience is testimony to that.

You may have noticed that there are a few key phrases that relate to the entire scam, also referred to in my previous book, *The Gold Man from the East*. Here they are again:

Request the borrower to pay his own cash to retention accounts before drawdown of the loan. This means a fund could be set up to receive money from other sources, or the fund could be used as the bank's own money to borrow through the credit creation system. So, the entire loan will not be using the bank's own balance sheet. This is possible because of the high level of the political party involved.

Then don't inform the borrower of the retention accounts' daily and monthly statements, so the borrower believes it's an untouchable cash deposit in the form of a pledge. No interest is earned and no financial statement needs to be given to auditors or borrower, so it can be designed to be used easily as the bank's own money under the borrower's account(s).

This short book explains how those systems were used to benefit the few, at the expense of the many. We must ensure it doesn't happen again!

At the time of the Mega Bank AML case, when Mega Bank was fined US$180 million by the NYDFS and an additional US$28 million by the Washington Fed for money laundering offences, Mega was the primary lender for TMT Group companies. TMT Group, part of which was involved in Chapter 11 bankruptcy, wants to know how Mega's improprieties may have negatively impacted on the company's fortunes. The many strange occurrences in the US Chapter 11 court were a joke, a soap opera, and I will never give up seeking the truth. After analysing the full scale of this scandal, TMT Group consulted Great Trust law firm to file a criminal case against three current and former Mega Commercial International Holdings officials. The scam may have not only involved Mega and other major Taiwanese banks, but also foreign entities. I am disappointed that, to date, Taiwan's financial authorities have not sufficiently investigated this potential wrongdoing in full. I am hoping out having filed this case will change that. As a global businessman and son of Taiwan, I am ashamed of the image that this series of sad events has portrayed of my country that I love so much. The true scale of scandal is still unknown and likely reaches beyond Taiwan's shores. That is why we need a full and thorough investigation.

## STATEMENT FROM NOBU SUE

This book is not only about what happened to TMT, a small shipping company that was set up as Taiwan Maritime Transportation in 1958, it is also a microcosm of the real history of Chinese Asia. The book is based on the facts, as I know them, and is not intended to have any political motive or to favour any particular political party, either in Taiwan or

# AFTERWORD

China. It is purely my neutral perspective, based on my own experiences and my own global investigations, in keeping with my lineage and how I was raised. Many issues are ongoing, which have their roots in British, American and Australian financial imperialism – how Chinese money was transferred to New York, London and many other centres of finance throughout the world. Writing this book has taken me on an amazing journey through many places and also time, from the last Chinese Emperor, to Chiang Kai-Shek and Madam Chiang and their successors and associates, to the Kuomintang Dynasty and how it controlled Taiwan. In doing so, it has opened a Pandora's Box of issues involving modern Chinese history, money, power and a focus on how the story is still evolving. In my opinion, the Taiwanese people had, and still have, a crisis of identity, just as other groups in greater China, Indonesia, Malaysia, Thailand and Vietnam struggle with the leitmotiv of colonisation and heritage. I don't know where the future will lead to, but perhaps when people read this book they will conclude that truth will only triumph over deception when it is sought out. I hope, therefore, that readers of this book will recognise truth from their past and take it with them into their future.

Nobu Sue

*Flags of New Power Party (l.) and Democratic Progressive Party (r.)*

# SUMMARY

I THINK A brief summary of the Retention Account, used for the money laundering, would be useful here.

In this case, it was used to open an 80-year US Trust Account – such as the Wilmington Trust N.A. in Delaware, who offer the largest services for trusts. There is another case in Deutsche Bank Trust America for three VLCC, built in DSME. This loan was organized by Peter Evensen, working with the DBTA banker I met once in the bank's dining room without him disclosing his name. His agenda was to make sure I did not know about the AML scheme to move KMT money to/from DBTA during the KMT money laundering. In this case, the Trust was set up for 125 years, as discovered.

The total first source of funds used to open the Trust was over US$53 million. Therefore, the funds did not have the dirty fingerprints of the Kuomintang. They used my signature to open the trust and used it freely to move the funds wherever and whenever they wanted.

The truth is, the Kuomintang made sure to put a KMT-influenced Chinese banker in DBTA who acted as the DBTA banker to handle the KMT funds.

The Chapter 11 case triggered all these US Trusts, set up by my signature and Retention Account cash paid before the drawdown of the 16 ships loan. These account details were never disclosed and the hijacked accounts' total amount transferred is unknown.

Furthermore, discovery found that the KMT set up a system of US Treasury investment from Taiwan to the USA.

## SUMMARY

The commissions and fees for those purchases were also withdrawn from the TMT Co. Ltd account. It was a simple case of using the TMT name to transfer the money as and when it wanted.

In order for it to be perfect, the KMT set up a pseudo-TMT name in Thailand, called Thai Master Transport Co. Ltd – and similar alias names in Vietnam and other places in order to facilitate money transfers. The TMT GMBH in Germany was also set up by two Russians in 2005 – which was the key account related to the Deutsche Bank money laundering, related to the Estonia branch of Danske Bank. Denmark was allowed to use Danish krone, similar to the British pound in the EU system. It was also discovered that professional accountants such as Deloitte fully backed the AML platform.

Fearing that this retention account, which was used for money-laundering between 2010 and 2012 would be exposed, the bank began to breach the loans at the end of December 2012. They began to arrest ships in order to ensure that the entire fraud would not be discovered by the Borrower. Who could have instructed the banks to do that? Very likely the highest level within the KMT.

Let me rephrase this –

The Borrower filed for Chapter 11 bankruptcy when the 180 days of deposit principal/interest was due to expire. TMT had no choice but to file for Chapter 11 in the US at around 170 days after the Lender breached the loan agreements. This was in order to ensure that the Borrower had never breached the loan, covered by two quarterly payments of principal plus interest. It was filed on 20 June 2013 and proved that it was the Lenders who had breached the entire loan contracts. It is almost unbelievable that they would kill the automatic stay, and any chance of restructuring the company, in order to save the Kuomintang system.

I said "almost".

Once the Chapter 11 case was filed, the sudden transfer of over US$500 billion caused problems. Each time the DOJ and regulators found the illegality. The solution was just to pay the fee and plead guilty – this has been the situation from 2014 until today.

# GLOSSARY 1 – TERMS

MANY OF THE terms (maritime, financial, legal, and otherwise) in this book will not be familiar to the lay reader. I attempted to explain such terminology as best I could in everyday language as I wrote, without interrupting the flow of the overall narrative. I hope this glossary will also be useful in negotiating the technical speak.

**Aframax:** Oil tanker capable of passing through the Panama Canal.

**AML:** Anti-money laundering. In August 2016, the New York Department of Financial Services ordered MICB of Taiwan to pay a $180 million penalty and install an independent monitor for violating New York's AML laws.

**ANZ:** Australia New Zealand Bank

**Arrest:** As in Ship's Arrest. Marine admiralty has this jurisdiction to prevent a ship from moving or trading legally as long as the resolution of a court action is pending. The ship, which has been authorized to be arrested by the pertained commission, is usually taken in charge in colligation with a claim rather than a warrant of arrest for its own sake. The ship is detained by judicial process to secure a maritime claim.

**BCC:** Broadcasting Corporation of China

**BP:** British Petroleum

**BSA:** Bank Secrecy Act

**CDO:** Collateralized Debt Obligation. A promise to pay investors cash from payments of interest and principal on loans. The mortgage or loan is the collateral. A CDO can contain a range of loans (car loans, credit cards, mortgages, etc.).

**CDS:** Credit Default SWAP. A financial contract where the buyer of a debt (mortgage) buys an insurance from the seller in an effort to eliminate possible loss from default.

CDSs are unregulated and anyone can buy them, even if they don't own the underlying loan.

**Central Bank of China:** Central Bank of the Republic of China (Taiwan) as opposed to the People's Bank of China. Located in the same building as Mega Commercial International Bank, New York branch.

**CEO:** Chief Executive Officer

**CFO:** Chief Financial Officer

**Chapter 11:** Chapter 11 is a chapter of Title 11 of the United States Bankruptcy Code, which permits reorganization under the bankruptcy laws of the United States. Chapter 11 bankruptcy is available to every business, whether organized as a corporation, partnership, or sole proprietorship, and to individuals, although it is most prominently used by corporate entities.

**China Investment Fund:** A conglomerate of KMT holding companies, overseen by Mega International Commercial Bank Co. Ltd.

**CMPC:** Central Motion Pictures Corporation

**CTB:** Chiao Tung Bank Co. Ltd.

**Designee:** The debtor designee manages the Chapter 11 bankruptcy proceedings under the debtor lawyer, as the debtor lawyer may not have enough experience of the business to run the operation or the restructuring requirements.

**DIP:** Debtor-in-possession. When a company files for Chapter 11 bankruptcy, the company's management and board of directors remain in possession of the business. For that reason, the company is called the debtor-in-possession.

**DIP Lender:** A Chapter 11 bankruptcy can provide certain options to facilitate financing for the debtor-in-possession. If the debtor company secures a lender to enable the business to continue during the bankruptcy proceedings, that lender is called the DIP lender. Unlike a loan outside bankruptcy, the DIP loan will not be subject to legal challenge. DIP loans are usually made by insiders or a "stalking horse," looking to buy the company's assets. DIP loans are expensive and highly lucrative for the DIP lender.

**Dodd-Frank:** The Dodd-Frank Wall Street Reform and Consumer Protection Act was a massive piece of US financial reform legislation passed by the Obama administration in 2010 in response to the financial crisis of 2008

**DPP:** The Democratic Progressive Party of Taiwan

**Error paper:** claim paper used by Deutsche Bank for 7% loans

**FCPA:** Foreign Corrupt Practices Act

**FFA:** Forward Freight Agreement

**FRB:** Federal Reserve Board

**FSC:** Financial Supervisory Commission

**FTV:** Formosa Television

**GDP:** Gross domestic product

**HHI:** Hyundai Heavy Industries

**HSBC:** Hongkong & Shanghai Banking Corporation

**ICBC:** International Commercial Bank of China or MICB—SWIFT Code ICBCUS33 (New York)—SWIFT Code ICBCTWTO011 (Taipei).

**IMF:** International Monetary Fund

**JPMC:** JPMorgan Chase

**KMT:** The Kuomintang of China (often translated as the Nationalist Party of China) is a major political party in the ROC or Taiwan). The predecessor of the KMT, the Revolutionary Alliance (Tongmenghui), was one of the major advocates of the overthrow of the Qing Dynasty and the establishment of the ROC. The KMT was founded by Song Jiaoren and Sun Yat-sen shortly after the Xinhai Revolution of 1911. Sun was the provisional president, but he later ceded the presidency to Yuan Shikai. Later led by Chiang Kai-shek.

**KYC:** Know your customer is the process of a business identifying and verifying the identity of its clients. The term is also used to refer to the bank and AML regulations which governs these activities. KYC processes are also employed by companies of all sizes for the purpose of ensuring their proposed agents, consultants, or distributors are anti-bribery compliant. Banks, insurers and export creditors are increasingly demanding that customers provide detailed anti-corruption due diligence information.

**Legislative Yuan:** The Legislative Yuan is the unicameral legislature of Republic of China (Taiwan). It is one of the five branches (五院; wǔyuàn) of government stipulated by the Constitution of the Republic of China (Taiwan), which follows Sun Yat-sen's Three Principles of the People. Although sometimes referred to as a

# GLOSSARY I: TERMS

parliament, the Legislative Yuan, under Sun's political theory, is a branch of government.

**LOC:** Letter of credit

**Maritime Lien:** The right of an individual to compel the sale of a ship because he or she has not been paid a debt on account of such a vessel.

**Mediation in Chapter 11:** Meaning settlement mediation, in which the goal is simple: find a settlement to the dispute, using the assistance of a neutral third party. Within bankruptcy, mediation varies by chapter. In Chapter 11, liquidation, partial or complete, of the debtor's assets may be involved, but the emphasis shifts to the preparation and confirmation of a plan that is feasible.

**MICB:** Mega International Commercial Bank

**MOA:** Memorandum of Association

**MOF:** Ministry of Finance

**MOR:** Management of risk

**New Power Party:** The New Power Party (NPP) is a political party in Taiwan formed in early 2015. The party emerged from the Sunflower Student Movement in 2014 and advocates for universal human rights, civil and political liberties, as well as Taiwan independence. The party is a part of the political phenomenon known as the Third Force," in which new political parties, unaligned with traditional Pan-Green or Pan-Blue Coalitions, sought to provide an alternative in Taiwanese politics.[

**NT$:** New Taiwan Dollar

**NYDFS:** The New York State Department of Financial Services is the department of the New York state government responsible for regulating financial services and products, including those subject to the New York insurance, banking and financial services laws

**OFAC:** Office of Foreign Assets Control

**Panamax:** The Panamax tankers operate in the region of Panama, especially the Panama Canal. The tanker size is designed as per the size regulations set by the Panama Canal Authority (ACP). The size aspect is very important when it comes to Panamax tankers because if the size is not monitored while the tanker is being constructed, then it could pose a lot of problems while the ship is in motion. The operation of the first Panamax tanker started in the year 1914 and they are still popular and useful as they were nine decades ago.

**PDCF:** Primary dealer credit facility

**POA:** Power of attorney

**PRC:** People's Republic of China, communist government of mainland China.

**Qing Dynasty:** Also known as the Qing Empire, officially the Great Qing, was the last imperial dynasty of China, established in 1636 and ruling China from 1644 to 1912. It was preceded by the Ming dynasty and succeeded by the ROC. The Qing multicultural empire lasted almost three centuries and formed the territorial base for the modern Chinese state. It was the fourth largest empire in world history.

**RBS:** Royal Bank of Scotland

**Regulation K:** Regulation K is one of the regulations set forth by the . It provides governance on the international banking front, offering guidelines for bank holding companies that engage in international trade and also foreign banks located domestically. It limits the kinds of business and financial practices and transactions that bank holding companies and foreign banks located domestically can participate in.

**Retention Account:** In bankruptcy or liquidation, a party who is facing an illiquid claim may retain in respect of an illiquid sum owed to him by the bankrupt and it is not necessary that the debts should arise out of the same contract.

**RO-RO/PCTC:** Roll-on-roll-off/pure car and truck carrier

**ROC:** The Republic of China, otherwise known as Taiwan—as opposed to the PRC, which refers to the Chinese mainland.

**SBSC:** Shanghai Commercial & Savings Bank

**SEC:** Securities and Exchange Commission

**Shell Company:** A non-trading company, used as a vehicle for various financial maneuvres or kept dormant for future use in some other capacity.

**Star Bulk Carriers:** Company owned by Petros Pappas, Greek shipowner.

**SWAP:** A derivative contract through which two parties exchange financial instruments—most are interest rate swaps and are not traded on exchanges, but are over-the-counter (OTC).

**SWIFT:** A SWIFT code is the standard format Bank Identifier Code (BIC), and is a unique identification code for a particular bank. SWIFT codes are used when transferring money and messages between banks. A SWIFT code consists of 8 or 11 characters. Generally, when 8-digit codes are given, it refers to the primary office.

**Syndication (loan):** Loan syndication is the process of involving several different lenders in providing various portions of a loan. Loan syndication most often occurs in situations where a borrower requires a large sum of capital that may be too much for a single lender to provide or outside the scope of a lender's risk exposure levels. Thus, multiple lenders work together to provide the borrower with the capital needed.

**TMT:** Taiwan Maritime Transportation—Nobu Sue's shipping company.

**UCC:** Unsecured Credit Committee

**UN:** United Nations

**VLCC:** Very large crude carrier.

**Vulture Fund:** A hedge fund, private equity fund or distressed debt fund, that invests in debt considered to be very weak or in default, known as distressed securities. Investors in the fund profit by buying debt at a discounted price on a secondary market and then using numerous methods to gain a larger amount than the purchasing price.

# GLOSSARY 2 – PEOPLE AND PARTICIPANTS

I ALSO APPRECIATE that there are many individuals, banks, law firms, shipping companies, financial organizations and other corporations named in this book. Consequently, I believe this second glossary of participants will be of use to the reader.

**BANKS**
ANZ Bank
Bank of America
Bank of Kaohsuing
Bank of New York Mellon
Bank SinoPac
Barclays Bank
BNP Paribas
Cathay United Bank
CBT Bank
Central Bank of China
Chang Hwa Bank
Chao Tong Bank
China Development Bank
Chinatrust
Citi Bank
Cortland Capital Services
Credit Suisse
Deutsche Bank
Federal Reserve Bank
First Bank
Goldman Sachs
Hua Nan Bank
HSBC
JPMorgan Chase
Macquarie Bank
Mega International Commercial Bank
Royal Bank of Scotland (RBS)
Shanghai Commercial & Savings Bank
Standard Chartered Bank
Ta Chong Bank
Taichung Commercial Bank
Taishin International Bank
Taiwan Cooperative Bank
Taiwan Land Bank
UBS
United Bank (Taiwan)

**LAWYERS**
AlixPartners

## GLOSSARY 2: PEOPLE AND PARTICIPANTS

Aries Law
Bracewell & Giuliani LLP
Ding & Ding
Johnson Stokes & Master
Kelley Drye LLP
Lee & Li LLP
Mayer Brown LLP
Morgan & Morgan PA
Norton Ross Fulbright LLP
Paul Weiss Rifkind Wharton & Garrison LLP
Quijano & Associates
Seward & Kissel LLP
Torrijos & Associates
Winston & Strawn LLP

## PEOPLE

Andy Case
Alan Donnelly
Albert Stein
Allen Pei-Jan Tsai
Bruce Paulson
Chan Tin-Hwa
Carl Chien
Charles Kelley
Chen Shui-bian
Chen Su Min
Chris Craig
Deirdre Brown
Esben Christensen
Evan Flaschen
George Panagopoulos
Hamish Norton
Jason Cohen
Jeffrey Koo
Judge Jones
Judge Marvin Isgur
Ken Leung
Kim Pu-tsung
Lien Chan
Lin Thon Yong
Lisa Donahue
Madam Chow
Ma Ying-jeou
McKinney Tsai
Michael Zolotas
Mister Shi
Paul Weiss
Petros Pappas
Priscilla Hsing
Randy Ray
Samson Wu
Charles Schreiber
Stephen Clark

## FUNDS AND FINANCIAL

China Investment Fund
CITIC
Cortland Capital Market Services
JPMorgan Chase
KGI Group
Monarch Capital
New Lead Holdings
Oaktree Capital Management
Oaktree Huntington (Cayman)
OCM Formosa Strait Holdings
SC Lowy Financial
SC Lowy Primary Investment
Solus Capital
Sovereign Strategy

## COMPANIES
Active Tankers
Hyundai Heavy Industries
Hyundai Mipo Shipyard
Hyundai Samho Industries
Onassis Holdings
ORIX
Ro-Ro Lines
Star Bulk Carriers (SBLK)

## GOVERNMENT
Democratic Progressive Party (DPP)
Dodd-Frank
Kuomintang (KMT)
NYDFS
SEC
FSC Taiwan

# ACKNOWLEDGMENTS

*DYNASTY ESCAPE* WOULD never have been written if I hadn't started investigating the Panama report and the US$180 million AML fine imposed on Mega Bank by the NYDFS. I didn't expect much when I first visited 60 Trinity Street, I thought it was just a small branch office. How surprised I was when I encountered the beautiful 100-year-old architecture near the heart of Wall Street. I was so surprised, I stood in front of the building for 30 minutes. During that time, the door never opened—there were no visitors, no clients. Yet the door was there, the bank was there. Then I noticed the Central Bank of China representative office, with an entrance into the same building. One building with two name plaques—two closed doors. What was this organization? It was Taiwan's Central Bank and had been the clearing house for US dollars and New Taiwan dollars for almost 70 years. I felt like Sherlock Holmes or his sidekick, Dr Watson, peering at a conundrum of financial complexity—as if it was laughing at me, daring me to find its long-hidden secrets.

My research started, and I feel I need to acknowledge the support of many people, directly and indirectly, over the years. I need to acknowledge my father and my grandfather for giving me my sense of responsibility and my determination to follow things through to the end, no matter what the consequences. I need to acknowledge the spirit of Taiwan, which comes from its people, back down through all the years of history. An island at the crossroads of the South China Sea and the North China Sea—unsinkable. Formosa!

I also have to acknowledge Tonic Lin and the team of Taiwan lawyers who helped explain the very complicated legal terms and processes that took me through the phases outlined in this book. Also, my writers and editors who shaped the language and put the myriad of complex research documents into some kind of legible format (I hope).

It's ironic, I know, but the cost and time spent in the Chapter 11 court helped me to write this book. Sitting there, day after day, watching millions of dollars being spent in what felt like a fiction drama. It inspired me in a way, it caused me to consider that it was a story that should be told—a story that might be of interest to others who might find themselves in the same situation at some time in the future. I hope this book makes sense to them and that they can take something from it—anything, even the smallest piece of assistance. If that happens, then it will have been worthwhile.

Barbara Bush died while I was writing this acknowledgment. Texas is the home of the Bush empire—the Bush Dynasty. George even has an airport named after him in Houston. How many times did I go through there, on the way in and on the way out. I lost count. One dynasty of many throughout the world—political dynasties, financial dynasties, royal dynasties, crime dynasties. And the dynasty this book is about. I acknowledge all dynasties past and present and future—and their downfall.

I acknowledge my friends of 35 years, Mr Daniel Olivares and Mrs Irena Olivares. Daniel assisted me in understanding Spanish, especially the system of language used in Panama and Mexico. It helped me so much in researching and finding out what was going on in Panama. Mr Yuzo Tobisaka from Tokyo assisted me in understanding the Japanese point of view. His 38 years of experience in the Mitsubishi Corporation were invaluable. You cannot exclude Japan when you're talking about Taiwan. The insight he gave me was amazing. Thank you so much.

# ACKNOWLEDGMENTS

All of the Chapter 11 records helped me to understand the strategy of that court, the drama, and the orchestration. There were over 30,000 dockets and lawyer Scott Goucher read them all—it took him two months, in the spring of 2018. He told me he'd never seen a Chapter 11 like it in all of his 30 years of bankruptcy law experience.

Finally, I would like to acknowledge my small team in Taiwan who collected information for me. They were steadfast and meticulous. Thank you.

This book could not have been written without a certain amount of courage, perhaps foolhardy, you may say. But it is also written with integrity and an inquiring mind that just wants to get at the truth. These days, the truth is hard to find, it is disguised and distorted by mores and media. However, having now written it, I believe this book is a reflection of the history of modern China. It will be of interest to Chinese people, whether they live in Greater China, or Hong Kong, or Taiwan. They will never have read a book like this before. Why not? Because a book like this has never been allowed to be written before.

The future to come depends on the generations to come. They must understand what happened over the last 100 years, since the fall of the last Chinese emperor and empress. Only by understanding what has gone past will they be able to understand what is to come—and change it.

The Chinese make up 20% of the world's population and this book may explain them in some small way to the rest of the world. They are still living under the dynasty system—but then, so are you!

Nobu Sue
April 2018

# APPENDIX OF EVIDENCE

*Confidential*

Date: Oct. 15, 2009 (V2.1)

## Senior Debt Term Sheet
## Approximately USD (532 to 745) Million Term Loan Facility
## Summary of Terms and Conditions

*This indicative term sheet (the "Term Sheet") has been prepared for the purpose of discussing the financing of seven VLOOs between TMT Group and Mega International Commercial Bank, which does not constitute any obligation of Mega International Commercial Bank to provide the financing accordingly, and is valid till Nov. 12, 2009 and subject to documentation reasonably satisfactory to the parties.*

| | | |
|---|---|---|
| Facility Purpose | : | To finance part of acquisition cost of seven VLOOs(Very large ore oilers) (the "Vessels" or "Vessel"), all 319,000 TDW, for delivery from February 2010 to February 2011 to be built by Hyundai Heavy Industries Co., Ltd.( "HHI") in Korea. The total contract price is USD 1,064.384 million. |
| Sponsors | : | Taiwan Maritime Transportation Co., Ltd., Great Elephant Corporation and their subsidiaries and affiliates (collectively the "Sponsors"). |
| Borrowers / Lessor | : | Tranche I – N Elephant Corporation. 1<br>Tranche II – Q Elephant Corporation. ↨<br>Tranche III – R Elephant Corporation. ʃ<br>Tranche IV – S Elephant Corporation. 4<br>Tranche V – T Elephant Corporation. 5<br>Tranche VI – U Elephant Corporation. 6<br>Tranche VII – V Elephant Corporation. 7<br><br>All Borrowers are special purpose vehicles incorporated in The Republic of Liberia and 100% directly or indirectly owned by the Sponsors or their major shareholders. |
| Lessee / Charters | : | UDH, companies under TMT group. |
| Final Time Charters | : | ( Wisco America Company Limited, Hunan Valin Xiang Tan Iron And Stell Co., Ltd., Corus group, Arcelor-Mittal group, BHP Billiton Marketing AG and Great Elephant Corporation or its affiliates ) .(the "Charters") |
| Facility | : | Secured Term Loan Facility :<br>Up to USD 〔532 to 745 or TBD〕 million in total of seven Tranches and in any event not more than the sum of〔( 50% to 70% )〕 the market value of each Vessel. |

*Ap.1: Senior debt term sheet*

 *Confidential*

the vessel at least until the scheduled maturity of the Facility.

| | |
|---|---|
| Representations and Warranties | : Representations and Warranties given by the Borrowers (subject to customary exceptions, cure periods and materiality thresholds as applicable) reasonable and customary for a facility of this type including with respect to incorporation and authority of the Borrowers, binding agreement, ownership of assets, due authority, litigation, ranking of credit, no material adverse changes, accuracy of information, no default, solvency, tax, and other regulatory compliance, no encumbrances, capacity, material contracts, no indebtedness, government approvals and the like |
| Covenants | : a. Usual covenants in a transaction of this type including material adverse change conditions as per Retention below; <br> b. All shareholders' or inter-company loans in respect of or relating to purchase of each Vessel to be fully subordinated in terms of payment and enforcement; <br> c. The loan outstandings shall not exceed 70% of aggregate amount of market value of the Vessels and other security acceptable to the lenders at any time during life of the Loan. Collateral coverage shall be reviewed annually when majority lenders require. Market value of the Vessels shall be determined in accordance with valuation by an independent broker or valuer acceptable to the Lenders. <br> d. No further mortgage to be granted on the mortgaged Vessels securing the Facility; <br> e. Each Time Charterparty will be kept in effect throughout the life of the Facility; <br> f. No change in control or ownership of the Borrowers without the Lenders' prior approval. |
| Flag | : Each Vessel will be registered in the ownership of each Borrower under the laws and flag of a jurisdiction acceptable to the lenders. |
| Events of Default | : The Loan Agreement will contain the usual events of default including but not limited to; <br><br> a. Failure to pay principal, interest and fees when due. <br> b. Failure to comply with covenants and undertakings. <br> c. Cross-default provisions relating to companies owned by Guarantors, unless the same in the opinion of the Lenders does not affect the ability of the Borrowers to perform their obligations with respect to the Facility. |
| Retention | : The Borrowers shall ensure that monthly payments be made to a designated account with the Agent in an amount equal to 1/3 |

*Ap.2: Mega International Commercial Bank contract*

| SC LOWY FINANCIAL (HK) LIMITED | OCM FORMOSA STRAIT HOLDINGS LTD. |
|---|---|
| By: *[signature]* | By: Oaktree Capital Management, L.P. |
| Name: Soo Cheon Lee | Its: Director |
| Title: Authorized Signatory | By: *[signature]* |
| | Name: GEORGE LEIVA |
| | Title: Authorized Signatory |
| By: *[signature]* | By: *[signature]* |
| Name: Steve Lyons | Name: WILLIAM MELANSON |
| Title: Authorized Signatory | Title: Authorized Signatory |

This Transfer Certificate is executed by the Agent and the Transfer Date is confirmed as 29 July, 2014.

Mega International Commercial Bank Co., Ltd. for itself and on behalf of each other Finance

*Ap.3: Evidence of signatures*

## APPENDIX

---

### NOTICE OF TRANSFER

From : Mega International Commercial Bank Co., Ltd. (as Agent)

To : C Whale Corporation
    Great Elephant Corporation
    Taiwan Maritime Transportation Co., Ltd.
    Hsin Chi Su

Dated : December 23, 2013

**US$84,000,000 Facility Agreement
dated June 21, 2010 (the "Facility Agreement")**

Dear Sirs :

Pursuant to Clause 24 *(Changes to the Parties)* of the Facility Agreement, we hereby inform you that a Lender has transferred all of its participation in the Loan together with related rights and obligations to a new lender (the "New Lender"). A copy of the Transfer Certificate executed by such Lender, the New Lender and the Agent is as attached.

Terms defined in the Facility Agreement shall have the same meaning herein.

Your sincerely,
For and on behalf of
MEGA INTERNATIONAL COMMERCIAL BANK CO., LTD.
(as Agent)

Name: Priscilla Hsing
Title: VP & DGM

---

*Ap. 4: Deed of Transfer—C Whale*

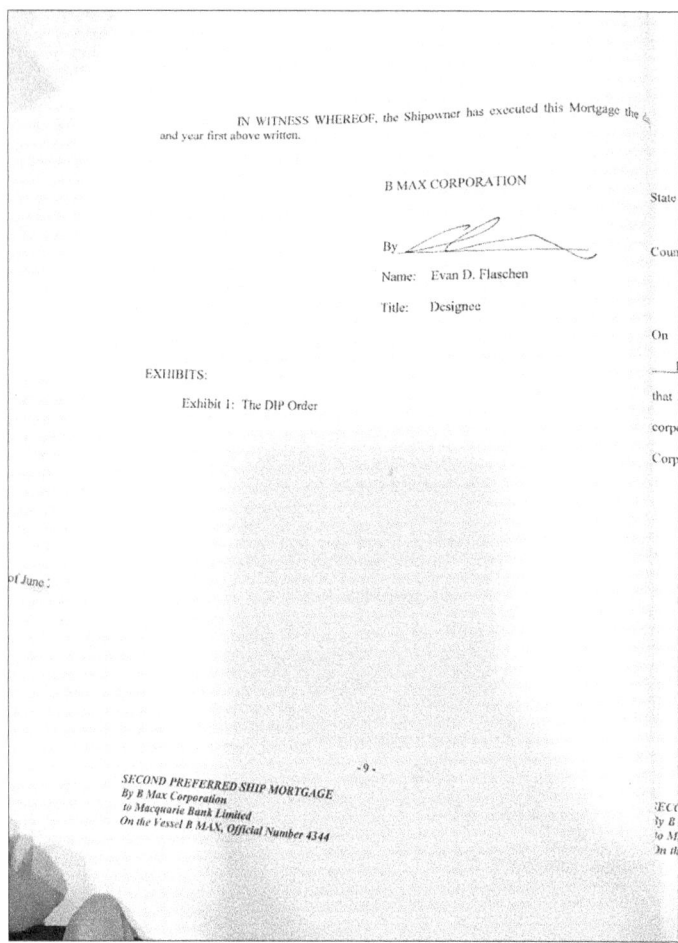

*Ap.5: B Max Exhibit—DIP Order*

PROVIDED ONLY, and the condition of these presents is such that if the Shipowner, its successors or assigns, or any other party liable therefor, shall pay or cause to be paid the Indebtedness Hereby Secured as and when the same shall become due and payable in accordance with the terms of the DIP Order, and shall perform, observe and comply with the covenants, terms and conditions in the DIP Order and in this Mortgage contained, expressed or implied, to be performed, observed or complied with by and on the part of the Shipowner, then these presents and the rights hereunder shall cease, determine and be void; otherwise to be and remain in full force and effect.

IT IS HEREBY COVENANTED, DECLARED AND AGREED that the Vessel is to be held subject to the further covenants, conditions, provisions, terms and uses hereinafter set forth:

## ARTICLE 1
## COVENANTS OF THE SHIPOWNER

The Shipowner represents to, and covenants and agrees with, the Mortgagee as follows:

**Section 1.1** **Performance of Obligations.** The Shipowner will fulfill its obligations under the DIP Order and such other orders of the Bankruptcy Court as are relevant to this Mortgage.

**Section 1.2** **Vessel Documentation.** The Shipowner was duly organized and is now validly existing as a Marshall Islands corporation. The Vessel is duly and validly registered in the name of the Shipowner under the laws and flag of the Republic of the Marshall Islands and shall so remain during the life of this Mortgage.

**Section 1.3** **Valid Mortgage.** The Shipowner has duly authorized the making, execution, and recordation of this Mortgage as a preferred ship mortgage under the laws of the Republic of the Marshall Islands.

**Section 1.4** **Due Recordation.** The Shipowner will cause and/or permit this Mortgage to be duly recorded in accordance with the provisions of the Marshall Islands Maritime Act, and will otherwise comply with and satisfy all of the provisions of the Marshall Islands Maritime Act to establish and maintain this Mortgage as a second preferred mortgage lien upon the Vessel and upon all renewals, replacements and improvements made in or to the same.

**Section 1.5** **Arrest of Vessel.** If a lien, libel or complaint is filed against the Vessel, or if the Vessel is attached or arrested, the Shipowner will promptly notify the Mortgagee in writing of such event.

- 4 -

SECOND PREFERRED SHIP MORTGAGE
By B Max Corporation
to Macquarie Bank Limited
On the Vessel B MAX, Official Number 4344

*Ap.6: B Max Exhibit—Article 1*

**Section 1.6  Access to Vessel.** The Shipowner, during normal business hours upon reasonable notice and at reasonable intervals, will afford the Mortgagee or its authorized representatives full and complete access to the Vessel, where located, for the purpose of inspecting the same and its cargoes and papers and, at the written request of the Mortgagee, will deliver for inspection copies of any and all vessel documentation for the Vessel.

**Section 1.7  Location of Vessel.** The Vessel shall not be abandoned in any port or place except as may be permitted in writing by the Mortgagee.

**Section 1.8  Notice of Mortgage.** The Shipowner will carry or cause to be carried on board the Vessel with its documents a properly certified copy of this Mortgage and will cause such certified copy and the documents of the Vessel to be exhibited to any and all persons having business with the Vessel which might give rise to a maritime lien thereon, other than liens for current crew's wages, salvage and for insurance premiums not in arrears, and to any representative of the Mortgagee; and will place and keep prominently displayed in the chart room and in the Master's cabin of the Vessel a framed and printed notice in plain type of such a size that the paragraph of the reading matter shall cover a space not less than six (6) inches wide by nine (9) inches high, and reading as follows:

> NOTICE OF SECOND PREFERRED SHIP MORTGAGE
>
> This Vessel is subject to a Second Preferred Mortgage in favor of Macquarie Bank Limited as Mortgagee, under authority of Chapter 3 of the Maritime Act 1990 of the Republic of the Marshall Islands. Under the terms of such Second Preferred Mortgage, neither the Shipowner, any charterer, the Master of this Vessel nor any other person shall have the right, power or authority to create, incur or permit to be placed or imposed upon this Vessel any lien whatsoever other than the lien of said Second Preferred Mortgage, a pre-existing First Preferred Ship Mortgage, and liens for crew's wages (including wages of the Master), liens for wages of stevedores employed directly by the Shipowner or the operator, Master, ship's husband or agent of this Vessel, general average and salvage (including contract salvage)."

## ARTICLE 2
## EVENTS OF DEFAULT AND REMEDIES

**Section 2.1  Event of Default.** Each of the following events are herein termed an *"Event of Default"*:

(a) Any representation or warranty by the Shipowner made or deemed made in this Mortgage shall prove to have been incorrect or misleading in any material respect when made; or

- 5 -

SECOND PREFERRED SHIP MORTGAGE
By B Max Corporation
to Macquarie Bank Limited
On the Vessel B MAX, Official Number 4344

*Ap.7: B Max Exhibit—Article 2*

(b) Any default under the DIP Order or the DIP Facility shall have occurred and be continuing unless such default is waived in writing by the Mortgagee;

(c) Any Termination of the DIP Facility; or

(d) Any arrest of the Vessel.

**Section 2.2  Consequences of Default.** If any Event of Default as specified herein shall have occurred and be continuing, then and in each and every such case the Mortgagee shall have the right to:

(a) Exercise all of the rights and remedies in foreclosure and otherwise given to mortgagees by the Marshall Islands Maritime Act;

(b) Exercise any other rights granted pursuant to the DIP Order or otherwise granted by the Bankruptcy Court; and

(c) Act as attorney-in-fact of the Shipowner with irrevocable power to take such action as may be permitted and reasonably necessary with regard to the exercise of the foregoing rights of the Mortgagee.

**Section 2.3  Possession of Vessel.** So long as no Event of Default has occurred and is continuing, the Shipowner shall be suffered and permitted to retain actual possession and use of the Vessel.

## ARTICLE 3
## SUNDRY PROVISIONS

**Section 3.1  Amount of Mortgage.** For purposes of filing and recording this Mortgage as required by the provisions of the Marshall Islands Maritime Act, the total amount of this Mortgage is twenty million two hundred thousand Dollars, United States currency (US$20,200,000).

**Section 3.2  Successors and Assigns.** All of the covenants, promises, stipulations and agreements of the Shipowner in this Mortgage contained shall bind the Shipowner and its successors and assigns and shall inure to the benefit of the Mortgagee and its successors and assigns and all persons claiming by, through or under it. The Shipowner recognizes that the Mortgagee may, consistent with applicable law, assign or otherwise transfer its rights under this Mortgage.

- 6 -

*SECOND PREFERRED SHIP MORTGAGE*
*By B Max Corporation*
*to Macquarie Bank Limited*
*On the Vessel B MAX, Official Number 4344*

*Ap.8: B Max Exhibit—Article 3*

## ACKNOWLEDGMENT

State of Connecticut )
) ss: Hartford
County of Hartford )

On the 14th day of March, 2014, before me personally came Evan D. Flaschen, to me known, who being by me duly sworn, did depose and say that he is a Designee of B Max Corporation, a Republic of the Marshall Islands corporation; that he executed the foregoing Second Preferred Mortgage in the name of B Max Corporation; and that he signed his name thereto by authority of his position with said company.

*Elizabeth L. Tyler*

Elizabeth L. Tyler
Notary Public-Connecticut
My Commission Expires
August 31, 2018

- 10 -

*SECOND PREFERRED SHIP MORTGAGE*
*By B Max Corporation*
*to Macquarie Bank Limited*
*On the Vessel B MAX, Official Number 4344*

*Ap.9: B Max Exhibit—Acknowledgment*

# APPENDIX

**SECOND PREFERRED SHIP MORTGAGE**

*Given By*

**C HANDY CORPORATION**
*Shipowner*

To

**MACQUARIE BANK LIMITED**
*Mortgagee*

WITNESSETH; THIS SECOND PREFERRED SHIP MORTGAGE, dated as of this 20th day of June, 2013 (this "*Mortgage*"), by C Handy Corporation, a Marshall Islands corporation (the "*Shipowner*"), with an office in care of TMT Co Ltd., 16th Floor, 200, Keelung Road, Section 1, Xinyi District, Taipei City, China, Republic of (Taiwan), to Macquarie Bank Limited (the "*Mortgagee*"), a bank and financial institution duly incorporated under the laws of Australia, having its registered office at 1 Martin Place, Sydney NSW 2000, Australia.

**WHEREAS:**

1. The Shipowner is the sole owner of the whole of the vessel named C HANDY (hereinafter called the "*Vessel*"), Official Number 4231, which Vessel is documented in the name of the Shipowner under the laws of the Republic of the Marshall Islands, of 22,683 gross tons or thereabouts; which Vessel is subject to that certain First Preferred Ship Mortgage dated September 16, 2011, granted by the Shipowner to The Shanghai Commercial & Savings Bank, Ltd. in the total amount of US$18,500,000, recorded on September 16, 2011 at 10:16 a.m. K.S.T. at Seoul, Korea (September 15, 2011 at 09:16 p.m. E.D.S.T. in the Central Office of the Maritime Administrator) in Book PM 22 at Page 395; as amended by that certain First Amendment to the First Preferred Mortgage dated May 11, 2012, recorded on May 17, 2012 at 11:51 a.m. H.K.T. (May 16, 2012 at 11:51 p.m. E.D.S.T. in the Central Office of the Maritime Administrator) in Book PM 23 at Page 470, as assigned by that certain Assignment of First Preferred Ship Mortgage dated December 9, 2013 to Deutsche Bank AG, London Branch except for the amount of U.S. $1.00, recorded on December 11, 2013 at 05:59 p.m. H.K.T. at Hong Kong (December 11, 2013 at 04:49 a.m. E.S.T. in the Central Office of the Maritime Administrator) in Book PM 24 at Page 1273; and as further assigned by that certain Assignment No. 2 of First Preferred Mortgage dated Dec. 12, 2013 to CVI CVF II Lux Master Sarl and its successors 85.65% of the right, title and interest of Deutsche Bank AG, London Branch, recorded on December 19, 2013 at 05:05 p.m. H.K.T. at Hong Kong (December 19, 2013 at 04:05 a.m. E.S.T. in the Central Office of the Maritime Administrator) in Book PM 24 at Page 1255.

*Ap.10: CarVal own only 85% of C Handy*

From: Russell Gardner <Russell.Gardner@hilldickinson.com>
Date: Wed, 25 Jun 2014 08:57:17 +0000
To: tony@gamingventures.co<tony@gamingventures.co>; nobu@blueskyfing.com<nobu@blueskyfing.com>
Cc: Albert Luoh<albert.luoh@tmtship.com>; Rebecca Maddison<Rebecca.Maddison@hilldickinson.com>; Edwin Cheyney<Edwin.Cheyney@hilldickinson.com>
Subject: Lakatamia v Nobu Su et al [HD-UK].IVE FID452107]

I refer to your emails last evening and, for ease of communication, I would be grateful if you could correspond with me – as partner in charge – henceforth with Rebecca copied in. I have the following comments:

1.

<br>

**Vidal Martinez collusion?**

2. ████████████████ but I am afraid that we are not going to respond to threats. The allegations of 'conspiracy' against Lakatamia in the Texas proceedings are in any event completely groundless. All that has happened is that we intervened in those proceedings to ensure that the court (and Vantage Drilling) were aware of the freezing orders which we had obtained so that our client's position was, so far as possible, protected. ████████████████ I suggest that you devote your efforts to achieving that instead of making unwarranted threats.

3. Tony's status is noted but it is inappropriate for us to communicate on substantive matters concerning the litigation with a solicitor who is not prepared to be on the Court record – and the Court would not expect us to. There is accordingly every basis for our position but, speaking wp, we would be interested to know what help it is anticipated Tony can give, in particular in relation to the matters set out in Rebecca's email dated 23rd June. If, as appears, our application to amend is going to be opposed, we will endeavour to arrange a convenient date in July but that cannot be guaranteed. That depends on our Counsel's and the Court's availability.

*Ap.11: Vidal Martinez/Vantage Exhibit*

EXHIBIT "D"
in the united states bankruptcy court
for the SOUTHERN district of TEXAS
HOUSTON division

| In Re: | § | Chapter 11 |
|---|---|---|
| TMT PROCUREMENT CORPORATION, | § | Case No. 13-33763 |
| et al., | § | |
| Debtors. | § | Jointly Administered |

TO ALL CREDITORS AND INTERESTED PARTIES:

Mr. Su encourages all creditors to vote in favor of the Plan. In addition, to the Debtors' Disclosure Statement, Mr. Su encourages creditors and interested parties to review the pleadings and other disclosure statements that have been filed in the case – all of which are available at http://dm.epiq11.com/#/case/TMT/info, as well as review the pleadings and briefs in the related cases pending before the United States District Court for the Southern District of Texas.

Mr. Su believes that this Chapter 11 was unique. Most Chapter 11 ships were not allowed to generate revenue so MOR became simple expenditure. The jointly administered Debtors had assets with a combined assets exceeding $1.2 billion, including some of the newer, most valuable and innovative vessels in the world. Mr. Su contends those vessels sold for a fraction of their value less than outstanding secured debts. In many instances, the sales were to the lenders and/or their affiliates by credit bid over the objection of Mr. Su.

Since the filing of the Bankruptcy, Mr. Su continues to learn more and more about the issues which may have been related and/or contributed to the Debtors' perceived need to file Bankruptcy and/or which may have impacted the success of the Bankruptcy. In particular, recent news reports regarding investigations of some of the Debtors' lenders have raised significant concern.

According to one Consent Order entered into by Mega International Commercial Bank ("Mega Bank") with NYDFS where Mega Bank was subject to a huge fine, NYDFS' investigation of Mega International Commercial Bank occurred between 2012 and later. The Debtors issues with lenders spanned the same timeframe.

Given the recent news, Mr. Su has a heightened concern regarding meetings certain Taiwanese lenders reportedly had in the period before the Bankruptcy was filed, as well as meetings he had with such lenders. For example, in or around April 2013, Mega Bank requested that the Debtors pay $20 million and, if paid, Mega Bank reportedly would work to restructure the TMT related companies.

By further example, Mr. Su is concerned regarding a loan between Mega Bank and TMT Procurement which was an unsecured loan. After the NYDFS was already apparently auditing Mega Bank, Mega Bank demanded a security interest in the Panamanian flag M/V A Ladybug which was owned by A Ladybug Corporation in Panama, a different debtor, less than a year prior to the Bankruptcy filing. Mr. Su is concerned that this loan, improper demand for security and the actions of Mega Bank could be related to criminal cases filed in Taiwan regarding McKinney Tsai and Mega Bank.

News reports represent that McKinney Tsai was indicted on charges of breach of trust, forgery, insider trading and other crimes.[1] These reports further triggered Mr. Su's concerns because he had analyzed the lenders' signatures on loan documents and proof of claims and found significant discrepancies. Su

---

1 See, http://www.taipeitimes.com/News/front/archives/2016/12/03/2003660471 and http://focustaiwan.tw/news/aeco/201704200019.aspx

Parties have also requested lenders voluntarily provide certified copies of loan documents attesting to the authenticity to no avail.

Mr. Su encourages the Plan Administrators to review and investigate issues related to the Debtors and all lenders, but especially with respect to Mega International Commercial Bank, First Commercial Bank, Chinatrust Commercial Bank Co., Ltd. a/k/a CTBC Bank, Shanghai Commercial & Savings Bank, Ltd., Cathay United Bank, Ltd., and Bank Sinopac, including but not limited to the sale of the debt by such lenders to SC Lowry, JP Morgan Chase Bank N.A., Macquarie Bank, Deutche Bank, Barclays Bank and Cortland Capital Services to the extent such debt was transferred to these parties as intermediaries for other lenders such as OCM Formosa Straight Holdings, Pacific Orca and Oaktree Capital or others as such transfers may have been contrary to Taiwanese financial public information and regulations.

In summary, Mr. Su is concerned that the Debtors' accounts and/or assets related to the loan facilities were improperly handled, including but not limited to: accounting irregularities; improper calculations; potentially improper use of intermediary Lenders when selling debt owed by the Debtors; ship flag mortgage registries: signatures on loan related documents and proof of claims which appear to be inconsistent; potentially improper default notices under English and/or Taiwanese law; etc. Further, on information and belief, entities with names similar to the Debtors or the Debtors' vessels were incorporated in foreign jurisdictions which Mr. Su believes appears odd and may be related to the Debtors' accounts or assets.

Mr. Su believed that authorizing the filing of Chapter 11 would provide an opportunity for the Debtors to restructure the business and continue operating.

In the end, the ships were sold. Mr. Su opposed the sale of the vessels because he believed they had substantial value and a life of at least 25 years which in a long-term plan could have provided value to creditors. For evidences, 16 vessels had earned over USD300mill EBITDA after ship sold until today. Others disagreed with him and the ships were sold. Contrarily, all banks started to auction Mr. Su personal assets and TMT Co, Ltd. assets without having proper audited deficiencies.

While Mr. Su is agreeing to release the Debtors as part of the settlement reached at mediation with the Debtors and UCC, such settlement in no way waives, prejudices or has any precedential effect on Mr. Su's patent claims against other parties. Mr. Su is preserving any and all rights, claims, interests and defenses he has related to all patent claims he may have against the vessels formerly owned by the Debtors, current owners, Debtors' lenders and/or other third parties. Mr. Su currently owns 3 granted patents related to estates ships as two of them were patent pending in 2014.

APPROVED BY:

_____     _____

HSIN CHI SU        DATE

*Ap.12: Exhibit "D"*

*Ap.13: A Duckling exhibit*

# APPENDIX

|   |                    | Anping Land   | Hualilen house | Dunhua house |
|---|--------------------|---------------|----------------|--------------|
|   |                    |               |                | Dollar: USD  |
| 1 | TaiChung Bank      | $20,583,261   |                |              |
| 2 | Bank of America    | 8,836,538     |                | $1,174,904   |
| 3 | MRMBS II LLC       |               |                | 331,818      |
| 4 | Wilmington Trust   |               | $187,945       | 2,045,098    |
| 5 | Shanghai Bank      |               | 1,853          | 625,720      |
| 6 | Cathay Bank        |               |                | 1,575,391    |
| 7 | Operation expense  | 4,643,164     | 35,869         | 117,440      |
|   | **Auction Total**  | $34,062,963   | $225,667       | $5,870,370   |

| No. | Subject | Date | Amounts of Transaction in USD | Counterparty | Loss or profit of transaction in USD |
|-----|---------|------|-------------------------------|--------------|---------------------------------------|
| 1 | Bad debts and accounts receivable | December 13, 2013 | 10,825,000 | SC Lowy Primary Investments, Ltd. | Loss approximately 6,654,012 |
| 2 | Bad debts | December 18, 2013 | 36,400,000 | Macquarie Bank Limited | Loss approximately 4,030,000 |

● 通匯銀行

| 別別 | 通匯銀行 | SWIFT CODE |
|------|---------|------------|
| 日幣 (JPY) | Bank of Japan, H.O., Tokyo (日本銀行)<br>The Bank of Tokyo-Mitsubishi UFJ, Ltd. Shinn-marunouchi Br. (三菱東京UFJ銀行新丸之內支店) | BOJPJPJT<br>BOTKJPJT |
| 美金 (USD) | Mega ICBC, New York (兆豐國際商業銀行紐約分行)<br>Mega ICBC, HOTRD (兆豐國際商業銀行財務部) | ICBCUS33<br>ICBCTWTP011 |
| 歐元 (EUR) | Mega ICBC, Amsterdam (兆豐國際商業銀行阿姆斯特丹分行) | ICBCNL2A |
| 人民幣 (CNY) | Mega ICBC, HongKong (兆豐國際商業銀行香港分行) | ICBCHKHH |

東京分行服務專線

○ 〒100-0005
東京都千代田丸之內2-2-1岸本大樓7樓
總機：03-3211-6688
傳真：03-3216-5686
SWIFT CODE：ICBCJPJT
E-mail：tokyo@megabank.com.tw

○ 存款：03-3211-1227
　放款：03-3211-2587
　外匯：03-3211-1240

どうぞ、お気軽に下記までご相談ください。

○ 〒100-0005
東京都千代田区丸の内2-2-1　岸本ビル7F
TEL：03-3211-6688（代）
FAX：03-3216-5686
SWIFT CODE：ICBCJPJT
E-mail：tokyo@megabank.com.tw

○ 預金：03-3211-1227
　貸付：03-3211-2587
　外為：03-3211-1240

○ 自2012年10月1日開始由台灣地區直接撥打東京分行免付費電話號碼：02-2181-1261

*Ap.14: Further evidence*

Dated 19 July 2012

"Certified true, accurate and complete copy of the original"

A LADYBUG CORPORATION
(as Owner)

to

MEGA INTERNATIONAL COMMERCIAL BANK CO., LTD
(as Mortgagee)

---

FIRST PREFERRED PANAMANIAN SHIP MORTGAGE

of

m.v. "A LADYBUG"

---

# MAYER·BROWN
JSM

HONG KONG

*Ap.15: A Ladybug exhibit*

# APPENDIX

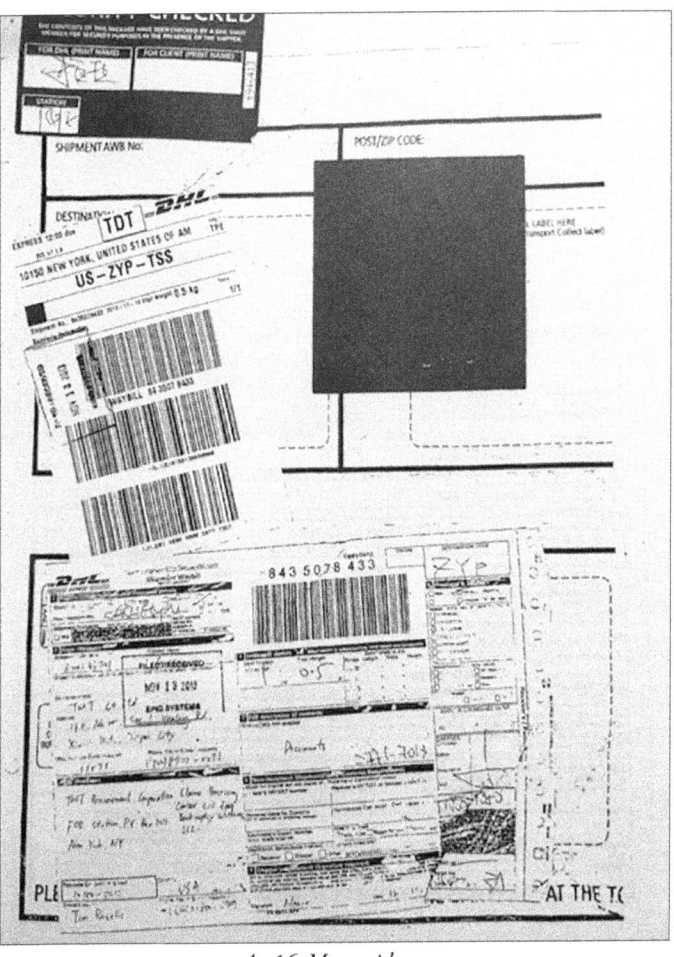

*Ap.16: More evidence*

# DYNASTY ESCAPE

| Claim no. | Creditor Name | Filed Date | Total Claim Value | Remark (Included continuing interest, costs, fees, expenses and carrying fees) |
|---|---|---|---|---|
| 371 | Hyundai Heavy Industries Co., Ltd | 13/11/2013 | US$6,939,047.00 | against A Whale Corporation / MV A Whale<br>*Unpaid interest from the period Jan 8, 2010 to Mar 1, 2010, amount to $ 6,023,333<br>*Additional insterest from period Mar 1, 2013 to Jun 20, 2013 amounts to $915,714 |
| 378 | Hyundai Heavy Industries Co., Ltd | 13/11/2013 | US$50,009,387.00 | against B Whale Corporation / MV B Whale<br>* as of the petition date, $ 29,785,358 principal of deferred amount + $ 6,448,928 in accrued interest<br>*as of the petition date, $ 11,300,200 in principal of the Deferred CI amount + $ 2,474,901 in accrued interest |
| 379 | Hyundai Heavy Industries Co., Ltd | 13/11/2013 | US$0.00 | against C Whale Corporation / MV C Whale |
| 380 | Hyundai Heavy Industries Co., Ltd | 13/11/2013 | US$5,955,545.00 | against D Whale Corporation/ MV D Whale<br>* as of the petition date, $5,049,330 in principal of the Deferred CI Amount + $ 906,215 in accrued interest |
| 381 | Hyundai Heavy Industries Co., Ltd | 13/11/2013 | US$5,893,761.00 | against E Whale Corporation/ MV E Whale<br>* as of the petition date, $5,019,230 in principal of the Deferred CI Amount + $874,531 in accured interest |
| 382 | Hyundai Heavy Industries Co., Ltd | 13/11/2013 | US$5,809,033.00 | against G whale Corporation / MV G Whale<br>*as of the petition date, $5,117,840 in principal of the Deferred CI amount + $691,193 in accured interest |
| 383 | Hyundai Heavy Industries Co., Ltd | 13/11/2013 | US$7,330,523.00 | against H Whale Corporation / MV H Whale<br>*as of the petition date, $6,476,840 in principal of the Deferred CI Amount + $853,683 in accured interest |
| 377 | Hyundai Mipo Dockyard Co., Ltd | 13/11/2013 | US$1,080,000.00 | against C Handy Corporation / MV C Handy<br>* as of the petition date, the deferred amount of $1,000,000 and $80,000 in accured interest |
| 372 | Hyundai Sambo Heavy Industries Co., Ltd | 13/11/2013 | US$8,754,439.00 | against F Elephant Inc / MV Forturn Elephant<br>*as of the petition date, the deferred CI amount of $ 7,541,242 in principal + $1,213,197 in accured interest |
| 373 | Hyundai Sambo Heavy Industries Co., Ltd | 13/11/2013 | US$57,437,266.00 | against A Ladybug Corporation/ MV A Ladybug<br>* as of the petition date, the defered amount of $40,000,000 in principal + $8,398,334 in accured interest<br>* as of the petition date, $7,807,420 in principal of the defered CI amount + $ 1,240,512 in accured interest |
| 374 | Hyundai Sambo Heavy Industries Co., Ltd | 13/11/2013 | US$14,254,958.00 | against C Ladybug Corporation/ MV C Ladybug<br>* as of the petition date, the deferred amount of $5,000,000 in principal + $ 635,556 in accured interest<br>* as of the petition date, $7,647,340 in principal of the deferred CI amount + $972,062 in accured interest |
| 375 | Hyundai Sambo Heavy Industries Co., Ltd | 13/11/2013 | US$13,996,808.00 | against D Ladybug Corporation/ MV D Ladybug<br>* as of the petition date, the deferred amount of $5,000,000 in principal + $ 467,639 in accured interest<br>* as of the petition date, $7,645,550 in principal of the deferred CI amount + $715,071 in accured interest<br>* as of the petition date, the delivery amount of$98,958 in principal + $29,858 in accured interest |
| 376 | Hyundai Sambo Heavy Industries Co., Ltd | 13/11/2013 | US$9,893,692.00 | against B Max Corporation/ MV B Max<br>* as of the petition date, the deferred amount of $9,023,661 in principal + $ 870,031 in accured interest |
|  |  |  | US$187,314,454.00 |  |

*Ap.17: Hyundai filed a Proof of Claim in Chapter 11*

# LOAN AGREEMENT

by and between

C Handy Corporation

as Borrower

and

The Shanghai Commercial & Savings Bank, Ltd.

as Lender

GUARANTEED by

Taiwan Maritime Transportation Co., Ltd.

and

Mr. Hsin Chi Su (蘇信吉)

Ding & Ding Law Offices
10<sup>th</sup> Fl., No. 563,
Chung Hsiao E. Rd., Sec. 4,
Taipei, Taiwan, R. O. C.

Tel: 886-2-2762-5659
Fax: 886-2-2761-7682
E-mail: ddinglaw@ms12.hinet.net

*Ap.18: Loan agreement between C Handy Corporation and Shanghai Bank, guaranteed by TMT*

FIRST PREFERRED MARSHALL ISLANDS SHIP MORTGAGE

of

m.v. "C Handy"

by

C Handy Corporation

As Owner and Mortgagor

to

The Shanghai Commercial & Savings Bank, Ltd.

As Mortgagee

To Secure

A US$18,500,000 Term Loan Facility

Under

A Loan Agreement

Ding & Ding Law Offices
10th Fl., No. 563,
Chung Hsiao E. Rd., Sec. 4,
Taipei, Taiwan, R. O. C.

Tel: 886-2-2762-5659
Fax: 886-2-2761-7682
E-mail: ddinglaw@ms12.hinet.net

*Ap.19: C Handy mortgage document*

## APPENDIX

## Notice of Assignment

### (to Borrower/Guarantors)

To: **C Handy Corporation** ("**Borrower**")
Attention: Greene Hung
Address: 12F, No. 167, Fu Hsin N. Rd., Taipei, Taiwan, ROC
Fax number: 886-2-8771-1559

**TAIWAN MARITIME TRANSPORTATION CO., LTD.** ("**Corporate Guarantor**").
Attention: Greene Hung
Address: 12F, No. 167, Fu Hsin N. Rd., Taipei, Taiwan, ROC
Fax number: 886-2-8771-1559

**HSIN CHI SU (蘇信吉)** ("**Personal Guarantor**")
Address: 12F, No. 167, Fu Hsin N. Rd., Taipei, Taiwan, ROC
Fax number: 886-2-8771-1559

From: Deutsche Bank AG, London Branch ("**Assignor**") and
CVI CVF II Lux Master S.a.r.l. ("**Assignee**")

12 December 2013

Dear Sirs

Loan Agreement dated 7 June 2011 (as amended from time to time) between Borrower and The Shanghai Commercial & Savings Bank, Ltd. ("SCSB"), together with any amendments, supplements to such Loan Agreement ("**Loan Agreement**") and all guarantees, promissory notes, mortgages, pledges, and other collaterals and securities provided by Borrower set forth in the Security Documents (as defined in the Loan Agreement) executed in connection with such Loan Agreement (collectively referred to the "**Assigned Related Agreements**")

1. On and with effect from 12 December 2013, Assignor assigned to Assignee pursuant to an Assignment Agreement dated 12 December 2013 (the "**Assignment**") any and all of Assignor's rights, titles, interests, benefits, entitlements, remedies, claims, and causes of action arising from and/or under the Assigned Related Agreements corresponding to an outstanding principal amount of Five Million Nine Hundred Three Thousand Seven Hundred Thirty-Six and Twenty-Seven Cent United States Dollars (USD5,903,736.27) ("**Outstanding Principal**") under SCSB's claim in the insolvency proceedings of the Borrower in connection with the Assigned Related Agreements (the "**Assigned Rights**"), including, without limitation:

   (a) the Guarantees issued by the Corporate Guarantor and Personal Guarantor to guarantee the performance of any and all the obligations under the Loan Agreement and Security Documents in favor of and to SCSB,

   (b) Assignor's rights and entitlements to collect the hire, freight and other payments under the charterparties of m.v. C Handy (if any), the rights and entitlements to claim and receive the insurance proceeds arising from the Hull and Machinery

*Ap.20a: SCSB error message print out*

Insurance, War Risk Insurance and other related insurances, and the protection and indemnity insurance coverage provided by mutual (i.e., co-operative) insurance association, the rights and entitlements to claim and receive Earnings and Requisition Compensation (as defined in the Assignment Agreement dated 7 June 2011 between Borrower and SCSB, which is part of the Security Documents);

(c) the rights and interests of the Assignor in and with respect to any and all the benefits of any payment orders (支付命令) and the certification of such payment orders being final and irrevocable (支付命令確定證明書) issued by the courts of the Republic of China and the promissory note enforcement order (本票裁定) and the certification of such enforcement orders being final and irrevocable (本票裁定確定證明書) (if any) issued by the courts of the Republic of China and any other court orders, court judgment awards, execution titles of the like obtained or to be obtained by SCSB against the Borrower and/or Corporate Guarantors and /or Personal Guarantors and the funds, proceeds and /or any recovery arising from or in connection with these orders, judgment awards, execution titles, or the like, including without limitation, the payment orders and promissory note enforcement orders listed in the **Schedule 1** attached hereto.

2. The details of Assignee's facility office are as follows:

    **CVI CVF II Lux Master S.a.r.l.**
    C/O Carval Investors UK Limited
    3rd Floor, 25 Great Pulteney Street
    London, W1F 9LT

    Attn: Annemarie Jacobsen/David Short
    Email: Annemarie.jacobsen@carval.com/ david.short@carval.com
    Tel: + 44 207 292 7720/21
    Fax: + 44 207 292 7777

3. With effect from the date of this notice, all payments due to Assignee (to the extent attributable to the Outstanding Principal) and required to be deposited to the Retention Account and Earnings Account (which account details are set out below) in accordance with the Assigned Related Agreements (i.e., the Loan Agreement and Security Documents) shall remain unchanged, and Borrower shall continue to abide by the Assigned Related Agreements and make and deposit the payments to these accounts just as Borrower has done before receipt of this notice of assignment:

    Retention Account
    Account Name: C Handy Corporation
    Account No.: 27108005507191
    Name of Bank: The Shanghai Commercial & Savings Bank, Ltd.
    Offshore Banking Unit

    Earnings Account
    Account Name: C Handy Corporation
    Account No.: 27108000305201
    Name of Bank: The Shanghai Commercial & Savings Bank, Ltd.

*Ap.20b: SCSB error message print out*

## APPENDIX

Offshore Banking Unit

For avoidance of any doubt, from the effective date of this notice of assignment, SCSB shall continue to act as the Agent in relation to the administration of the facility and security under and in accordance with the Assigned Related Agreements and account bank for the Retention Account and Earnings Account.

4. Except for the payments required to be deposited into the Retention Account and Earning Account as set forth in paragraph (3) above, with effect from the date of this notice, all other payments (if any) due to Assignor in respect of the Assigned Rights (to the extent attributable to the Outstanding Principal) shall be directly paid to Assignee. The details of Assignee's account for these purposes are as follows:

   Account Name: CVI CVF II Lux Master Sárl
   Account Number: 486347003
   Beneficiary Bank: JP Morgan Chase, New York
   BIC: CHASUS33

5. Terms defined in the Assignment have the same meanings when used in this notice.

6. Assignor assigned to Assignee pursuant to the ASSIGNMENT OF A FIRST PREFERRED MORTGAGE dated on or around the date hereof Assignor's rights, interest and benefit (to the extend attributable to the Outstanding Principal) in the First Preferred Mortgage established and registered on m.v. C Handy.

Sandeep Chandak / Heng Cheam
Director
**Deutsche Bank AG, London Branch**

CVI CVF II Lux Master S.a.r.l.
BY CARVAL INVESTORS UK LIMITED
DAVID SHORT
OPERATIONS MANAGER

Schedule 1:
List in conjunction with the enforcement orders and payment orders

*Ap.20c: SCSB error message print out*

C Handy

Account Name: C Handy Corporation
Account No.: 27108000305201
Name of Bank: The Shanghai Commercial & Savings Bank, Ltd.
Offshore Banking Unit

For avoidance of any doubt, from the effective date of this notice of assignment, Assignor shall continue to act as the Agent in relation to the administration of the facility and security under and in accordance with the Assigned Related Agreements and Account Bank for the Retention Account and Earnings Account, and the Agent shall only, to the extent permitted by applicable laws and/or court orders and the terms of the Assigned Related Agreements and the account opening agreements in respect of the Retention Account and Earning Account between Account Bank and the account holder, operate these two accounts in accordance with the instructions of majority of Assignee and Syndicated Members Banks (as defined in the Assignment); Account Bank shall not exercise any right of combination, consolidation, or set-off against the accounts without Assignee's prior written consent; nor shall Account Bank amend or vary any rights attaching to the accounts without the prior written consent of a majority of Assignee and Syndicated Members Banks.

4. Except for the payments required to be deposited into the Retention Account and Earning Account as set forth in paragraph (3) above, with effect from the date of this notice, all other payments (if any) due to Assignor in respect of the Assigned Rights shall be directly paid to Assignee. The details of Assignee's account for these purposes are as follows:

   Deutsche Bank Trust Americas, New York (ABA 021001033)
   Account Number: 04411739
   Beneficiary: Deutsche Bank AG London (SWIFT - DEUT GB 2L)
   Reference: TMT / SCSB
   Attention: London Loans Admin / Yvonne Choo
   Email: yvonne.choo@db.com

5. Terms defined in the Assignment have the same meanings when used in this notice.

6. Assignor, in its capacity as a lender, assigned to Assignee pursuant to the ASSIGNMENT OF A FIRST PREFERRED MORTGAGE dated on or around the date hereof Assignor's First Preferred Mortgage established and registered on m.v. C Handy.

.................................................
The Shanghai Commercial & Savings
Bank, Ltd.  Kevin Shiao
Senior Vice President

.................................................
Deutsche Bank AG, London
Branch  Sandeep Chandak
Director

Jack Tsai
Director

Schedule 1:
List in conjunction with the enforcement orders and payment orders

錯誤! 無法識別文件屬性名稱。

*Ap.20d: SCSB error message print out*

# APPENDIX

C Handy

## Schedule 1

### List in conjunction with the enforcement orders and payment orders

The status of orders granted until 2013.10.15

**C HANDY**

| | Order Number | Principal Payable | Interest and Fees Payable | Status |
|---|---|---|---|---|
| C HANDY promissory note enforcement order | Taipei District Court, Year 102 Si-PiaoTze No.8605 | USD 16,496,703.19 | Interest is 6% per year with the principal of USD 16,453,692.32 and calculated from May 4, 2013, until payment in full + Procedural fee NTD5,000. | Not final |
| TMT promissory note enforcement order | Taipei District Court, Year 102 Si-PiaoTze No.8604 | USD 16,496,703.19 | Interest is 6% per year with the principal of USD 16,453,692.32 and calculated from May 4, 2013, until payment in full + Procedural fee NTD5,000. | Final and Binding |
| TMT payment order | Taipei District Court, Year 102 Si-Tzu-Tze No.12390 | USD 16,496,703.19 | Interest: 4.0058% per year with the principal of USD 16,453,692.32 and calculated from May 4, 2013, until payment in full. Default Penalties: (See the annex of the payment order). Procedural fee NTD500. | Final and Binding |

錯誤! 無法識別文件屬性名稱。

*Ap.20e: SCSB error message print out*

Case 13-33763   Document 1195   Filed in TXSB on 03/07/14   Page 1 of 4

IN THE UNITED STATES BANKRUPTCY COURT
FOR THE SOUTHERN DISTRICT OF TEXAS
HOUSTON DIVISION

| In re: | § | Chapter 11 |
|---|---|---|
| | § | |
| TMT PROCUREMENT CORP., et al.,[1] | § | Case No. 13-33763 |
| | § | |
| | § | |
| DEBTORS. | § | Jointly Administered |

**EMERGENCY MOTION FOR ENTRY OF FINAL ORDER (I) AUTHORIZING POST-PETITION SECURED FINANCING TO B MAX CORPORATION AND (II) PROVIDING RELATED RELIEF WITH RESPECT THERETO**

THERE WILL BE A HEARING ON THIS MOTION ON MARCH 10, 2014 AT 9:00 A.M. IN COURTROOM 404 AT THE U.S. BANKRUPTCY COURT, 515 RUSK AVENUE, HOUSTON, TEXAS 77002.

THIS MOTION SEEKS AN ORDER THAT MAY ADVERSELY AFFECT YOU. IF YOU OPPOSE THE MOTION, YOU SHOULD IMMEDIATELY CONTACT THE MOVING PARTY TO RESOLVE THE DISPUTE. IF YOU AND THE MOVING PARTY CANNOT AGREE, YOU MUST FILE A RESPONSE AND SEND A COPY TO THE MOVING PARTY. YOU MUST FILE AND SERVE YOUR RESPONSE WITHIN 14 DAYS OF THE DATE THIS WAS SERVED ON YOU. YOUR RESPONSE MUST STATE WHY THE MOTION SHOULD NOT BE GRANTED. IF YOU DO NOT FILE A TIMELY RESPONSE, THE RELIEF MAY BE GRANTED WITHOUT FURTHER NOTICE TO YOU. IF YOU OPPOSE THE MOTION AND HAVE NOT REACHED AN AGREEMENT, YOU MUST ATTEND THE HEARING. UNLESS THE PARTIES AGREE OTHERWISE, THE COURT MAY CONSIDER EVIDENCE AT THE HEARING AND MAY DECIDE THE MOTION AT THE HEARING.

THIS MOTION SEEKS A WAIVER OF THE NORMAL REQUIREMENT FOR SEPARATE INTERIM AND FINAL HEARINGS ON PROPOSED POST-PETITION FINANCING. EMERGENCY RELIEF HAS BEEN REQUESTED. IF THE COURT CONSIDERS THE MOTION ON AN EMERGENCY BASIS, THEN YOU WILL HAVE LESS THAN 14 DAYS

---

[1] The Debtors in these chapter 11 cases are: (1) A Whale Corporation; (2) B Whale Corporation; (3) C Whale Corporation; (4) D Whale Corporation; (5) E Whale Corporation; (6) G Whale Corporation; (7) H Whale Corporation; (8) A Duckling Corporation; (9) F Elephant Inc.; (10) A Ladybug Corporation; (11) C Ladybug Corporation; (12) D Ladybug Corporation; (13) A Handy Corporation; (14) B Handy Corporation; (15) C Handy Corporation; (16) B Max Corporation; (17) New Flagship Investment Co., Ltd; (18) RoRo Line Corporation; (19) Ugly Duckling Holding Corporation; (20) Great Elephant Corporation; and (21) TMT Procurement Corporation.

*Ap.21: Chapter 11, emergency motion*

## APPENDIX

### DECLARATION OF JOHAN SUDIMAN

I, Johan Sudiman, declare as follows:

1. I am employed as Executive Director of J.P. Morgan Securities (Asia Pacific) Limited. All statements of fact contained herein are true and correct and are based upon my personal knowledge, or based upon a review of defendant JPMorgan Chase Bank, N.A.'s ("JPMorgan") records where ownership of the "Debt," as defined below, would reasonably be expected to be reflected.

2. Transfer Certificates dated various dates in January 2014 were executed pursuant to which the holders of various tranches of loans secured by certain vessels known as the *M.V. C Whale*, the *M.V. D Whale*, the *M.V. G Whale* and the *M.V. H Whale* transferred such tranches to JPMorgan, as set forth below (the "Debt"):

*M.V. C Whale*

- A Transfer Certificate dated January 17, 2014 was executed pursuant to which CTBC Bank Co. Ltd. transferred to JPMorgan $7,500,000 of a loan designated as US$84,000,000 Facility Agreement for C Whale Corporation dated June 21, 2010. (Ex. A.)

- A Transfer Certificate dated January 20, 2014 was executed pursuant to which Ta Chong Bank Ltd. transferred to JPMorgan $4,125,000 of a loan designated as US$84,000,000 Facility Agreement for C Whale Corporation dated June 21, 2010. (Ex. B.)

- A Transfer Certificate dated January 21, 2014 was executed pursuant to which First Commercial Bank Co., Ltd. transferred to JPMorgan $2,625,000 of a loan designated as US$84,000,000 Facility Agreement dated June 21, 2010. (Ex. C.)

- A Transfer Certificate dated January 29, 2014 was executed pursuant to which a syndicate of lenders transferred to JPMorgan $38,624,999 of a loan designated as US$84,000,000 Facility Agreement dated June 21, 2010. (Ex. D.)

Exhibit B

*Ap.22a–e: JPMorgan Chase declaration*

*M.V. D Whale*

- A Transfer Certificate dated January 17, 2014 was executed pursuant to which CTBC Bank Co. Ltd. transferred to JPMorgan $7,200,000 of a loan designated as US$91,600,000 Facility Agreement for D Whale Corporation dated September 28, 2010. (Ex. E.)

- A Transfer Certificate dated January 20, 2014 was executed pursuant to which Ta Chong Bank Ltd. transferred to JPMorgan $5,520,000 of a loan designated as US$91,600,000 Facility Agreement for D Whale Corporation dated September 28, 2010. (Ex. F.)

- A Transfer Certificate dated January 21, 2014 was executed pursuant to which First Commercial Bank Co., Ltd. transferred to JPMorgan $5,520,000 of a loan designated as US$91,600,000 Facility Agreement dated September 28, 2010. (Ex. G.)

- A Transfer Certificate dated January 29, 2014 was executed pursuant to which a syndicate of lenders transferred to JPMorgan $44,839,999 of a loan designated as US$91,600,000 Facility Agreement dated September 28, 2010. (Ex. H.)

*M.V. G Whale*

- A Transfer Certificate dated January 17, 2014 was executed pursuant to which CTBC Bank Co. Ltd. transferred to JPMorgan $10,284,999 of a loan designated as US$90,000,000 Facility Agreement for G Whale Corporation dated March 9, 201[1]. (Ex. I.)

- A Transfer Certificate dated January 20, 2014 was executed pursuant to which Ta Chong Bank Ltd. transferred to JPMorgan $7,225,000 of a loan designated as US$90,000,000 Facility Agreement for G Whale Corporation dated March 9, 201[1]. (Ex. J.)

- A Transfer Certificate dated January 21, 2014 was executed pursuant to which First Commercial Bank Co., Ltd. transferred to JPMorgan $10,285,000 of a loan designated as US$90,000,000 Facility Agreement dated March 9, 2011. (Ex. K.)

- A Transfer Certificate dated January 29, 2014 was executed pursuant to which a syndicate of lenders transferred to JPMorgan $41,480,000 of a loan designated as US$90,000,000 Facility Agreement dated March 9, 2011. (Ex. L.)

*M.V. H Whale*

- A Transfer Certificate dated January 17, 2014 was executed pursuant to which CTBC Bank Co. Ltd. transferred to JPMorgan $10,285,000 of a loan designated as US$90,000,000 Facility Agreement for H Whale Corporation dated June 7, 2011. (Ex. M.)

- A Transfer Certificate dated January 20, 2014 was executed pursuant to which Ta Chong Bank Ltd. transferred to JPMorgan $7,225,000 of a loan designated as US$90,000,000 Facility Agreement for H Whale Corporation dated June 7, 201[1]. (Ex. N.)

- A Transfer Certificate dated January 21, 2014 was executed pursuant to which First Commercial Bank Co., Ltd. transferred to JPMorgan $10,284,999 of a loan designated as US$90,000,000 Facility Agreement dated June 7, 2011. (Ex. O.)

- A Transfer Certificate dated January 29, 2014 was executed pursuant to which a syndicate of lenders transferred to JPMorgan $41,480,000 of a loan designated as US$90,000,000 Facility Agreement dated June 7, 2011. (Ex. P.)

3. Transfer Certificates dated various dates in January 2014 were executed pursuant to which the Debt was transferred from JPM to OCM Formosa Strait Holdings, Ltd. ("OCM"), as set forth below:

*M.V. C Whale*

- A Transfer Certificate dated January 21, 2014 was executed pursuant to which JPMorgan transferred to OCM $11,625,000 of a loan designated as US$84,000,000 Facility Agreement for C Whale Corporation dated June 21, 2010. (Ex. Q.)

- A Transfer Certificate dated January 23, 2014 was executed pursuant to which JPMorgan transferred to OCM $2,625,000 of a loan designated as US$84,000,000 Facility Agreement for C Whale Corporation dated June 21, 2010. (Ex. R.)

- A Transfer Certificate dated January 29, 2014 was executed pursuant to which JPMorgan transferred to OCM $38,624,999 of a loan designated as US$84,000,000 Facility Agreement dated June 21, 2010. (Ex. S.)

*M.V. D Whale*

- A Transfer Certificate dated January 21, 2014 was executed pursuant to which JPMorgan transferred to OCM $12,720,000 of a loan designated as US$91,600,000 Facility Agreement for D Whale Corporation dated September 28, 2010. (Ex. T.)

- A Transfer Certificate dated January 23, 2014 was executed pursuant to which JPMorgan transferred to OCM $5,520,000 of a loan designated as US$91,600,000 Facility Agreement for D Whale Corporation dated September 28, 2010. (Ex. U.)

- A Transfer Certificate dated January 29, 2014 was executed pursuant to which JPMorgan transferred to OCM $44,839,999 of a loan designated as US$91,600,000 Facility Agreement dated September 28, 2010. (Ex. V.)

*M.V. G Whale*

- A Transfer Certificate dated January 21, 2014 was executed pursuant to which JPMorgan transferred to OCM $17,509,999 of a loan designated as US$90,000,000 Facility Agreement dated March 9, 2011. (Ex. W.)

- A Transfer Certificate dated January 23, 2014 was executed pursuant to which JPMorgan transferred to OCM $10,285,000 of a loan designated as US$90,000,000 Facility Agreement for G Whale Corporation dated March 9, 2011. (Ex. X.)

- A Transfer Certificate dated January 29, 2014 was executed pursuant to which JPMorgan transferred to OCM $41,480,000 of a loan designated as US$90,000,000 Facility Agreement dated March 9, 2011. (Ex. Y.)

*M.V. H Whale*

- A Transfer Certificate dated January 21, 2014 was executed pursuant to which JPMorgan transferred to OCM $17,510,000 of a loan designated as US$90,000,000 Facility Agreement dated June 7, 2011. (Ex. Z.)

- A Transfer Certificate dated January 23, 2014 was executed pursuant to which JPMorgan transferred to OCM $10,284,999 of a loan designated as US$90,000,000 Facility Agreement for H Whale Corporation dated June 7, 2011. (Ex. AA.)

- A Transfer Certificate dated January 29, 2014 was executed pursuant to which JPMorgan transferred to OCM $41,480,000 of a loan designated as US$90,000,000 Facility Agreement dated June 7, 2011. (Ex. BB.)

4. JPMorgan's business records described in Paragraph 1 above were searched for records that reflect the ownership or transfer of the Debt. Such records reflect the Transfer Certificates described in Paragraphs 2 and 3 above. Such records do not reflect, nor am I aware of, (a) any current ownership of the Debt; (b) any other ownership or transfer of the Debt; or (c) any agreement by JPMorgan to retain any right, title, interest, benefit, claim, cause of action, obligation or liability related to the Debt.

I declare under penalty of perjury under the laws of the United States of America that the foregoing is true and correct.

Executed on: 26th March 2015

# APPENDIX

Historical Information

Provided by: CTBC FINANCIAL HOLDING CO., LTD.

| | | | | | |
|---|---|---|---|---|---|
| SEQ_NO | 3 | Date of announcement | 2013/11/12 | Time of announcement | 19:12:55 |

Subject: Announced by CTBC Financial Holding Co., Ltd. on behalf of CTBC Bank Co., Ltd. (CTBC Bank) regarding the sales of distressed assets

Date of events: 2013/11/12   To which item it meets: paragraph 20

Statement:

1. Name and nature of the subject matter (if preferred shares, the terms and conditions of issuance shall also be indicated, e.g.dividend yield): Non-Performing Loan of CTBC Bank
2. Date of occurrence of the event: 2013/11/12
3. Volume, unit price, and total monetary amount of the transaction:
   (1) Volume: NA
   (2) Unit Price: NA
   (3) Total monetary amount: USD$29,198,001.25
4. Counterpart to the trade and its relationship to the Company (if the trading counterpart is a natural person and furthermore is not an actual related party of the Company, the name of the trading counterpart is not required to be disclosed):
   J.P. Morgan Chase Bank N.A.
5. Where the counterpart to the trade is an actual related party, a public announcement shall also be made of the reason for choosing the related party as trading counterpart and the identity of the previous owner (including its relationship with the company and the trading counterpart), price of transfer, and date of acquisition: NA
6. Where a person who owned the property within the past five years has been an actual related person of the company, a public announcement shall also include the dates and prices of acquisition and disposal by the related person and the person's relationship to the company at those times: NA
7. Matters related to the creditor's rights currently being disposed of (including types of collateral of the disposed creditor's rights; if the creditor's rights are creditor's rights toward a related person, the name of the related person and the book amount of the creditor's rights toward such related person currently being disposed of must also be announced):
   (1) Type of collateral of the disposed: Secured loans' collaterals are vessels and interest rate swap loans are unsecured loans;
   (2) Creditor's right toward a related person: NA
8. Anticipated profit or loss from the disposal (not applicable in cases of acquisition of securities) (where originally deferred, the status or recognition shall be stated and explained):
   Anticipated loss of USD 25,330,160.69
9. Terms of delivery or payment (including payment period and monetary amount), restrictive covenants in the contract, and other important stipulations:
   Based on the terms of Sales Agreement
10. The manner in which the current transaction was decided, the reference basis for the decision on price, and the decision-making department:
    (1) The manner in which the current transaction was decided: Negotiating the transaction price directly with the counter parties
    (2) The reference basis for the decision on price and the decision-making department: BOD of CTBC Bank Co., Ltd.
11. Current cumulative volume, amount, and shareholding percentage of holdings of the security being traded (including the current trade) and status of any restriction of rights (e.g.pledges): NA
12. Current ratio of long or short term securities investment (including the current trade) to the total assets and shareholder's equity as shown in the most recent financial statement and the operating capital as shown in the most recent financial statement: NA
13. Broker and broker's fee: NA
14. Concrete purpose or use of the acquisition or disposition: For Accelerating disposal of Non-Performing Loans.
15. Net worth per share of company underlying securities acquired or disposed of: NA
16. Do the directors have any objection to the present transaction?: NA
17. Has the CPA issued an opinion on the unreasonableness of the price of the current transaction?: NA

Historical Information

18. Any other matters that need to be specified:
The above related transaction is recorded and traded in USD. The exchange rate. USD 1= NTD 29.61
The Buyer will pay CTBC Bank Ltd., related fees USD 373,000.

# BIBLIOGRAPHY

Financial Times, September 2009
NYDFS, August 2016
Reuters, August 2005
South China Morning Post, November 2016
Süddentsche Zeitung, December 2016
Su, Nobu (2017) *The Gold Man from the East*, Gatecrasher Publications: London
TradeWinds, November 2013
Wikipedia articles

# ILLUSTRATIONS

All illustrations in *Dynasty Escape* have been sent to, commissioned by or are copyright of Nobu Sue, except as stated.

Frontispiece The Author—Nobu Sue (© Odette Sugerman)

p.41    5.1. McKinney Tsai (© Liberty Times)

p.113   13.1. Pure theatre (© stocksnapper/123RF)

p.176   17.1. Destroying the evidence (© orangeline/123RF)

p.205   22.1. JPMorgan Chase sign (© Felix Lipov/123RF)

p.210   22.2. Bribery and corruption (© Andriy Popov/123RF)

www.ingramcontent.com/pod-product-compliance
Lightning Source LLC
Chambersburg PA
CBHW042123100526
44587CB00025B/4162